New Orleans Cuisine

With contributions by

KAREN TRAHAN LEATHEM

PATRICIA KENNEDY LIVINGSTON

MICHAEL MIZELL-NELSON

CYNTHIA LEJEUNE NOBLES

SHARON STALLWORTH NOSSITER

SARA ROAHEN

CONTENTS

FOREWORD

There is nothing quite like this book. On the one hand, it is assertively not a cookbook, yet it provides some wonderful and workable recipes and rich insights on fully fourteen iconic New Orleans dishes. On the other hand, it is not a monograph of anthropology, history, sociology, or economics, although it draws on all these fields and more besides. In it, seven talented authors combine evidence from printed texts, oral interviews, literature, travelers' accounts, economic and social history, and their own taste buds. They have not merely "read ten books and written the eleventh," but produced something absolutely original and, in an understated way, important.

This book is a kind of renovation project, an effort to reclaim the vital essence of a living art that has suffered from familiarity. As such, it bears comparison with the restoration of an ancient but timeworn New Orleans house. To do this right, you need to know as much as possible about those who first built and inhabited the structure. This will help us understand why it was made the way it was. It is also important to identify and deal with all the later changes and additions. Some are best torn away, leaving the bold original exposed for the first time in generations. But other additions should be kept, for they may offer something innovative and valid in themselves. This, in essence, is what the authors have done here, not with buildings but with some renowned New Orleans dishes. Thanks to their careful research, we understand better how each of these culinary classics came to be and why they are the way they are. Along the way, we gain fresh understanding of the city that gave rise to them.

And that is itself an important part of the story. Through example after example the authors show us that the New Orleans culinary tradition belongs to the city as such, in all its bewildering diversity, and not to any one or few of its many constituent groups, however much each may have contributed over time.

Yes, there were strong influences from France, the West Indies, and, through them, Africa. But we also see how many other peoples and groups contributed centrally to the Crescent City's rich culinary culture. A near constant among them were the Germans, who began arriving in the early eighteenth century and by the 1860s were one of the largest groups in the city. Then came the Sicilians (mainly from two towns outside Palermo), with their bountiful gastronomic heritage, who called on it to rework and enrich what they found in their new homeland. Other key contributors included the Cubans, Canary Islanders, Croatians, and even Chinese. As early as the 1880s Lafcadio Hearn, the city's greatest nineteenth-century writer and author of one of the earliest local cookbooks, was singing the praises of an inexpensive downtown Chinese restaurant he frequented.

Anyone with even the most superficial acquaintance with any of the many foreign and ethnic food traditions that contributed over the centuries to New Orleans cookery knows that New Orleans cuisine differs sharply from all of them. True, one can detect distinct and specific echoes of each of the contributing cuisines in the local fare. But the food of New Orleans is not just a mixture of what went into it. As the various contributing food cultures interacted with each other, each was fundamentally transformed. Through a process akin to a chemical reaction (as opposed to a mere compound) there arose something entirely new, a single, if highly diverse, cuisine that transcended and supplanted all the cuisines that went into its making.

This is scarcely surprising. After all, every group arriving at the Mississippi Delta found unfamiliar vegetables, fruits, and meats, as well as unanticipated new spices. Mirlitons, red fish, local turtles, the abundant fowl that astonished Audubon, plantains, cane sugar raised on nearby plantations, hot peppers like those the McIlhenny family came to appreciate during their Civil War–era stay in the Mexican province of Tabasco, or a dozen other indigenous foods posed equal challenges to all newcomers. Add to these the variegated palates and gastronomic wisdom of a dozen nations, all of which were quickly shared throughout the community, and you had one of the most challenging culinary environments anywhere. No wonder it gave rise to a new cuisine that was indebted to all the cuisines that went into it but was at the same time independent of them all.

Note the past tense. As Susan Tucker ruefully acknowledges in her introduction, the food culture that reached its glory in the century after 1850 began to change fundamentally in the 1960s. Improved transportation brought food-stuffs from far away, undercutting the market for fresher produce grown locally. A younger generation grew accustomed to generic dishes, precooked frozen meals, and fast food. A few decades ago local food stores stocked aisles full of beans, rice, and other local basics, but now they carry the same fare available in Milwaukee, Hartford, or Portland. At the same time, locally reared men and women whose parents were content to serve as cooks in neighborhood eater-ies or chefs in restaurants or private homes now aspired to careers in the big world.

No less important, the rise of mass tourism threatened to turn New Or-leans cuisine into a standardized commodity. The ranks of knowledgeable and exacting local natives shrank as a percentage of total patrons at New Orleans eateries, their places taken increasingly by less-demanding folks who arrived in tour buses. Inevitably, the gastronomic repertoire shrank precipitously. Subtle old classics like *courtbouillon*, grits and *grillades*, or *daube* spaghetti gave way to overspiced and oversized portions of the same few dishes that signified New Orleans to tourist agents in Tampa or Albuquerque.

As this occurred, a curious countermovement arose, under the banner of "celebrity chefs." These often talented entrepreneurs, mainly "from elsewhere," marketed nationally their "interpretations" of iconic local dishes through tele-vision shows, cookbooks, and their own lines of food products. A handful of national food impresarios appropriated what had been created and sustained for a century by thousands of anonymous local chefs. At a lower level, ersatz powdered gumbos appeared, complete with instructions to "just add water and boil."

But the masters of South Louisiana kitchens took their subtle revenge by mastering a process akin to cloning. Beginning in 1972 Alvin Copeland, a manic high-school dropout, parlayed his locally derived chicken recipe from a low-end eatery in the impoverished suburb of Arabi into the seven-hundred-store Pop-eyes franchise. Paul Prudhomme, a farm boy from Opelousas, marketed rural Cajun cuisine so successfully that many Americans now consider it the essence of what is, in fact, the quite different traditional urban cuisine of New Orleans. A justly admired celebrity chef, Prudhomme grew rich on his cookbooks and line of "Magic Spices." In the same years Ruth Fertel, a tireless and gracious sin-gle mother of two, transformed her Ruth's Chris Steakhouse from a local haunt on Broad Street into a chain of more than a hundred restaurants.

Do these developments mark the end of the line for New Orleans cooking? Far from it, if this book is any guide. Over and over again the authors show us that New Orleans food culture has never been static. In the same way in which refugees from Saint-Domingue (now Haiti), Germany, and Sicily once reworked the recipes they found in their new environment, so other groups are doing the same today. Devastation following Hurricane Katrina forced a large community of Vietnamese from their isolation on the eastern edges of New Orleans into the mainstream, bringing their cuisine with them. Who knows what this amalgamation might bring? In the same period since 2005 tens of thousands of Mexicans and Hondurans have arrived on the banks of the Mississippi, where they are helping not only to rebuild the city but, inevitably, to extend its culinary horizons in a southerly direction. Nor is this a break with the past. Back in 1926 New Orleans Jazz cornetist Freddie Keppard paid a bravura tribute to Mexicans in the Crescent City with his recording of "Here Comes the Hot Tamale Man." The city council may fulminate against the many sidewalk *taquerias* of today, but tomorrow these same establishments on wheels could give rise to yet another manifestation of the classic New Orleans cuisine. Stay tuned!

Finally, a word on the social environment in which all this culinary intermingling has occurred over the centuries. Good food was, and remains, only one among many components of "the good life" as that term is understood in South Louisiana. Alcohol, whether beer, wine, rye whiskey, rum, or bourbon, has always been a central ingredient in that recipe for living. It is therefore fitting that this book should start with a chapter on the Sazerac cocktail. Perhaps there should also be an appendix on cigars, which were produced locally by the millions in huge, factory-like buildings. And others on music, dancing, gambling, and carousing.

As in all great cultures, every aspect of life in New Orleans is intimately and inseparably linked with food. For a century the vegetable-based green *gumbo z'herbes* marked the austerity of Lent in the Crescent City, and as recently as the 1980s it was still offered as Lenten fare at Eddie's on Law Street. The famous Japanese Room at Antoine's, long sealed up but then rediscovered a generation ago, marked America's growing internationalism a century ago. And key developments of the civil rights movement in New Orleans were launched over dinner meetings in the upstairs room of Dooky and Leah Chase's restaurant on Orleans Avenue.

These and many other examples remind us that food is not a mere adorn-
ment of life in New Orleans but a core part of life itself. Which is why this book
is important, timely, and much worth pondering, even as one enjoys it.

—S. FREDERICK STARR
New Orleans, 2008

ACKNOWLEDGMENTS

New Orleans Cuisine: Fourteen Signature Dishes and Their Histories was developed from a project of the New Orleans Culinary History Group.

Like the food of New Orleans, this book would not have been possible without the help of many people and institutions. Archival and research assistance from the Historic New Orleans Collection, especially from Gerald Patout, was essential to our analyses. Gerald provided extensive research material, answered bibliographic queries with grace and speed, and passionately joined in tastings and discussions. We also found invaluable information in the Special Collections at Earl K. Long Library at the University of New Orleans, in Louisiana State University's Hill Memorial Library and Special Collections, in the Amistad Research Center, and in the Howard-Tilton Memorial Library at Tulane University. The archivists at the State Library of Louisiana and at the Baton Rouge Public Library both went out of their way to locate newspaper articles and magazines, as did the librarians at the New Orleans Public Library. Many thanks also go to student workers at the Newcomb Center for Research on Women: Kenneth Balla, Dawn Lucas, Patricia Neves, Avram Penner, Allyson Mackay, and Dawn Chadwick. Stephanie Bordy was an excellent archivist for us all. The Newcomb Center's Vorhoff Library's cookbook collection provided the basis for most of our research.

Groups like the Southern Foodways Alliance and the Southern Food and Beverage Museum provided important information. From the latter, Elizabeth Williams assisted in the beginning of this project when she wanted to do more than have just a bibliography of New Orleans food. Poppy Tooker with Slow Food New Orleans lent her knowledge, passion, and vision to the project. Special thanks also to Savvy Gourmet for allowing us the use of their wonderful store and kitchen for tastings. Dr. Randy Sparks and Dr. Shana Walton encouraged our beginnings, and to them we also owe our deepest gratitude.

Within our own group, Maureen Detweiler coordinated the tastings. Maureen provided extraordinary charm, generosity, organizational skills, and culinary expertise. Faun Fenderson likewise arranged for much of our success. For more than seven years she has served as Web mistress for our bibliography and provided legal help. Kevin McCaffrey first coordinated the work of oral history; his expertise, willingness, and encouragement allowed a smooth beginning to almost all our work. Mildred Covert also helped in our initial endeavors, providing memories, oral history interviews, and knowledge of food in the city. Pat Gloriosa was a willing taster, reader, and supporter. Ann Maylie Bruce lent materials, memories, expertise, and fun. Similarly, Dolores Martins de Barros enchanted us with her studies of Sicily and New Orleans and her own magic way of seeing the world. Finally, Phyllis Marquart fits into the category of dream researcher. Not only did she edit with great precision, but she also always presented our own foodways back to us in a careful and wholehearted way that was never less than absolutely astounding.

Completion of the project was also aided by the gracious assistance of Sal Serio at the American Italian Renaissance Foundation Museum. Others who aided our proofreading and fact-finding were Rebecca Jordan, Elizabeth Pearce, Clive Wilson, Harriet Swift, Peg Kohlepp, and Richard Coram.

Although we learned much history about New Orleans food from diaries, letters, reports, oral histories, scholarly essays, and newspaper articles, our research would not have been complete without conversations with chefs, food writers, and those who love to eat and cook. Special appreciation goes to Chef John Folse, Michaela York, Martin Spindel, Warren Smith, Mike and Kathy Sansovich, Mikel and Octavia Sansovich, Carolise Rosen, Sally K. Reeves, Brett Anderson, Patrick and Françoise Perié, Lolis Eric Elie, Sue Laudeman, Pat Stevens, Judy Walker, and David Wondrich.

We especially thank our families and friends for carrying pots, tasting dishes, and joining us in celebration and sharing of New Orleans food. Within the Culinary History Group, this would be the help of Howard Nobles, Franny Tucker, Linda Lehmil, Antoine Perié, William Detweiler, Michael Leathem, and Adam Nossiter.

New Orleans Cuis

SETTING THE TABLE
IN NEW ORLEANS

Susan Tucker, with Cynthia LeJeune Nobles,
Karen Trahan Leathem, and Sharon Stallworth Nossiter

New Orleans is a city of extremes and always has been. Visitors and residents alike have remarked upon the wretched state of its infrastructure (from streets to levees), its underbelly of poverty, and the great wealth visible today in its mansions and sometimes subtle, sometimes overt class divisions. Scarcity and plenty have lived side by side since 1718. With a reputation for richness, many of the city's most famous dishes evolved from a resourcefulness born of deprivation. They were born of adaptability, but they also reflected the exuberant excess of colorful public celebrations enjoyed by most citizens.

This book is about both these extremes brought together on the table at which New Orleanians eat. The authors present specialties common to New Orleans cuisine: fourteen iconic dishes chosen because they tell the stages of adaptability, the centrality of public encounters with food, the passion for ingredients and talk of food, manners of serving, and social and economic forces that lie behind the way New Orleanians cook. The fourteen dishes are those foods for which the traces of historical documents, recipes, and other written and oral accounts show how cooking became a hallmark of the city. They are symbolic of the social history of New Orleans.

Cuisine everywhere is defined around available "ingredients, techniques, and flavorings," and New Orleans is no different in this respect. The ingredients of New Orleans cuisine rest upon the location of the city at the mouth of the Mississippi River. For the Native Americans and the first Europeans and Africans, the nearby bayous, lakes, and the Gulf of Mexico provided fish and shellfish. The interior lands were home to turkeys, partridges, and hares; the alluvial soil yielded produce. The African slave traders brought rice and okra, and their human cargo brought the knowledge to grow these foods that became so indispensable to many New Orleans dishes. By 1722, the first generation of Africans was cultivating rice on "the Kolly concession on the Chapitoulas coast just north of New Orleans." Other experienced farmers, the colonial Germans (and later Sicilians), stocked city homes with sugar, meat, fresh produce, and butter. Nearby neighbors (Southerners, both African American and white) who moved to the city brought the staples of what has been aptly called "the great triumvirate of southern vegetables . . . turnips, cowpeas, and sweet potatoes." Grace of the port, flour and olive oil could be added to these basic ingredients, and the fundamental elements of New Orleans cuisine were established.

The same colonial groups and later immigrants to the city learned from the Native Americans and from one another, always blending various preparation techniques. From the people of the Choctaws, Chickasaws, Natchez, Chitimachas, and other tribes, the settlers learned to find the fruit to dry, became familiar with filé to thicken soup, and gained (more) skill in making hominy (*sagamité*) and what the French called its "younger sister," grits from ground corn.[1] Although most early settlers survived on a diet of corn and beans, the later French introduced the creation of roux and directions for sauces and stocks. The Spanish combined foods in a rice mixture, added many spices, and were fond of slowly simmering their foods. The French, Spanish, and Germans (from the Rhineland, from Alsace, and from elsewhere) were all expert sausage makers; the same Rhinelanders, Alsatians, and, later, Sicilians were proficient bakers. The Sicilians popularized tomato-based gravies and were not afraid of using French as often as their native Sicilian, Italian, or any other language to describe their foods, foregoing their *arrosti y pasta* or *stracotto* for daube and spaghetti, for example. In the 1920s, Turci's Italian Garden served many pasta dishes but also offered *paté de foie gras* and many other dishes *à la Créole*. The Congolese, Senegalese, Gambians, French, and Spanish all had a tradition of

---

1. Although a New World crop, maize was widely used among French peasants and poor West Africans by the middle of the seventeenth century. Some settlers, then, arrived knowing how to make a cornmeal mush similar to what the Native Americans ate.

one-pot cooking. An iron pot became the recognized symbol of their cooking practices, one that is still a romanticized prerequisite of the city's kitchens.

Flavor principles came from all the settlers and the ingredients available to them. The Native American sassafras leaves, dried and ground into filé powder, lent an earthy, herbaceous taste. The African, and later southern, taste for the slightly astringent texture of okra was also added. The sweet butter of French sauces formed the base of many of the dishes in the fine restaurants as well as the simple fish dishes served at home. There remained also, on the other extreme, the more economical (and thus ecumenical) use of lard, which is heavier than butter but similarly sumptuous on the tongue and suitable for smothering dishes of vegetables. The Spanish flavors associated with the slow sautéing of onions, bell peppers, garlic, and seasonings became a fundamental part of the city's foods. Later, Mexican capsicum peppers would be found in nearly every cupboard of the city, in a bottle of hot sauce, whose makers always credited a returning soldier from the Mexican War (1846–48). Finally, all the groups that settled the city passed down a liking for garlic and for the acidity and sweetness of tomatoes. Using the schemata developed by a cataloger of the world's great cuisines, Elisabeth Rozin, New Orleans food can be understood as relying on fat plus bell peppers plus celery plus onions plus garlic plus spices (filé, bay leaf, cayenne and other peppers, sometimes thyme) plus tomatoes, and sometimes alcohol.

The blending of culinary habits was critical to survival for all the early settlers. However, old New Orleans was said to be not a part of the "melting pot," but the "boiling pot," and it was the Africans and African Americans who tended this cauldron. By necessity, they chose from the ingredients available, the skills they had or learned from others, and affinities of all the people they met.[2] Their descendants, especially those free persons of color who became property owners and leaders, and African Americans who later arrived from other parts of the South extended the contributions of persons of African descent to New Orleans cuisine. Their own adaptability was enriched by those of their neighbors—French, Spanish, Native American, Saint-Dominguean, German, Sicilian, Croatian, and other cultures. The history of all these groups in the passage

---

2. Slaves were not as numerous in the city as in the rural areas, though one can learn from the way the slaves in these other areas shaped cuisine. All over the Americas, the slaves knew well the varieties and provisions available and thus influenced the whole of the food cultures in the societies in which they lived and worked. See Genovese; Northup; and Mintz, *Tasting Food.*

between hunger and affluence made what came to be called Creole food, for the mixing of people who ate at the tables of the city. Together, they crafted the rules of preparing and serving this food: how to choose a seasoning meat, how to make a roux, when to choose to sauté rather than fry one's fish, when to eat red beans and rice, when to drink café brûlot, and much more.

Because of early hunger and later affluence of a port filled with food, eating became the key pleasure of both daily life and special occasions. But the centrality of food came in other ways, too. The Native Americans traded with the earliest Europeans and Africans at markets. The public nature of these markets meant the exchange of recipes and talk about food as well as the sale of small game, poultry, and produce. The commencement of these markets can be tied to many cultures in Africa and Europe. The earliest slaves came from Senegambia and the Senegal River basin and were part of the Bambara culture, a society that thrived around a tradition of trading. The first Europeans in the city were building their entire culture around the movement of products. When they arrived in the New World, these groups brought their model of marketing food. The Sunday markets became one of the first examples of the centrality of New Orleanians' approach to food, a combination of people and ideas, a "setting" of cuisine. The Spanish institutionalized this setting by establishing official markets, thus easing access to food, ensuring food safety, and placing food in the center of not only daily life but also governmental oversight of this life. Present in the names of foods and preparation techniques, the French of the late eighteenth and early nineteenth centuries extended the centrality as part of the growth of French culinary expertise, a haute cuisine.

Other immigrants in later years also brought ideas about hospitality and food, setting a bountiful table for guests. Besides the southern African Americans who came from rural areas, many white Southerners and Midwesterners also brought families to work and live in New Orleans. Even New Englanders and other East Coast migrants should not be left out of New Orleans and its preoccupation with food. Cookbook writer Natalie Scott and the authors of *The Picayune Creole Cook Book* mention the English ancestors of many of those who married into Creole cooking. These settlers, especially those who came after the Civil War to buy land and businesses, brought an interest in puddings and various types of breads as well as a source of money to develop many food-related businesses. They employed New Orleanians as cooks—African Americans for the most part.

The Mexicans (stationed in New Orleans as early as the 1760s by the Spanish); the Cubans and Jamaicans (always in a small minority); the Hondurans, Vietnamese, and Cambodians who arrived in the twentieth century; the Mexicans and other Central Americans again in the early twenty-first century; and others—all are part of the adaptability of the city's eating habits. In short, many groups came over a long period of time, each adding variations, small or large, to the idea that food could be pleasure within reach, crafted with adjustments here and there, discussed along the way to work and home again.

The word *Creole* derives from the Latin *creare* (to create) and then from the Portuguese word *crioulo,* meaning a slave of African descent born in the New World. The variant *criollo* was used by the Spanish to name all Africans and Europeans born in the colonies. Some scholars tell us that anything Creole must come from French, Spanish, or African extraction, or a combination of these three.

There are dozens of definitions of, and controversies over, the word *Creole.* But the most basic meaning is the most appropriate: *Creole,* used as a noun or adjective, means "new to the southern French and Spanish colonies" or "born here."

Traditional Creole cuisine even today retains the flavor principles of the early settlers noted above: fat, bell peppers, celery, onions, garlic, spices (filé, bay leaf, cayenne pepper, sometimes thyme), tomatoes, and sometimes alcohol. The shelves and refrigerators of most New Orleans cooks contain these spices and vegetables along with butter and olive oil. The city's residents call bell peppers, celery, and onions the "holy trinity." And some of them call garlic "the pope." In the hampers of New Orleans cooks, there are likely to be sweet potatoes, red and white beans, and, in season, butter beans. In their refrigerators, they will have some okra and some sampling of fish and shellfish, beef, pork, and poultry. They will use wine to flavor sauces for the special occasion dishes they craft, and a good number will know the classical French sauces such as marchand de vin, béarnaise, bordelaise, and ravigôte.

There are, of course, many definitions of Creole cuisine and many arguments about whether the adaptability of its basic background, along with social and economic forces, has also meant its undoing. Today in many of the city's restaurants, *fusion cuisine,* a term widely used all over the world to mean a blending of culinary traditions, coexists with the older Creole cuisine also formed from a blending. In the homes of some New Orleanians, too, the pantries have changed. In a project of the History Channel and the Historic New Orleans Collection, diaries kept by New Orleans public schoolchildren in early 2005 and in 2007 show that many of the staples of the city's pantries have disappeared. Day to day, children in the city recorded eating the same sorts of food their contemporaries in other North American cities ate: cereals, dried fruits, macaroni and cheese prepared from a mix, chips, and cookies. Only one or two days a week and for all holidays they ate with grandmothers or in large family gatherings. At those times, they ate "lots of red beans and rice, lots of shrimp, a multitude of gumbos, okra, and here and there mirlitons and crawfish bisque." One family among the nine hundred odd diary-keepers ate daube glacée, and one left an account of the family's turtle soup.

No doubt this sort of pattern of homogenization and the periodic, ritualistic return to old ways would be found in Baltimore, Los Angeles, Minneapolis, New York, and any number of other places. About New Orleans food, however, there remains more written discussion than about food in other cities, according to Richard Campanella in his richly detailed study of the city's geography and urban habits, *Geographies of New Orleans*. This documentation of interest is significant to the deciphering of the many opinions that remain vital to New Orleanians' daily conversations. No set rules, or even opinions, hold firm in Creole cuisine, except an acknowledgment of a passion for food and a shared agreement that food can be adjusted to a particular circumstance and can be the topic of many a conversation.

Passion and adaptability, again, were born of hunger. The many passages between poverty and wealth were felt throughout the city's governance by the French (1718–1762), the Spanish (1762–1800), the French again (1800–1803, although they were not formally in control), and the Americans (1803 to the present). The first European settlers in the city had not learned much about growing food in their years along the Gulf Coast since 1701. The climate was wildly different than anything they had experienced in Europe or Canada and did not permit the raising of their accustomed staple, wheat. Popular history recounts times of starvation, great need and great laziness, and ultimate reliance on Native Americans. The first colonists waited for supplies to come from France, but their saviors arrived in the 1720s: as noted above, Africans who knew how to grow rice and Rhinelanders and, later, Alsatians who settled upriver, in what today is still called the German Coast. "By the mid-1700s the river-front was an open-air exchange and commodities were sold either on the levee or in the streets by pushcart" by the African Americans selling for themselves or their masters and German farmers who brought their produce to the city by boat.

Beginning in the 1760s, the Spanish control of the city meant improvements in this availability of food. In 1779, the Spanish authorities built the city's first central public market, a wooden structure to shade butchers and their meat. *Cabildo* (town council) members also inspected flour shipments and warehouses, posted weekly bread prices that were fixed by law, and prosecuted sellers who cheated customers. Other public markets soon followed to serve a population that grew steadily (from approximately 3,000 in the 1760s to some 8,500 people by 1803). The public markets were charged with the exclusive sale of perishables. Their vendors attained a certain status, and various groups came to dominate particular sales. Alongside these purveyors, women and men of all ethnicities, but especially the free women of color who rented from whites, maintained small stands in the markets where gumbo, oysters, and, of course, coffee could be purchased.[3] The Spanish period, particularly, witnessed the growth of a three-tiered social order of whites, slaves, and free persons of color. This latter group held many different places in society. In the study of food, especially that of the late eighteenth and early nineteenth centuries, they can be seen as representative of the crossovers of traditions.[4]

All the while, vegetables and small game also were sold from unregulated vendors around the city. The food that some city dwellers could not raise or afford to purchase at the markets came from these local sellers, for example, fish from the river and mutton and veal from small farms near the city. The poor (African American, free persons of color, and white) created, by necessity, the dishes today considered part of the haute cuisine as they learned to make do

---

3. In what is now called the French Market, a series of different markets was built, as told in various chapters in this book. The most elaborate building (constructed in 1813 after the first "palazzo-like monument" [Reeves, "History of Markets"]) was destroyed in the hurricane of 1812) still stands in the site occupied by Café du Monde (2008). Until the 1860s, this was always known as the meat market, or *les halles de boucheries*. In the 1880s, the French Market consisted of four other divisions, as well: the Bazaar, where dry goods were sold; the fruit and flower market, where poultry was also sold; the vegetable market; and the fish market. During market hours the streets between the markets also had stands of vendors selling such things as filé. See Reeves, "Making Groceries," 28, 33; and Horner, 46f.

4. Later the prominence of some of the Creoles of color and the cohesion almost all of them attained (and still retain) as a group would contribute much to the lasting habits of eating traditional foods described in this book.

with the poor cuts of meat, the cast-off fish, the milk that would sour, and the bread that would soon be too hard to eat.

Refugees from revolutionary France and especially from Saint-Domingue (which became Haiti in 1804) began arriving at the end of the eighteenth century and brought with them their own standards of a Creole cuisine, born of the amalgamation of French, Caribbean, African, and other eating traditions. Saint-Domingue was the wealthiest of the French colonies and the one with the largest numbers of free persons of color. Even before 1790, the colony had produced a distinctive culinary explosion.[5] Their ways of cooking rice and beans and their tastes in, and ways of serving, various vegetables came with these (until then) relatively well-off refugees, also people of a three-tiered society. Their cuisine enriched the food of New Orleans and made it solidly Creole. Before coming to the city, some of the Saint-Domingue refugees had fled first to Jamaica, Cuba, or other parts of the Caribbean, and so they also added traditions from these cultures to Creole cuisine. The oldest recorded public eating place in New Orleans dates from 1791 and was called the Café des Emigrés for the first of the "refugees from West Indian uprisings."

The Creoles from Saint-Domingue felt at home in the French-speaking city. Throughout the Spanish period, New Orleans remained French in various customs. Local historian Mary Gehman has speculated that this was so because most of the Spaniards did not bring wives. French-speaking women governed family life as they married Spanish men.

Food in the home, too, may well have been governed by French more than Spanish customs. But in terms of survival, it was the mix of the Creoles, those from all groups, who were more critical to eighteenth-century Louisiana. Yet they were not able to erase the shortages completely. The last French colonial prefect, Pierre-Clément de Laussat, describes a homely scene from 1803 that even he, a member of the elite, experienced in New Orleans:

> The difficulties one encountered during the summer in procuring the necessities of life were hardly in keeping with the wealth and civilization of the city. Provisions were lacking in the market and were had only at prohibitive prices. . . . We

---

5. As the chapters in this book show, the people of Saint-Domingue would add their tastes to the city, but many of the sources that allow some speculation on how this happened can be found more often in records on Cuba, Charleston, Philadelphia, and even France, than on New Orleans.

imitated the colonists. Almost like farmers ourselves, we drew as they did upon our own resources, and our poultry yard came alive with hens, roosters, chicks, fatted pullets, turkeys (both domesticated ones raised in our aviary or wild ones hunted in the woods), domestic and wild geese, peacocks, bustards, ducks, sheep, deer and raccoons. We set up a useful managerie [*sic*] that was prolific, made a pretty sight, and provided amusement below our galleries.

Distrusting the city's monitoring of butchers, Laussat would only buy meat directly from the farmer. He considered poultry sold in the market "disgusting." Vegetables did not meet French standards. On the other hand, *papabots* (also spelled *papabotte*, the French name for the upland plover), grasset, and partridges were excellent. Sea turtle was prepared "perfectly" by local cooks. Redfish, eel, and sea perch were "greatly prized." The pecan, unknown to him in France, was better than any nut he had tasted; and "the best fruit of the country is without question the orange." The fact that the orange had been brought first by other colonists shows how quickly foods became assimilated into the culture. Around such creativity and innovations, New Orleanians would shape their survival diet, their simple meals, and, later, their haute cuisine.

Food scarcities would be resolved, Laussat wrote, by the "enterprising spirit of the United States . . . already showing itself in Louisiana" in 1804 as he was preparing to leave. But his account of his own efforts also showed all the attributes that would figure heavily in later descriptions by New Orleanians of their French and, especially, Creole food. He was pleased with his own resourcefulness, and he enjoyed giving his opinions on food. These two responses formed another setting in the development of the city's cuisine: talk of food was fun and amusing; and finding the best food in times of trouble, a mark of character.

The vitality that Laussat saw in the Americans came quickly. As a traveler named Henry Whipple remarked in the early 1840s, New Orleans became the "grand reservoir of the great West." And as agricultural historian Wendell H. Stephenson noted in an insightful essay from 1941, "It was with pardonable pride that New Orleanians witnessed the agricultural surplus of the Mississippi Valley deposited in their city. The valley . . . poured its wealth at their doors."[6] The

---

6. Whipple's account tells of the city as "the hottest, the dirtiest, the most sickly, and at times the most healthy, the busiest and the most dull, the most wicked & most orderly" (118) and much more. Stephenson uses Whipple to introduce the history of the "agricultural focus" that the city became and the many "transcendent phrases and rhetorical frills" used to describe the city (Stephenson, 301, 302).

river current floated hundreds and eventually thousands of flatboats, barges, and keelboats carrying food down to the city. On the levees could be found sugar, molasses, corn, flour, whiskey, butter, "kegs of lard, puncheons of rum, . . . sacks of wheat, tierces of flaxseed, . . . 'mountains of grain sacks' [including oats, wheat, and rye]."

Equally important for the city and its food, European New Orleans remained mostly intact until at least 1810. New Orleans writer Lyle Saxon would even claim it remained so until the Civil War. Saxon and others describe a distinctly European appreciation of food as one of the blessings of eating in New Orleans. The merging of this awareness with African American cooking would remain prevalent.

Again, the food habits were transformed through the mixing of cultures as more plentiful waves of newcomers made their way to the nineteenth-century city. The first mixing in the nineteenth-century city centered around migrations from the Caribbean, Mexico, and South America. In 1809 alone, the arrival of over nine thousand more Saint-Domingue refugees, "roughly evenly divided among white, free people of color, and enslaved black," doubled the overall city population and "revived" the "city's Francophone culture." Certainly, as noted above, these later arrivals of those fleeing Saint-Domingue brought their own richly developed Creole cuisine. This way of eating is present in the many foods that remain to this day French in name (*bouilli, courtbouillon, etouffée, meunière,* as examples of some of the two dozen French names in New Orleans cookbooks, even in 2008). The Mexicans, Hondurans, Cubans, and other Hispanics in the nineteenth and twentieth centuries added their own customs. *The Picayune Creole Cook Book* uses the word Mexican-Creole to describe tamales, for example. Pork dishes and other sausage-making traditions from Central and South America were also added to those of the French, German, Spanish, and, later, Creoles of color discussed elsewhere in this book.

Concurrent with this fusion of American cultures, New Orleans became one of the United States' largest cities (seventh in population in 1810, fifth in 1820 and 1830, and third in 1840). More important to its European character, New Orleans was the second busiest port of immigration to the United States. By 1850, German was more apt to be spoken than French, and German newspapers and schools rivaled those exclusive to the French and Americans. But like the Saint-Domingueans, these Germans quickly saw themselves as part of the city. The arrival of Irish immigrants also in this period (1830 to 1850) extended the layers of ethnic complexity begun in the earlier century. In these new immigrant groups, New Orleans resembled the cities of the Northeast, an aspect that made its cuisine all the more mythical to travelers, relatives, and friends from neighboring states.

The markets particularly enhanced the romance with food enjoyed by residents and visitors alike. Such public markets were not unique to New Orleans, but here they joined together the port, the multicultural inhabitants, and the restaurant culture in a way that lasted far longer than in other cities. The French Market became one of the most drawn, painted, and photographed sites in the United States. Twelve more public markets were built by the mid-nineteenth century, most in the rapidly growing part of town called the American Sector.[7] The French Market captured the most attention, but other city markets were the daily meeting place of housewives, servants, and suppliers of all sorts. The meat concessions in these markets were generally controlled by men born in Gascony, France, or descendants of these men. They spoke to one another in Creole French or in the French they brought from Gascony well into the early twentieth century, thus adding to the aura of a Francophone city.

Sunday mornings brought out many who missed this commerce of food during the week. Guidebook writer Benjamin Norman in 1845 commented on this, "The greatest market day . . . youth and age, beauty and not-so-beautiful—all colors, nations and tongues . . . commingled in one heterogeneous mass of delightful confusion." Markets opened every day at dawn and a closing bell rang at noon (or 10 a.m. in summer) with vendors locking up for the day. This was a safety measure as well as a labor policy: food could not withstand long hours in the market, and farmers and vendors, who had arrived as early as 3 a.m., needed a break.

The combination of local food and the corn, wheat, coffee, and other products shipped through the port governed what was available at markets, the meals that could be served, and what visitors and journalists would describe. The city was the final stop for goods and people traversing the United States down the Mississippi River. The journey was enlivened by the presence of investors, boat hands, and travelers; their arrival and their ideas, in turn, made the city all the more memorable. The exoticism expected by the travelers, coupled with the

---

7. In the mid-nineteenth century, over 1,000 people worked in the meat markets, and in the 1880s those centers of commerce generated $200,000 in revenues for the city. See Reeves, "Making Groceries," 30.

lingering French language and other languages as the city grew, transformed the word *Creole.* The visitors came to apply this term to "everything coming from Louisiana . . . Creole eggs, Creole ponies, Creole cows, Creole butter, and so forth." As a trademark *Creole* came to signify "the home-raised or home-made, the better and fresher goods in contrast to those imported from the West, from the north, or from Europe." No longer even were Creoles the descendants of the firstborn Africans, French, or Spanish. Creole Germans, too, joined in the reshaping of this word and in the presentation of New Orleans food.

These New Orleanians made a city that had a reputation for a variety of foods and a joy in finding them. In 1821 at the public markets, artist John James Audubon could buy for his work six kinds of wild waterfowl, nine kinds of wild birds, and many squirrels. In 1833, a traveler named Catherine Busstry could delight in the transformation of the city because she could eat well: "Even New Orleans seemed to have lost something of its dinginess, when, after a three days' voyage, I found myself comfortably seated at the French restaurateur's and saw the waiter enter with a most tempting dish of becaficas, or some bird very much like them, and very nearly as good."

Busstry was probably eating in a hotel. By 1830, the dining rooms of the Tremoulet, St. Charles, St. Louis, and Verandah hotels provided elegant meals to southern plantation families, businessmen, and other wealthy visitors. The menus of the hotels contained most of the elaborate dishes one would expect in similar hotels in France. Creole New Orleans continued to send some of its most elite and wealthy to France for education, and in turn, France sent its best ideas, including its developing ideas on cooking, to its former colony. But here, too, was the bustling city of American businessmen: historian William Cowan writes of these repasts and the "free lunch . . . served to bibbers who came in for a noontime potion." Local seafood, game birds, and produce, along with imported exotic spices and delicacies graced these tables.

Most other eateries in the bustling city served only men.[8] One French Quarter establishment that housed businessmen was a small pension established in April 1840 by Antoine Alciatore. Because of his training as a chef, this boardinghouse dining room, called Antoine's, thrived and can boast of being

---

8. Gender segregation was prevalent until the early twentieth century. In many small neighborhood restaurants, a separate entrance for women was created so they would not have to pass men seated at bar counters. The sidewalk tiles showing the women's entrance where once Brocato's stood in the French Quarter can be seen in front of Croissant d'Or in 2008.

one of the oldest continually operating restaurants in the United States. Given Alciatore's culinary training and his prior work at the St. Charles Hotel, it is safe to say that his restaurant was among the first stand-alone establishments in the line of haute cuisine in the city. As anthropologist Sidney Mintz notes, to have *haute cuisine*, a culture first must have in place *cuisine*. Thus, Alciatore's beginning serves as one of the first markers of a fine-dining culture in which distinctive New Orleans food was consciously created and sustained.[9]

Most New Orleans restaurants grew from a different incarnation of nineteenth-century commerce—from bars, usually called exchanges or cafés, where men drank and discussed business. The exchanges had strong connections with the public markets, and their proprietors and workers had strong connections with one another. One establishment, Tujague's, was founded in 1856 by Guillaume and Marie Abadie Tujague. Like their neighbor, the famous Madame Bégué, the couple sold breakfast and lunch to riverfront and French Market laborers. Tujague descendants, in a fashion typical of other city restaurant owners past and present, came to run other establishments such as Des Chênes Verts, which later became Tavern on the Park. This latter restaurant was associated also with those who worked in the Tremé Exchange, the coffee stand of the working-class Tremé Market. Here, too, were the small stands of the Creoles of color. All of these small bars, vendors, and the meals they served worked in tandem with the market economy: food would rot if not used quickly.

The lingering Francophone world included a vast array of people whose lives revolved around marketing, cooking, and serving food and who identified themselves as French. There were those, like Alciatore of Antoine's, who had trained as chefs in France. There was the network of Gascon-born butchers, with their brothers, sisters, in-laws, and descendants. There were the French-identified Creoles of color, a good number of whom worked as food purveyors, many in public markets. New Orleans food, then, was seen as French.[10] This identification occurred just as the mother country of France was successfully building its global domination of food preparation in the great hotels of Europe

9. One could argue that the haute cuisine served there came mainly in 1880s when Jules Alciatore took over operation. Jules had been sent to France and England for training. However, Italian-born but Marseilles-raised Antoine Alciatore had apprenticed in hotel kitchens, and he certainly was familiar with the then-spreading rules of French haute cuisine.

10. To be called "French" here one was either Creole-French speaking or French speaking; attached to the various French benevolent societies; or born in France, a category that such people themselves and English-speaking New Orleanians called "the Foreign French."

and all the Americas. The rules of Antonin Carême, the urgings of Alexis Soyer, and the codifications of Auguste Escoffier all coincided with the richness available on New Orleans tables via the very healthy economy and a good number of French-identified establishments. In the French monopoly of gastronomy, New Orleans was part of this larger diffusion of ideas and people in a singularly focused way not found in other U.S. cities.

The city's wealth was built largely on another kind of network, however—that born of the shipment of southern agricultural products. Who ate the elegant food on the well-laden tables of the hotels? This would have been, in large part, the planters who worked slaves to produce the great southern crops, the commission merchants who sold their products, and the slave traders who oversaw the thousands of people treated as property. In the elegant hotels and along the streets where the vendors sold their wares, businessmen also participated in, or at least saw, the exchanges that were literally slave auctions.

Much about the lives of New Orleanians of all colors would change during and after the Civil War. Banking, manufacturing, trade in foodstuffs from the Ohio and Missouri valleys, science and medicine were, however, all economic fallbacks for the loss of trade in southern agricultural crops. This wealth aided the continuing evolution of restaurants, markets, and home cooking in the city. Creole cooking survived because its founding characteristics were built around adaptations and blendings of many cultures. African adaptability and French thriftiness became the mottos of New Orleans housewives and their cooking. For visitors to the World's Industrial and Cotton Centennial (1884–1885), two cookbooks were compiled and published, both of which articulate these responses. The first by the Christian Woman's Exchange, *The Creole Cookery Book*, and the second by Lafcadio Hearn, *La Cuisine Creole*, provided extensive listings of recipes considered to be those of the city alone, and especially of the housewife, making the most of her dollar. By the end of the nineteenth century, the New Orleans table had been set by a history that went from poverty to wealth, back to some semblance of poverty again.

The pairing of New Orleans haute cuisine and *bonne femme* emerged fully articulated in the early twentieth century just as New Orleans were fashioning themselves as part of the New South.[11] Restaurants serving French and

---

11. Both Mary Land and Richard Collin talk of the two forms of New Orleans food, the one of classical French training and the other of economy. Land remarked upon the comfortable uniting of grand restaurant food and the food of home, the *bonne femme* in her kitchen (Land, *New Orleans Cuisine*, 9). For Collin in the 1970s, New Orleans was "one of the great eating cities of the world" precisely because of "two distinct genres of Creole cooking." The first was "more nearly French, with its love of deli-

Creole food, such as Galatoire's (1905), Arnaud's (1918), and Broussard's (1920), joined Antoine's in cementing the primacy of French conceptions of eating in an elite restaurant. Tortorici's (1900) and Kolb's (1909) were just two of the early Italian and German restaurants that added their own versions of European dining to the city.

Within this grand tradition of a developing Creole haute cuisine stood an older Genoese tradition, Solari's (founded in 1864 and closed in 1961), which represented and purveyed luxury: "fancy and staple groceries" and "fine wines and liquors." From its French Quarter corner, Solari's delivered groceries, served patrons at the counter ("no reading . . . between 12 and 1"), brought imported delicacies, and created its gumbos, roasted chickens, layer cakes (favorites were jelly cake and a layer cake with orange-custard filling), and much more for takeout. A candy counter filled with chocolates and "elephants, violins, or watches" shaped in marzipan made this emporium all the more opulent.

More modest traditions proved equally memorable, however, and more significant to the adaptive characteristics of New Orleans food. One example from this early twentieth-century period was the "decidedly unfussy space that even today doubles as both bar and main dining room" of Mandina's, born in 1920 in a grocery store turned neighborhood restaurant. Mandina's and many other eating places continued in the pattern of connections established in the nineteenth century: families, public markets, bars, and small groceries joined together in shaping the public sale and consumption of food.

It was an uneasy alliance, however. For more than one hundred years, the public markets, by law, maintained a monopoly over the sale of all perishables. The small grocery stores were restricted even in where they could be located. And only the elite and perhaps a few restaurants and butchers could avail themselves of ice, a precious commodity that arrived in the city from the Northeast in ships that would return with cotton and other products.

But by the late 1880s, Edison and Westinghouse had begun wiring the city for electricity. Local icehouses then could create block ice, which rested in the bottom of iceboxes. And, as refrigeration became the norm for small stores, all sorts of government regulations of markets began to be questioned and revised. By the 1930s, small grocers could be located within nine blocks of the nearest

cate and subtle sauces and its affinity for expensive haute dining in sumptuous surroundings." The other was "the poorer and earthier cooking, with its emphasis on cheapness as well as on robust spicing, which produces the great New Orleans Creole gumbo . . . as well as the traditional boiled seafood . . . in peppery sauces" (Collin, *Revised New Orleans*, 17–18).

public market. For some people, the public markets were no longer necessary, and for the city, no longer lucrative. The Poydras Market, for example, established in 1838, was torn down in the 1930s. By 1935, only nineteen public markets were operating, and in 1946 the city decided to sell or lease sixteen of them.

The small stores began to sell not only meat and other perishables, but also sandwiches. Eventually, many of them became small restaurants and bars, the neighborhood restaurants so very popular in the period 1940–1990. In 1900, nearly fifty small grocery stores were in the French Quarter alone, including Central Grocery (1906), famous for an enduring sandwich, the muffuletta. Like the Bégués and the Tujagues of the nineteenth century, Central Grocery owner Salvatore Lupo literally looked across the street to the market and dockworkers for his livelihood. He sold them bread and watched as they put together meats, cheeses, and olives.[12] From these ingredients, Lupo created the muffuletta—a plate-sized round sandwich, named for the bread that encloses it. The sandwich is more famous today than the other example that makes Central Grocery more unusual: it never became a full-fledged restaurant.

Segregation by race governed even these small restaurants, prohibiting African Americans from eating in white-only establishments, many of which employed them as cooks. In the African American community, windows offered takeout food for blacks and whites, who otherwise would not sit down at adjacent tables. Yet men and women, African Americans and whites in New Orleans, for the most part, ate the same types of food.

Practices of a common cuisine for a specific locale existed, of course, all over the world. What remained different about New Orleans was that food—in all its presentations—had a prominence in the culture, a public side, and a near disregard for the amalgamation of cultures that shaped its preparation for New Orleans tables. The public side came from the port, the markets, and the habits of shopping and discussing food. Alice Toklas, companion to Gertrude Stein, wrote of her 1930s visit to the city: "In New Orleans I walked down to the market every morning realizing that I would have to live in a dream of it for the rest of my life. How with such perfection, variety and abundance of material could one not be inspired to creative cooking?"

---

12. The seed-topped *muffuletta* loaf is filled with Genoa salami or mortadella and Cappicola ham and three cheeses, usually layers of sliced Provolone, mozzarella, and Swiss. The crucial ingredient is olive salad, a mixture of green, unstuffed olives, pimentos, celery, garlic, cocktail onions, capers, oregano, parsley, olive oil, red wine vinegar, salt, and pepper.

Most notable among early-twentieth-century food writings was *The Pica-yune Creole Cook Book* or, as it was entitled in its first four editions from 1900 to 1910 and its last (1987), *The Picayune's Creole Cook Book*. Compiled and edited anonymously, the *Picayune* became to countless men and women a compendium of food customs, race relations, religious observations, and festivals. Published in fifteen different editions over the whole of the twentieth century, the cook-book professed to aid the new woman, both white and "Negro." At the same time, the anonymous compilers always emphasized the "old-time Mammy." As scholar Jessica Harris has pointed out, the centrality of African-derived cook-ing is evident in much of the book, despite the authors' decided emphasis on a French heritage.

The book is still a useful manual, still in many ways "definitive." In authori-tative and ethnocentric tone, the compilers give lengthy statements about foods both familiar and unusual. About sweetbreads, for example, they write: "Scarcely one person in ten, if the question is put directly, can tell just what a sweetbread is, and they can scarcely be blamed, for the most distinguished lexicographers, from Webster down to the late compiler of the *New Century*, fail to give the correct definition. . . . Every old French dictionary . . . define[s] sweetbreads as the glands in the throat of any young animal, more generally the sucking calf. . . . The old Creole gourmets have had infinite amusement over the defini-tions given by American dictionary makers." And for pork chops, the *Picayune* is similarly pleasurable in its straightforward pronouncement: "The Creoles will never eat a broiled pork chop." For many other dishes, the *Picayune* both de-lights in its vocabulary and gives clues about the longevity of recipes. As the compilers say of Sassafras Mead: "Drink while effervescing. . . . The above recipe has been in use in Creole homes for generations." Chapters on regular fare as well as Lenten soups, the *bouilli*, sweet *entrements*, and many others make the book a dictionary itself not only of food but also of language and culture.

Of course, the people who staffed and frequented the restaurants, the cus-tomers who might order from and visit Solari's, and the housewives and cooks who governed home cooking also contended with other modifications. By the twentieth century, railways crisscrossed the United States and diverted traffic from the Mississippi River and the port of New Orleans. The city had not been queen of the South since the 1850s and was, by the early twentieth century, no longer one of the nation's biggest metropolitan areas. Instead, a new mixture of creativity, poverty, decay, and economic growth reinvigorated eating as still central to New Orleans culture. More than thirty breweries operated in this period. In 1898, there were eight hundred places one could drink beer, wine, or other alcoholic beverages.[13] The development of jazz in some of these places alongside the older, classical musical traditions also made for a different city. The centrality of jazz to the later tourist industry and to serious jazz enthusiasts would mean more eyes upon the city and, ultimately, its food. Jazz, like the city's official markets, was also a public enjoyment, a passion of the streets.

The French Quarter was no longer quaint, but seedy and crumbling, and at times, raucous. In 1912, the English novelist and essayist John Galsworthy described the domed room of the St. Louis Hotel, as a "fine—yea, even a splendid room" now with "the vivid strength of things—gone all gone!" Galsworthy found a horse rambling inside the disintegrating dining place and also recalled that it had once accommodated the sale of slaves. Instead of the Creoles and the affluent businessmen as neighbors of the old hotel, new immigrants populated the French Quarter. Many were Sicilian, like Lupo of Central Grocery.

The Sicilians experienced prejudice as well, adding to the layers of inequities within the city. But alongside the Creoles of color who dominated several of the vegetable markets within the public market system and some of their butchers who have remained leaders in the sausage-making traditions of the city, the Sicilians came to dominate the fruit markets. They also owned many of the small grocery stores in the city: 19 percent in 1900 and 49 percent by 1920, according to sources found by Chef John Folse. The term *Creole-Italian* came into parlance to describe seafood, meats, and vegetable dishes, many involving tomato sauces, but also the use of eggplants, peppers, squash of various kinds, and artichokes.

World War I brought increased attention on the city. Those Americans who once spent time in Europe now came to New Orleans. The new tourists wrote home about the picturesqueness: the Roman Candy Man driving his mule-drawn wagon, African American women crying out in French the names of their products, Native Americans selling their herbs, and vendors on mule carts, marketing their produce through the city streets. The traveler John Martin Hammond recalled the simplicity of "the restaurants and eating houses . . .

---

13. Further study is needed on how such establishments shaped the city and its food. In late-eighteenth-century America, New Orleans had 1 tavern keeper for every 71 residents as compared to Boston (1 for every 694) and Philadelphia (1 for every 429) (Price, quoted in Hanger, 65). In the early period, Hanger also reports, several free women of color operated taverns.

a bare room with pine tables and a sanded or saw-dusted floor. Not much for looks are they, but the food they serve is most delicious. Old Antoine's, indeed, has a reputation for quality even in far Paris."

The downfall in the economy that came after the 1927 flood, the Great Depression, and then rationing during World War II limited food choices. Typical New Orleanians praised the rules of thriftiness advocated in their cookbooks and practiced it, by necessity, in their small restaurants, more than they complained about what they lacked. Writer Mary Lou Widmer described this sentiment when she noted that New Orleanians could visit numerous "small ma-and-pa family restaurants all over town, where you could get a meal of fried chicken, beans and rice, and turnip greens for a dollar or so." Here again were the southern and the African American influences combined with those of the Creoles of color. The ingredients they preferred were "not rationed, hard to get, or expensive." Relative plenty in a time of deprivation may well have been because the old ways (fishing, for example) still meant that individuals could bring food home at the end of the day or even sell to other homes and restaurants. As in the earliest history, the cast-off foods (the odd fish, the tough meat) were valued in commonly known soups and distinctive New Orleans dishes such as *grillades*.

In these traditions of making-do and the work of the family as an economic unit came other small restaurants, some that gained considerable fame and brought down-home cooking styles closer and closer to that of haute cuisine. The two types of cuisine became recognizable embodiments of one another. Bread pudding, for example, that could be found at the windows of many take-out restaurants and the sweet shops all over the city, became a dessert, slightly embellished, served at the "old line" restaurants.

One restaurant that began as a family-run sandwich shop emerged in 1941 as Dooky Chase's Restaurant. With the Creole cooking and warm hospitality of Leah Chase, it grew into a respected fine-dining establishment, sought after by local African Americans and visiting military, then later by many others who wanted to taste her distinctive dark gumbo and other New Orleans dishes. Another restaurant that opened in this period was that of Helen Dejan Pollack, later called Chez Helene, first on Perdido Street. Others of a similar nature are now mostly forgotten. Jackie Pressner Gothard's family, for example, ran a Jewish delicatessen that had grown from her grandparents' and then her parents' grocery store. During World War II, homesick soldiers from New York found on the Pressner's tables familiar foods with a New Orleans flair.

World War II shipbuilding created prosperity for New Orleans that continued into the 1950s. That growth also brought widespread attention to Creole cuisine. A writer for the *New York Herald Tribune*, Clementine Paddleford, especially spotlighted New Orleans food. Paddleford had first turned her attention to New Orleans in the late 1930s, when she spotted the genius of African American Lena Richard and her gumbo shops, cooking schools, and catering businesses. Paddleford helped Richard secure a contract for the second printing of her locally published cookbook, *The New Orleans Cook Book* (1940), with prestigious Houghton Mifflin. But the bulk of the New York journalist's work on the city began in the late 1940s. In 1948, she wrote a small cookbook, *Recipes from Antoine's Kitchen*, proclaiming, "Nowhere else in the world is eating so surrounded by mystery, by legend." For her columns, she interviewed Creoles of all backgrounds and was not adverse to giving them full credit for unusual traditions like *croxignolles* (or, as called elsewhere, krullers, crullers, frogs, or doughnuts). In this way, she encouraged New Orleanians to preserve their foodways and persuaded the national community to take notice of the city, just as more writing on food across the United States in general was beginning to appear.

In his wide-ranging book on the city's growth, Peirce Lewis argues for a quiet and steady nonchalance that New Orleanians brought to their love of the city in the 1970s and earlier. New Orleanians do not love their city because of any "boosterism," according to him. Their love of the city was not of the type that needed broadcasting to the world. But national and local reporting in the 1940s through the 1960s, along with the downturn in the economy and the threat of an unwanted superhighway through the Vieux Carré, mobilized citizens in a new way. This mobilization grew into this very "boosterism," at least in terms of what has today come to be the city's main focus on tourism.

In this campaign, the French Quarter was saved but the mostly African American and Creole businesses along portions of Claiborne and St. Claude avenues were destroyed. The saving of the French Quarter meant revitalization but also the beginning of a focused era of tourism. One key player in this was Owen Edward Brennan. In 1946, he founded his namesake restaurant on a dare from his friend "Count" Arnaud (of Arnaud's Restaurant) that an Irishman could not run a French restaurant. Brennan shaped a successful venture that continued even after his early death. The remarkable Brennan family food dynasty eventually vaulted Commander's Palace and other restaurants to world prominence, to positions that spoke for New Orleans *and* the nation.

The period between the 1950s and the 1980s also saw the popularity of more neighborhood restaurants, such as Eddie's in the Seventh Ward and the still-revered Willie Mae's Scotch House on St. Ann Street, and the continuing vitality of older ones like Casamento's on Magazine Street and the aforementioned Chez Helene. In a new location on North Robertson, Chez Helene gained national fame when *Frank's Place*, the short-lived but critically acclaimed television show inspired by Chef Austin Leslie, aired in 1988. CBS liked the series since it combined both the public and the private lives of characters. For New Orleanians, such restaurants kept "alive and vigorous many of the city's most traditional dishes."

At the end of the twentieth century, home-style small establishments and the grand restaurants grew to represent New Orleans to the world and to present tourists with the food they expected. Ruth's Chris Steak House (1965) and Popeyes Fried Chicken (1972), both of which might have once been safely put into the down-home category, were so successful that they spurred national franchises. A group of Uptown and Mid-City bistros evolved in small houses and abandoned corner groceries. These establishments imitated traditions of neighborhood restaurants but employed adventuresome chefs trained elsewhere in the United States and willing to serve new dishes.

It was in this environment that Acadiana-born Chef Paul Prudhomme changed much about the way New Orleans food is eaten and discussed. Prudhomme was the first to experiment with "Nouvelle Creole"—contemporary New Orleans cooking that borrows from local customs while using a broader ingredient palette, evolving methods of food preparation, and simple but formal presentations. Prudhomme's success brought books, television appearances, and recipes that initiated the era of the New Orleans celebrity chef. Emeril Lagasse, Susan Spicer, John Besh, and others today follow Prudhomme in teaching the world about New Orleans. Prudhomme himself trained a bevy of other chefs: Frank Brigtsen and Greg Sonnier, to name just two who gained attention of their own. Prudhomme's ideas about food built upon the role of New Orleans as one of the few representative regional cuisines in North America, but he also changed much about North American food in general. Although the public often confused Creole and Cajun, food historian Sylvia Lovegren credits Prudhomme as teaching an appreciation of local food everywhere and showing that dining-out need not be in "a traditional flocked-velvet dining room."

The late twentieth century also saw the ascendancy of New Orleans dining experts with long ties to the city and others from "away" (as New Orleanians say). The anonymous female home economists employed by New Orleans Public Service, Inc. (NOPSI) compiled small brochures of recipes distributed in utility bills, on streetcars, and on buses. In newspaper columns, in blogs, in reference questions to libraries, and on the street, countless residents still seek these old-time favorites accommodated to include canned goods and shortcuts of various types.[14]

Adding to the canon of New Orleans culinary traditions in the same way that the Christian Woman's Exchange and the *Times-Picayune* had were local writers such as Deirdre Stanforth, Nathaniel Burton, Peter Feibleman, Marcelle Bienvenu, Gene Bourg, the members of the Junior League, John DeMers, Lolis Eric Elie, and Poppy Tooker. All these attracted and still attract national attention for the city's foodways. Notably, too, there is a radio show, three hours a day, six days a week, where food writer Tom Fitzmorris keeps New Orleanians themselves talking of restaurants, cooking, wine, and any type of dish they wish to discuss. In the tradition of the outsider Lafcadio Hearn and his consultation with locals, William Kaufman and Sister Mary Ursula Cooper and Emeril Lagasse garnered acclaim for their New Orleans cookbooks.[15] More often than not, these writers were interested in home cooking. As food editor of the *Times-Picayune* Judy Walker pointed out in 2007, New Orleanians eat well at home. Most "actually cook," an activity that surprised her upon her arrival in the city in 2000 from Phoenix.

The complexity of New Orleans food continues. In one final example, consider Schwegmann's grocery stores and their progression within the history of food in the city. John G. Schwegmann Jr., the visionary supermarket developer, was the grandson of a German-born small grocer who established his store in 1869 just downriver of the French Quarter in the neighborhood now called Bywater. In the late 1940s, the younger Schwegmann and his two brothers opened

---

14. NOPSI and the company that came next, Entergy, collected some of these recipes in publications such as *Creole Cuisine* (1951), *Creole Favorites* (1966, 1971), and *From Woodstoves to Microwaves—Cooking with Entergy* (1997).

15. In the period 1970 to the present, over 250 cookbooks on New Orleans food were published, almost three times the number of cookbooks published before 1969. While this is reflective of a national trend, this figure, too, needs further study to show how food traditions are continued or disrupted by various forces.

the first Schwegmann Brothers Giant Super Market on St. Claude Avenue. Expanding from this Eighth Ward base, Schwegmann's many stores sold everything from groceries to fishing gear and liquor.

They introduced a local version of self-service shopping to New Orleanians.[16] As market historian Sally K. Reeves recalled, for some families as late as the 1960s "food arrived in a wooden crate, atop shaved ice" after being ordered and often delivered from the store. Schwegmann's offered a 10 percent discount to those foregoing delivery, and the incentive to "make groceries" (as New Orleanians call grocery shopping) at Schwegmann's became all the rage. In this way, Schwegmann's almost monopolized the city's grocery shopping. At one time, the 155,000-square-foot Old Gentilly Road location was the largest supermarket in the world. Its uniquely New Orleans qualities were not lost on tourists or newcomers. Historian Joseph Logsdon recalled one of the defining moments of his baptism into the city in 1964 as he watched people buying "beers when they walked into Schwegmann's" to drink while shopping. Schwegmann's distributed lists in the order of their shelves to make shopping easier. In the 1980s, law firms and other businesses handed out these lists, considered a benefit to their employees. Schwegmann's success (and those of national chains that moved into the area in the 1980s) precipitated the decline in the corner groceries. But financial troubles forced the family to sell the chain in 1996.

To bring the story full circle to 2008, the Louisiana-based Rouses Supermarket chain recently bought out the New Orleans stores run by A&P, one of the first national grocery chains. Rouses' publicity promotes stocking what locals want as well as local products. There are also a number of small groceries (some are small chains) that still exist, to which New Orleanians remain so fiercely loyal that some apologize for entering the nationally based Whole Foods. No doubt there are many grocery and food stories still to tell.

With all such changes, culinary New Orleans reshapes itself, a continual process throughout the city's history but one now with daunting challenges. As H. L. Mencken said of Baltimore in 1927, there is now "increasing standardization and devitalization." Mencken was talking about how hard it was to find *local* dishes. With characteristic pomp, he proclaimed that "the American people have become the dullest and least happy race in Christendom. There was a time when even the poorest man, in such a place as Baltimore, at least

---

16. National chain Piggly Wiggly, which had arrived in 1919, was not nearly as adventuresome or appealing.

ate decent food." For Mencken, the city had slipped to some very disappointing levels.

There are ways of seeing New Orleans being reduced to some incarnation of this same predicament. As New Orleans poet Kalamu ya Salaam once said, "Living poor and Black in Big Easy is never as much fun as our music, food, smiles and laughter make it seem." Most New Orleanians believe that food here is no longer as distinctive as it once was. The availability of cheap food from other places threatens at every turn the farmer who can grow and sell food locally. Besides the lack of corner stores, gone, too, are many of the small neighborhood restaurants and bars that made possible not only the merging of food traditions but also discussions of the best ingredients between persons of diverse backgrounds. Hurricanes Katrina and Rita and the levee failures did major damage to these restaurants; to farmers, fishermen, and hunters; and to a whole way of living.

But what remains may well be what always saved Creole food, its adaptability and the passion of New Orleanians for this attribute. These two, adaptability and passion, were always the foundation of the city's cuisine. These two were always the work of the community as a whole: the socialization of an active engagement in what to eat, when to eat, and, especially, how what was being eaten tasted. To be called a "cuisine," anthropologist Sidney Mintz once noted, a culture must have "a population that eats that cuisine with sufficient frequency to consider themselves experts on it. They all believe, and care that they believe, that they know what it consists of, how it is made, and how it should taste. In short, a genuine cuisine has common social roots: it is the food of a community—albeit often a very large community."

Today in New Orleans there are still large pockets of such a community. In the fourteen dishes given in this book, people are joined mainly in the celebratory meals or special, once-weekly menus—not in the everyday. However, the dishes are all recognizable, all part of the knowledge New Orleanians bring to their tables, now usually filled with other ingredients available in sufficient quantity for fair prices.[17] Most importantly, food remains central and public to New Orleanians. Along with music, it is a defining characteristic of the twenty-first-century economy. Some residents are cynical about this, and their skepticism is another healthy form of adaptability. But in discussing food of times

---

17. Recent books by Elsa Hahne and Sara Roahen tell exclusively how New Orleanians eat today.

gone by and foods today, it is the residents more so than the tourists who still find an easy way to use food, in reality or in talk, as a way of creating goodwill. Most New Orleanians view finding and creating good food as part of their responsibilities as citizens of the city, as neighbors to one another. At the end of a meal or mention of a particular food, the final question is evaluative and inclusive. They ask, "So, how was it?"

SAZERAC

Sara Roahen

The Sazerac is New Orleans' most emblematic cocktail, first, because of its longevity and, second, because its chronological permutations help to recount key moments in the city's own history. Today's Sazerac is a chilled blend of rye whiskey or bourbon, a touch of anise-flavored liqueur, dashes from one or two bitters formulas, sugar, and a twist of lemon, which is either left in the glass or not. The cocktail has traveled a lengthy road to this current incarnation.

The story, as it is more or less told in New Orleans–based writings and in folklore, begins with Antoine Amédée Peychaud, a son of French colonialists, who was born on the Caribbean island of Saint-Domingue (now Haiti) and who escaped that country as a young child during violent slave rebellions. According to many writings and the research of Phil Greene, one of Peychaud's descendents, Peychaud was separated from his parents during the chaotic evacuation; it is not known whether he came directly to New Orleans or whether he first spent some time in Jamaica (where one branch of his family settled temporarily), Cuba (where other evacuees found refuge), or elsewhere.

It is almost certain that Peychaud ultimately arrived in New Orleans when he was still a child. Eventually, he became an apothecary and operated a drug store at 437 Royal Street (then 123 Royal Street) in the French Quarter, where he dispensed a bitters formula that was perhaps integral to the making of the first Sazeracs. Peychaud's Aromatic Cocktail Bitters, his legacy, remains a key Sazerac ingredient today.

In a 2005 article, "Antoine Amedee Peychaud, Pharmacist and New Orleans Cocktail Legend," published in *Mixologist: Journal of the American Cocktail*, Phil Greene writes that while Peychaud no doubt existed, he has perhaps become "an admixture of fact and folklore in the tradition of Johnny Appleseed, Paul Bunyan and even George Washington." It is with this in mind that we must consider the less-corroborated aspects of Peychaud's—and thus the Sazerac's—history. Some accounts, for example, posit that Peychaud made his bitters according to a recipe that he brought with him from Saint-Domingue. While his bitters may well have evolved from a family recipe or from a recipe that originated on the island of his birth, it is unlikely that a child would have had the foresight to pack such an item during a frenzied escape. According to Greene's research, Peychaud was born in 1803 (Greene cites a correspondence with Michel Peychaud of Bordeaux, France, and also two newspaper death notices). As the Haitian Revolution and the associated violence ended the following year, in 1804, it is possible that Peychaud was only an infant when he left the colony.

Additionally up for question is the claim—common in scantily researched writings and in New Orleans folklore—that Peychaud single-handedly invented the American cocktail. It is probably true that in addition to dispensing medicines and healing tonics at his pharmacy, Peychaud dribbled his bitters into portions of cognac. Greene (and before him, the author Stanley Clisby Arthur) describes him as a "joiner" and a member of a Masonic order, and he writes that Peychaud's "cronies" would retreat to the pharmacy on Royal Street to drink following meetings of the Masonic Lodge.

The running story, an account of which can be found in Arthur's *Famous New Orleans Drinks and How to Mix 'Em*, published in 1937, is that Peychaud served his brandy-and-bitters concoctions in double-ended egg cups, or *coquetiers*. English mispronunciations of the French resulted in a word that sounded close to "cocktail"; thus was the American cocktail born in Peychaud's pharmacy, both the product and the name. It is a good story, and it may contain some element of truth. But the English-language word "cocktail" appeared in an 1806 newspaper editorial in Hudson, New York, referencing a mixture of spirits, sugar, water, and bitters. This was long before Peychaud reached adulthood and entered the pharmacy trade.

There are other claims to the coining of "cocktail" and to the concept's invention. While listing them is unnecessary to our exploration of the Sazerac, let their existence cast some doubt onto whether Peychaud invented the American cocktail. Such doubt lessens neither his bitters' contribution to the Sazerac, nor his own contribution to New Orleans' native cocktail culture.

By most accounts the first drinks called Sazeracs were served in a bar located at 13 Exchange Alley (the building is, in 2008, a Walgreen's pharmacy) and owned by John B. Schiller, a local importer of the French brandies of Sazerac de Forge et Fils. Although a few sources contend that a Sewell Taylor owned the business, Schiller's name is more often associated with the bar that opened in 1859 and was named the Sazerac Coffee House. Again, by most accounts, the signature cocktail there incorporated brandy and bitters and, eventually, a drib-ble of absinthe: the original Sazerac cocktail.

During his presentation at the October 2007 Southern Foodways Alli-ance symposium in Oxford, Mississippi, contemporary cocktail historian David Wondrich countered these previous accounts, and with them much of the Sazerac lore that is accepted as gospel in New Orleans. According to Wondrich, the Sazerac cocktail wasn't a fixed entity as far back as New Orleanians tend to imagine. The Sazerac Coffee House was, indeed, famous for its Sazerac cocktails. Until around 1910, however, a "Sazerac cocktail" was most likely either simply a cocktail made with Sazerac label brandy and/or any number of cocktails pre-pared in the signature style of the Sazerac Coffee House. During a telephone interview in November 2007, Wondrich explained that the descriptions of Sazerac cocktails before 1910 or so were too varied for them all to be referring to a single cocktail preparation.

Wondrich offered Lafcadio Hearn's *La Cuisine Creole* cookbook as evidence that the Sazerac as we know it today was not a significant player in nineteenth-century New Orleans. Regarded as representative of eating and drinking in Creole New Orleans—including the French Quarter—at the time of its print-ing in 1885, the book's section on drinks is absent a recipe for a cocktail called Sazerac. It does, by the way, include instructions for making whiskey, brandy, or gin cocktails "New Orleans Style," and these do closely resemble the form of today's Sazerac, minus the important anise flavor: "Two dashes of Boker's, Angostura or Peychaud bitters—either will make a fine cocktail. One lump of sugar, one piece of lemon peel, one tablespoonful of water, one wine-glassful of liquor, etc., with plenty of ice. Stir well and strain into a cocktail glass."

It was in the 1880s when the owner of the Sazerac Coffee House (then a man named William McQuoid, according to Wondrich) began to market a line of bottled cocktails nationwide under the Sazerac name. The line included a whiskey cocktail. By 1900, the Sazerac Coffee House was widely known as a cocktail destination. "It's the usual story of commerce coming into it," Wondrich said during the telephone interview.

It is interesting to note that at the time of Wondrich's 2007 lecture, which he titled "You Call That a Sazerac? The Curious and the Contradictory History of New Orleans' Signature Cocktail," his extensive research had yielded scant mention of any cocktails whatsoever served in the French Quarter prior to 1900. Juleps and slings, yes, but cocktails seemed to be relegated primarily to the American sector of the city (upriver, or west of Canal Street) rather than the Creole sector, which included the French Quarter. Additionally, Wondrich reported that in the early 1900s, when the name Sazerac became affixed to the recipe we know today, the whiskey/bitters/anise cocktail was just as popular in other parts of the country as it was in New Orleans; it remains a classic American cocktail in the minds and recipe books of all traditional cocktail makers in this country. Why, then, did the Sazerac become this city's signature drink even while relatively falling off the radar in others? Why do New Orleanians take such pride in claiming the Sazerac as their own?[1] "Because in New Orleans they didn't change and follow trends. They found something good and stuck to it," Wondrich answered, adding that he has not finished exploring the complicated history of the Sazerac. "The problem is there's so much myth and the myth is so entrenched."

Most sources assert that absinthe was added to the Sazerac around 1870. Certainly, it was served in bars such as the Sazerac Coffee House during that era, as it was a popular spirit throughout New Orleans. Absinthe was invented near the end of the eighteenth century, in Switzerland, by a Frenchman aspiring to create a digestive that contained wormwood and other herbs with medicinal quantities. By the mid-nineteenth century, absinthe was the favored drink in bohemian Paris, where cocktail hour became known as *l'heure verte*, or "the green hour," so named for absinthe's distinctive color. In their book *Absinthe, Sip of Seduction: A Contemporary Guide* (2003), Betina Wittels and Robert Hermesch write that "the popularity of the drink stretched across to America, spanning from New York to San Francisco. But absinthe received perhaps its most enthusiastic American welcome in the 'Little Paris of America,' New Orleans." They continue, "New Orleans and absinthe seemed to be made for each other—both sinfully delectable and equally enamored by some, as abhorred by others."

The Old Absinthe House Bar at the corner of Bourbon and Bienville streets was renowned for its patrons—Walt Whitman, Andrew Jackson, and

---

1. In April 2008, Senator Ed Murray introduced a bill in the Louisiana legislature to make the Sazerac the state cocktail.

Mark Twain reportedly among them—as well as for a marble fountain faucet on its bar from which water dripped into glasses of absinthe. (A traditional preparation involves placing a lump of sugar on a flat spoon with holes, balancing the spoon over the mouth of a tall glass containing absinthe, and then letting cold water drip slowly over the sugar until it dissolves. The cold sugar water turns the absinthe an opalescent green or grayish color—the transformation is called *louche*—and pries open the liqueur's strong anise bouquet.)

During this period, local companies such as Green Opal and Milky Way began to produce absinthe in New Orleans, and many drinks were fashioned with the liqueur as their chief ingredient. Among them were the absinthe frappé (absinthe, water, and simple syrup stirred vigorously in a glass with crushed ice), absinthe Suissesse (absinthe, vermouth, and sugar shaken with egg white and poured over crème de menthe), and the Ojen cocktail (absinthe, Peychaud's bitters, and soda). All three of these drinks are still served in New Orleans in classic restaurants and bars or in newer restaurants and bars that have a mission to carry on tradition. But, as with the Sazerac, these drinks today are made with wormwood-free absinthe substitutes.

After two murder cases occasioned the outlaw of absinthe in Switzerland in 1910, the liqueur was banned in the United States in 1912. The consensus was that the ingredient wormwood contained dangerous psychoactive properties. Absinthe producers, such as Pernod in France, responded by removing the wormwood from their products; the contemporary result is *pastis*, an anise-flavored liqueur. However, beverage recipes using absinthe and wormwood were still published in the fifth edition of *The Picayune Creole Cook* book in 1916 and were not dropped until the sixth edition, after Prohibition eliminated references to the use of wines and liquors in the cookbook.

Anise flavor is essential to the Sazerac; and Legendre Herbsaint, today produced by the Sazerac Company in Kentucky, is commonly used by New Orleans bartenders. The accepted method is to swirl a splash of pastis around the inside of a glass in which the Sazerac will be served and then to pour the pastis out. What is left clinging to the interior wall of the glass will be enough to properly flavor the cocktail.

Many countries worldwide have since legalized the production, sale, and consumption of wormwood-inclusive absinthe. At the time of this writing, the U.S. government has begun to relax its absinthe regulations; two wormwood-inclusive absinthes are currently on the market. Of note is the native Louisianian

Ted Breaux, an environmental chemist, who legally produces artisanal varieties of absinthe in France, in a distillery designed by Gustave Eiffel. Breaux sources his herbs from growers all over that country.

Besides the Sazerac, absinthe's licorice-flavored legacy in New Orleans extends to some savory recipes, including perhaps oysters Rockefeller, which was first served at Antoine's Restaurant. While the dish's inventor, Jules Alciatore, never divulged his original recipe—a tradition continued by Alciatore's descendents more than a century later—the preparation of oysters Rockefeller at Antoine's and elsewhere does by definition display a subtle anise flavor, as discussed later in this book.

At least as far back as Mary Moore Bremer's 1932 cookbook, *New Orleans Recipes*, New Orleanians were mixing their Sazeracs with Angostura as well as Peychaud's bitters. In fact, Bremer used Angostura and orange bitters in hers— no Peychaud's bitters at all. The two bitters contribute different characteristics to the cocktail. Angostura bitters, which according to the company's Web site were invented in 1824 and are currently distilled in Trinidad, have a dark, clove-and-bark-like flavor with orange rind and other earthy undertones. Peychaud's bitters, meanwhile, are brighter in color and flavor; they have an anise edge and a peppercorn quality.

It is no coincidence that the question of how the first American cocktail came to be (was it Peychaud's invention or not?) is caught up with a bitters maker at least in part. In his 2001 book, *Straight Up or On the Rocks: The Story of the American Cocktail*, William Grimes writes:

> Early observers seem to agree that the key ingredient defining a cocktail was bitters [made by infusing distilled spirits with spices, fruits, and botanical ingredients]. When Edward Henry Durrell, visiting New Orleans in the 1840s, expressed puzzlement at the term "brandy cocktail," an obliging native gave him a quick tutorial: "Now the difference between a brandy cocktail and a brandy toddy is this: a brandy toddy is made by adding together a little water, a little sugar, and a great deal of brandy—mix well and drink. A brandy cocktail is composed of the same ingredients, with the addition of a shade of Stoughton's bitters; so that the bitters draw the line of demarcation."

Angostura and orange bitters were not the only market competition for Peychaud during his lifetime. His descendant, Greene, found advertisements for more than a dozen different bitters and patent medicines besides Peychaud's in a single issue of the *New Orleans Bee*, published on March 1, 1859, including Dr. J. Hostetter's Celebrated Stomach Bitters, Richardson's Sherry Wine Bitters, and Dr. Ham's Aromatic Invigorating Spirit. Greene also located one of Peychaud's own ads, which appeared in an 1857 issue of the *Bee*, that mentioned a "cordial introduced into general use" at the Sazerac Coffee House that incorporated his bitters, thus verifying that Peychaud's bitters were, indeed, used at the oft-alleged birthplace of the Sazerac.

Over time, domestic rye whiskey replaced brandy as the brown liquor of choice in New Orleans. This was true at the Sazerac Coffee House, which eventually came to be known as just the Sazerac House. Arthur leads the reader to believe that the switch from brandy to whiskey at the Sazerac House occurred around the time that the bar changed hands from John B. Schiller to his bookkeeper, Thomas Handy. (Arthur writes that Handy's rye of choice was Maryland Club.) Handy also eventually purchased the rights to Peychaud's Aromatic Cocktail Bitters, which he later sold to McQuoid.

Other sources assert that the switch from brandy to rye occurred slightly earlier, during the Civil War, when imports were cost prohibitive. Mary Land includes a comprehensive chapter about beverages and bartending in her 1954 cookbook, *Louisiana Cookery*, in which she expresses her distaste for the switch and a possible reason for it: "As time passed brandy was replaced by whisky to suit the plebeian taste of the Americans who had infiltrated the Creole city."

It should be noted that until Hurricane Katrina forced him into retirement in August 2005, Martin Sawyer, the octogenarian bartender at the Rib Room in the Omni Royal Orleans Hotel, mixed his famous Sazeracs with both rye whiskey and brandy, in homage to the original recipe and the modern one. During an oral history interview conducted by Amy Evans for the Southern Foodways Alliance in March 2005, Sawyer correctly acknowledged that some bartenders in New Orleans today stray yet further from the original recipe, using ordinary bourbon whiskey instead of rye. He also stated his preference for using homemade simple syrup over a muddled sugar cube; for stirring and straining his Sazeracs instead of shaking them; for always serving a Sazerac up, never on the rocks; and for dropping his lemon twist into the cocktail to slowly release its oils, rather than simply twisting a lemon peel over a Sazerac and then discarding it. "In my opinion, it's supposed to have a brownish-reddish-looking color. You know what I mean? Not pale," Sawyer said. Other than the addition of brandy, which is rare, Sawyer's formula/opinion jibes with—or at least comes close to—the method by which the majority of the city's Sazeracs are constructed today.

Of course, the earliest cocktails in New Orleans, as elsewhere, were neither chilled nor contained ice. In his *Straight Up or On the Rocks*, the aforementioned Grimes writes that "before commercial ice harvesting began in the mid-nineteenth century, only substantial estates or hotels maintained icehouses." Grimes credits the 1930s invention of the ice plow for making ice a commercial proposition. "Production soared and the price dropped—enough to influence the preparation of mixed drinks."

Sometime in the first part of the twentieth century, the Sazerac House relocated, and its name was changed to the Sazerac Bar. At this point, women were allowed to patronize the Sazerac Bar only one day per year. The author Robert Kinney reveled in this policy of discrimination in his 1942 writing *The Bachelor in New Orleans*: "At 300 Carondelet Street, is man's domain and dear to the heart of every male Bachelor in New Orleans worthy of the name. Here is served the Sazerac Cocktail as it is made from the original and now secret recipe. Ladies are not welcome—save on Mardi Gras Day." However, on September 26, 1949, a group of brave women entered the bar and broke the tradition.

In 1949, the Sazerac Bar moved inside the Roosevelt Hotel, where the Ramos Gin Fizz, another classic New Orleans cocktail, became a house specialty. A Ramos Gin Fizz is made by vigorously shaking crushed ice with gin, powdered sugar, orange flower water, citrus juices, egg white, soda, milk or cream, and, optionally, vanilla extract; the whole is then strained into a tall glass. The Roosevelt eventually became the Fairmont Hotel; the Sazerac Bar remained there until Hurricane Katrina closed the entire operation. While the Sazerac lives on in other establishments, it is remarkably more difficult to find a bartender to mix the more time-consuming Ramos Gin Fizz.

Other classic New Orleans cocktails include chilled brandy milk punch, which is often drunk during the day; the Hurricane, a strong rum punch and currently the house drink at Pat O'Brien's bar; the mint julep; and café brûlot, for which sugar, spices, and lemon rind are steeped in brandy, which is then dramatically lit on fire and added to hot, strong, dripped coffee, as described later in this book.

Recent years have brought about a nationwide resurgence of interest in classic cocktails and the people who make them; it is *au courant* to call serious bartenders mixologists. It is also customary to pay the modern mixologist well for his expertise—it is not unusual to spend fifteen to twenty dollars on a well-made cocktail in a major city like New York. Though any mixologist of merit knows how to mix a Sazerac, regardless of his or her geographical location, the drink today makes most sense in New Orleans, where it is not merely the drink of the moment but a cocktail of the centuries.

One recipe appears on the Web site of the Sazerac Company, maker of Peychaud's Aromatic Cocktail Bitters and Herbsaint. Note that as it contains rye whiskey instead of brandy, and Herbsaint instead of absinthe, it is hardly "original," though its name is the "Original Sazerac Cocktail." It begins by instructing the maker to take two heavy-bottomed 3^1/$_2$-ounce bar glasses and to fill one with ice. The other glass will be filled with "a lump of sugar and just enough water to moisten it." The maker should then "crush the saturated lump of sugar with a bar spoon. Add a few drops of Peychaud's Bitters, a jigger of rye whisky [*sic*] and several lumps of ice and stir briskly. Empty the first glass of ice, dash in several drops of Herbsaint, twirl the glass rapidly and shake out the Herbsaint. Enough of it will cling to the glass to impart the desired flavor. Strain into this glass the rye whisky mixture prepared in the other glass. Twist a lemon peel over the glass, but do not put it in the drink."

Mary Land's recipe, from *Louisiana Cookery*, contains Angostura as well as Peychaud's bitters:

THE SAZERAC

"To make a sazerac [*sic*], muddle together a teaspoon of sugar and a few dashes of Peychaud bitters with a teaspoon of water. Add a dash of Angostura bitters and two jiggers of rye whisky [*sic*]. Rinse the inside of a short, heavy glass with absinthe. Place two ice cubes in this glass and pour the mixed sazerac ingredients over the ice. A small drop of lemon peel squeezing may be added if desired. Some mixers rub the edge of the glass with lemon."

One recipe favored by the Culinary History Group does not involve the long process of cracking the ice just so. Indeed, it is ice-free and a modification of various recipes, such as that in Bremer's book cited above and in *Brennan's New Orleans Cookbook:*

SAZERAC

Two to three dashes simple syrup

Two dashes Peychaud's Bitters

One dash Angostura Bitters

One and one/fourth ounces bourbon (or if none available, whiskey)

After stirring these ingredients, add three dashes of Herbsaint or another pastis. This is best done in a chilled measuring glass. Roll around to coat inside of glass. Then strain the drink into an Old Fashioned glass. Add a twist of lemon peel.

FRENCH BREAD

Michael Mizell-Nelson

Bread symbolizes maintenance of life as well as deprivation, as in a bread-and-water diet. A staple throughout the world, bread figures prominently throughout New Orleans culinary history as variations on the French cap loaf and other styles. It accompanied the finest meals, and stale loaves from the same bakeries fed the poor. New Orleanians could build a day's meals around loaves: *pain perdu* (lost bread or French toast) for breakfast, a poor boy sandwich for lunch, and *pistolet* (a smaller oval roll) with dinner, which one could end with either bread pudding or Russian cake, amalgamations of leftover bread and cake, respectively. Fittingly, the history of bread in New Orleans cuisine demonstrates a culinary mixing, with German and Italian bakers making essential contributions.

The first baker in the city accompanied the move of Louisiana's colonial headquarters from Mobile in 1718 to the area that developed into New Orleans' old quarter. François Lemesle, working under the alias Bellegarde, had by the early 1720s sited his bakery at the corner of St. Ann and Chartres streets. Food and flour shortages presented two of the early colony's most regular hardships. Lemesle's bakery recovered from the devastating 1722 hurricane, but a rival baker went into debt. Lemesle purchased the baker's business and equipment at auction in 1725. The next year the Superior Council found Lemesle guilty of "running short-weight loaves" and had the bread dumped into the Mississippi, despite flour's scarcity and high cost. Flour shortages, concern over pricing, and underweight loaves dominated colonial records regarding bread bakeries. Corn and rice flour as filler and, at times, substitute, proved to be a useful if unpalatable alternative to wheat flour.

The earliest loaves produced in the colony resembled the standards of early-eighteenth-century France. Unlike the more familiar and lighter baguette or "stick" loaves introduced later, these were the heavier, round, "cap" style available in one-, two-, or four-pound loaves. Humid conditions made it difficult for bakers to produce hard crusts and capture yeast from the air. Producing this elemental part of life generated too much heat and required too much physical stamina and skill for most New Orleanians to attempt.[1] Since so few households produced their own bread, the gathering of this staple, along with produce and meats, represented one of the city's communal acts from its earliest days.

Bread production separated the community, too. The Company of the Indies takeover of the colony in the late 1710s introduced en masse enslaved Africans, who handled the most difficult parts of the work. They carried water in buckets from the Mississippi River to their owners' shops; many developed into skilled bread artisans. Slaves owned by bakers regularly distributed bread orders in wicker baskets balanced upon their heads. Advertisements for a baker's business and equipment included his slaves and lease among the bargain.

The transition from French to Spanish rule in the 1760s was marked by more than the local elites' ill-fated rebellion and the familiar French cultural holdovers. General Alejandro O'Reilly had been dispatched in 1769 to put down the rebellion and end the smuggling trade between colonists and English merchants. O'Reilly's earlier relationship with Scots-Irish merchant Oliver Pollock proved mutually beneficial. After the latter offered a cargo of precious flour at a reasonable price, O'Reilly provided Pollock free-trade status and contracted with him to supply the garrison. A weak military presence allowed the free trade to continue with little interference, especially since grain from North America's French and British colonies proved essential to maintaining the colony. Pollock's flour bargain and the subsequent supply of North American flour also factored into the success of Governor Bernardo de Galvez's military campaigns against the British in Baton Rouge and other areas of the Gulf Coast during the American Revolution.

In periods of scarcity, colonial governing officials often set prices to prevent gouging. In 1772, the government purchased all available flour and resold the supply at cost to individual bakers. In the 1790s, Spanish officials worked with two bakers to determine the exact amount of rice one could add to flour without

---

1. Brick ovens fueled by wood fire produced a hellacious job of cleaning out the embers every Saturday, the one day providing a lull in baking. The later development of oil-burning ovens also produced a mess, so it was not until the arrival of natural gas in the 1920s that bakeries benefited from clean burning fuel.

jeopardizing the loaves. The disastrous fire of 1794 destroyed not just buildings, but the system of taxation based on each structure's number of chimneys. In order to maintain funding for night watchmen and street lighting, Governor Hector Carondelet imposed a tax on other items, including bread.

Shortly after Louisiana's transfer to the United States, bakers protested the introduction of a tax applied only to their profession. Post-colonial government continued its oversight of this crucial business. A few years later the mayor fixed the price of flour barrels and ordered all bakeries to supply thirty-one ounces of bread for a "bitt." Another ordinance established the position of a flour inspector who was authorized to dump into the Mississippi River any flour deemed unfit for humans. Neither the decades of Spanish governance nor the early period of the American era affected the taste for French bread-baking style. By 1820, almost sixty bakers—most of whom were French—ran small- to medium-sized businesses. A few bakeries were large enough to afford horse-and-wagon delivery, but the majority continued to dispatch slaves carrying bread loaves in wicker baskets.

During the 1830s, Germans began to proliferate in the baking trade, which the early arriving Americans had never done. Notice of monthly bakers club meetings held in Louis Stein's bakery began to appear in the German-language newspaper, *Tagliche Deutsche Zeitung*, in 1851. These meetings led to the development of the New Orleans Bakers Benevolent Society. Quick to mature, the society dedicated its burial grounds in 1869. The German presence also furnished the first major alteration in bread-baking style.

Exactly when lighter, longer loaves displaced the rounded and heavier cap-style bread in popularity remains unclear in New Orleans culinary history. However, French culinary history provides some insight. When the Louisiana colony was founded, even the Parisian poor were developing a taste for the refined white flour once only available to the wealthy. The hearty breads associated with peasant culture were rapidly declining in popularity. "The round shape had been associated with firm dough that boasted a compact crumb and as little crust as possible," notes leading French bread historian Steven Kaplan. The transition to softer "dough required a flatter shape and more crust, and thus became elongated." By the mid-1700s, Parisian bakers increasingly used softer dough and produced more elongated loaves than round ones. Fourth-generation New Orleans baker John Gendusa has described this traditional French bread loaf as "fat in the middle and narrow at the ends." Considered symbolic of France, the much longer "stick loaf," or baguette, is depicted by some researchers as a fairly recent development. Some accounts suggest that "the very thin long baguette" was introduced to urban diners in the nineteenth century and to the provinces in the twentieth century. Increasing popular preference for white bread and Parisians' fondness for crust figured into the evolution of the elongated French bread loaf and, eventually, the baguette.

By the mid-nineteenth century, Viennese bread and other baked goods rather than French bread were renowned throughout Europe. Vienna's 1873 International Exposition introduced many Americans to Austria's "peerless baked goods." One U.S. official prepared a report on Vienna bread, and the 1876 Philadelphia Centennial featured a "working Viennese-style bakery." The rapidly developing presence of German bakers in antebellum New Orleans may have brought the Vienna-style bread and other Germanic baking techniques to Louisiana earlier than to other parts of the United States. The use of milk in the dough of Vienna bread is noted as one key difference between the Austrian and the French styles. By the early 1900s, both Vienna bread and French bread were widely available in the United States; the former was noted for being "made of the same dough used in France for the *pain riche*" loaves, which featured milk in the dough.

Milk is not added to traditional New Orleans French bread, but many observers suggest that German and Austrian influences have made New Orleans loaves much less dense and significantly lighter than traditional French bread. François Poupart, a master French baker with experience in both France and Louisiana, suggested in a 1979 interview that bakers in his native country did not add "shortening or sugar as they do in New Orleans." Poupart's further comments may signal the reason for the difference: "Some of the New Orleans French bread reminds me of the kind they make in Marseilles. There they add the sugar and the shortening. That does keep the bread fresher a little longer, that's true. They need that there because the fishermen take the bread out in their boats, and it might be a while before they get to eat it. It's good, of course, but it does taste different." The harsh experience of baking in humid conditions and trying to maintain fresh loaves in that same damp environment may be the rationale for the inclusion of sugar and shortening. Another bread authority, Rima Collin, noted that French bakers use unbleached and much less glutenous flour, whereas the New Orleans bakers "use a special hard wheat flour."

New Orleanians create a new yeast culture when preparing each new batch of dough, while the French generally use a *levain*, or "starter," taken from an earlier batch. These differences are evident in the thinner crust and lighter loaves associated with New Orleans bread. The French loaves are "chewy, slightly sour, and invariably served at room temperature." The differing needs of bakery customers also have determined the texture of the final product. For retail sales that demand more shelf life, New Orleans bakeries generally prepare a par-baked loaf, which requires a few more minutes of baking for a crisp loaf, while loaves meant for use only hours later in a restaurant might be fully cooked. By late twentieth century, baker John Gendusa reported many more requests for softer loaves, which he attributes to the increasing numbers of conventions and other events bringing out-of-town palates to the city.

Many New Orleans bakers refer to the special qualities of the hard Mississippi River water to explain local French bread's unique qualities. Until the flooding following Hurricane Katrina, the John Gendusa Bakery displayed on a bakery wall a list of the ingredients known by his family as "the formula" for making batches of dough. Visitors often asked for permission to photograph the formula and then stated that they would make their own loaf of French bread. John Gendusa would remark: "You take that formula and about ten years, and you might make a loaf of bread out of it. It's just a feel; it's just getting acquainted with [the process]. Time and temperature are very essential—the timing all the way along is essential. All through the process we take the temperature, and if it's not right, we know whether the bread will come out good or not. The weather changes at night, so we have to change the mix—put less water in it, more ice, more water—depending on the weather."

Sandy Whann, the fourth-generation family member who heads Leidenheimer Baking Company, believes that "New Orleans French bread evolved based on the variety of ingredients used to make poor boys. The delicate balance of a thin, crisp crust with enough firmness to stand up to brown and red gravy and a lightness that would not compete with Gulf seafood made the poor boy loaf the perfect base. Restaurants needed a loaf that diners could readily bite into without cutting the roof of their mouth as might happen with traditional French bread; however, the loaf had to be strong enough to hold up to gravy, mayonnaise, and other 'dressings.'"

The artisanship of individual bakers is also evident in the range of table breads or loaves meant for individual consumption. Some speculate that the name *pistolet,* a term first attributed to bread in 1850s Belgium, stems from the small loaf's resemblance to the shape of a small pistol. Another explanation may be that the pistolet, known as a stuffed roll or stuffed bread in Acadian cuisine, may refer to the way in which one loads a pistol or "loads" a roll with seafood or other meat. Many dinner rolls lack any connection to the shape of a gun. Some table loaves appear to be small versions of cap bread or the traditional French bread loaf while others appeared in the shape and size of a softball or even the toy known as Mr. Potato Head. Waiters at several New Orleans French Quarter restaurants often imitated the latter, decorating each loaf with condiments from the bar as impromptu centerpieces. A waiter at Brennan's created his "Gizmo" using orange slices for ears, olives for eyes, and so forth.

Despite the introduction of machinery to the process, baking in New Orleans retained some of its artisanal nature because so many of the bakeries remained small, family-owned businesses. In the 1850s, the Poincy Bakery boasted of the arrival of one of New Orleans' first machines used to produce bread: the *Pétrin Mécanique,* a mechanical kneader imported from France. In announcing the innovation, the bakery graphically described how the machine prevented perspiration as well as "body humors from a sick worker" from affecting the dough. While making hygienic strides forward, this early move to automation did not herald an end to artisanship.

The largest French bread producer in the Gulf South as well as contemporary New Orleans, Leidenheimer Baking Company, and the much smaller scale John Gendusa Bakery share the belief that the application of steam in the newer commercial ovens plays an important role in producing the crisp crust while preserving the soft interior. Leidenheimer chief executive Whann argues that technological improvements in the latest-generation bread ovens allow for much more consistent application of steam, which is crucial for producing the thin, crisp crust New Orleanians expect. Amid an upsurge in artisan bakeries, Whann joined the movement by returning to methods used in his great-grandfather's day and working with renowned chef Susan Spicer to form Wild Flour Breads (an independent company co-owned by Spicer and Whann). After purchasing Reising and Angelo Gendusa Bakeries, Leidenheimer added each bakery's most popular breads to their production line. Many local customers continue to enjoy those breads without knowing that those bakeries no longer exist. Gendusa and Leidenheimer demonstrate that the human skills and attention to detail needed to fashion good bread remain to a great extent despite the replacement of manual labor with machine kneading and brick ovens with modern ones.

Bread and poverty associated closely with one another well before the term *poor boy* was applied to loaves. Bakers donated stale loaves to charitable institutions and some produced bread under government contract for Charity Hospital. Bakeries made involuntary contributions of bread to the poor if government officials caught them shorting their loaves. The most memorable example of philanthropy tied to bread is found in Margaret Gaffney Haughery, who was celebrated as the "Breadwoman of New Orleans." Her charitable efforts included donating both bread and funds to serve the city's poor. Orphaned as a child, the immigrant married and lost both her husband and her infant during New Orleans' 1853 yellow fever and cholera outbreak. Acutely aware of the difficulties facing widows and orphans, Haughery dedicated her life to creating and sustaining institutions meant to serve their needs. Everyone in the city addressed her simply as Margaret, a practice continued in this work. Despite an emphasis on her giving nature, only her remarkable business acumen in a trade dominated by men made such acts possible. Margaret began her charitable pursuits using funds earned in traditional women's work, such as hotel work and laundries. Living frugally and investing her earnings provided her start as a businesswoman. When the owner of D'Aquin's Bakery could not repay a loan she had made to him, Margaret took over the large-scale bakery and quickly made it a success producing "sea biscuits" and other crackers, as did a number of other New Orleans bakeries, especially for the maritime industry and the military. Her bakery was one of the city's first to be "mechanically equipped, because the machines were operated by overhead pulleys and belts, powered by a steam engine." She was also one of the earliest bakers to advertise, and one of her display ads featured a side-wheel steamboat, reflecting the fact that Margaret's Steam and Mechanical Bakery was technologically advanced.

The dire conditions facing New Orleanians during the Civil War propelled Margaret's development into the city's most respected figure. Bread shortages and shorted loaves were prevalent during and following the war. Margaret donated bread and flour to diverse groups, including Confederate prisoners, despite the efforts of Federal authorities to stop her. During at least one flood, her workers brought her by boat to deliver loaves to the homes of the poor. When Union forces blockaded the city, prices rose considerably. During the Federal occupation, the military commander set prices for the bread, and giveaways of bread typically resulted from confiscations of underweight loaves. Early in the Reconstruction period, a legislative effort to force bakers to mark each loaf with the exact weight caused bakers to protest. The bill's proponent reported having purchased five dime loaves of bread from five separate bakers and discovering that not one loaf came close to the mandated weight of twenty-seven ounces. The loaves varied from seven to twelve ounces below the required weight. The plan's originator had envisioned using "a sharp die that will cut the surface of the dough, and which widens with the fire and cannot be effaced, or with a punching die, with pins projecting, which will make holes in the loaf as we see in biscuits."

Amid shortages and shorted customers, Margaret's generosity proved to be extraordinary. Her dress and demeanor never reflected her success as a businesswoman. Upon her death in 1882, her estate was distributed among several institutions serving widows and orphans. A statue erected represented her in a typically modest and informal wardrobe, seated, with a child at her side. One of the nation's first monuments honoring a woman, the statue remains at the intersection of Prytania and Camp near one of the institutions she had helped to establish, St. Vincent De Paul Infant Asylum.

The demise of enslaved labor confronted bakers with wholly new issues regarding the workplace. For centuries, the European tradition of bakery guilds had required each apprentice to work for nine years before being designated a master baker and affording him the privilege to set out on his own. That system had adjusted rather smoothly to the perpetual enslavement of most bakery workers in New Orleans. One of the largest and most technologically advanced bakeries in the 1840s and 1850s included "eight certain negroes, and certain other property" as part of its lease agreement. The transition to free labor led to new complications. One of the first developments among the freedmen community was a cooperative organization in which skilled laborers sought to build upon their hard-won talents. Late in 1865, the "Commercial Association of the Laborers of Louisiana" published their constitution regarding plans to establish cooperative enterprises, beginning with the "People's Bakery." Undercapitalized, the experiment joining socialism with skilled former slaves did not survive.

Labor problems forced the artisan employers to confront workplace issues together despite their tradition of baking secrecy and independence. An upsurge of union victories in trades throughout the city in 1892, the year of the New Orleans General Strike, helped the Union of Journeymen Bakers and Confectioners win their demands for "an amelioration of their hard conditions." The "Boss Bakers Union" quickly agreed to a twelve-hour workday ("give and take half an hour") with a fifteen-hour day on Fridays in order to accommodate Saturday as the workers' one day off. Another condition forbade any boss baker from requiring "his journeymen to board and lodge on his, the employer's premises." These negotiations and a common threat posed by organized laborers forced the artisans to organize and led directly to the founding of the New Orleans Master Bakers' Association. Many of the nineteenth- and early-twentieth-century bakeries remained small and peopled by family, but several blossomed into large-scale bakeries with unionized workers and regional distribution. The family-run shops that developed into industrial-scale bakeries tended to be of German origin; Reising, Leidenheimer, Heebe, and Weil's Bakery (later, Holsum, producer of Sunbeam bread) were the most prominent ones.

The history of the poor boy sandwich is marked by the same sorts of legends surrounding many culinary innovations. In approaching the poor boy genesis, one might expect only to isolate some of the more interesting myths. However, documentary evidence confirms the oral history accounts regarding the role of one particular restaurant.

Brothers Bennie and Clovis Martin left their Raceland, Louisiana, home in the Acadiana region in the mid-1910s and settled in New Orleans. Both worked as streetcar conductors for New Orleans Railway and Light Company until they opened Martin Brothers Coffee Stand and Restaurant in the French Market in 1922. The oldest and largest city market paralleled the wharves in the lower section of the old city center or French Quarter, which at the time was a working-class neighborhood filled with struggling Italian American and African American residents.

Throughout the 1920s, the Martins primarily served longshoremen and workers in the produce, fish, meat, and other markets. Their reputation for creating carryout sandwiches began to eclipse their focus on serving coffee. By the start of the Great Depression, their coffee stand had been transformed into a restaurant. By 1931, they had relocated to the 2000 block of St. Claude Avenue, a main business corridor serving the Seventh, Eighth, and Ninth Ward neighborhoods. The larger space of this fully developed restaurant offered table seating as well as counter service. The Martins chose this spot to be close to their bread supplier, John Gendusa Bakery, located two blocks away on Touro Street. The Martins and Gendusa collaborated to create what is now known as the poor boy loaf, and John Gendusa provided its birthing facility.[2]

Gendusa family history suggests that the Martins approached their baker about solving the problem of serving many more sandwiches than they had in the past. French bread's characteristically narrowed tips meant that the ends would be lopped off and only the broader mid-section used for sandwiches. Restaurants customarily served the tips with plates of red beans, bowls of gumbo, and other dishes. As the Martins sold an increasing number of sandwiches, they were left with the problem of too many bread tips. The Martins requested that Gendusa develop a longer loaf that would also be more uniform in shape. Customized for the sandwich trade, Gendusa's forty-inch loaf represented one culinary response to the quickening pace of life in industrial-age New Orleans. This much longer loaf of French bread accompanied the nation's rapid urbanization and the evolution of baking from family shop to industrial manufacturing. Restaurants throughout the nation's cities developed especially large sandwiches during the early twentieth century.

Gendusa recalled having seen similarly long loaves of bread while a child in Sicily, and he set out to make a longer, more rectangular-shaped bread. The original loaf shrunk. (Most now range between thirty-two to thirty-six inches in length.) Gendusa named the Martin's sandwich loaf the "Special," which still appears on the bakery's bread sleeves. His customers called them "Long Johns" in reference to Gendusa's above-average height. Neither name endured. The loaves presented a stunning departure from the size and shape of most French bread; they also allowed for even more sandwiches, furthering the Martins' renown.

Gendusa produced the key feature of what later came to be known as the poor boy loaf, but the sandwich name developed through its association with the street railway workers. While working as streetcar conductors, both Martins had belonged to the streetcar workers' union: the Amalgamated Association of Electric Street Railway Employees, Division 194. Streetcar conductors and motormen provided city residents with one of the most visible glimpses of

---

2. The first Gendusa Bakery had been established in the City Park neighborhood in the early 1900s by Sicilian immigrants Emanuel and Conchetta Gendusa. Their two sons, John and Angelo, formed the Gendusa Brothers Bakery on Touro Street in the mid-1920s. Late in the decade, Angelo developed his own bakery at a new location, and John remained on Touro Street.

union labor in any city, and their very public workplace led to long-lived relations with passengers. Veteran operator pairs enjoyed seniority, so passengers might commute to work with the same pair of men for many years.

Simultaneous with the rise of the street railway union in the early 1900s was the consolidation of the independently owned car lines into one privately held utility. The human representatives of the streetcar company endeared themselves to most passengers, while the utility company that collected five-cent fares as well as gas and electric bill payments grew increasingly unpopular.

Throughout the 1920s, the carmen's union disputed bitterly with New Orleans Public Service Inc. (NOPSI) managers over survival of the union during a period when many companies used "welfare capitalism" to compete against the power of trade unions. Management introduced employee benefits in the hopes of eroding the strength of unions. Employers often competed directly with organized labor by creating rival or "company unions" closely affiliated with the employer. NOPSI created the "Progressive Benevolent Association," whose leadership battled against the union throughout the 1920s. Following increasingly heated contract negotiations, the carmen struck, beginning July 1, 1929. The survival of the carmen's union and eleven hundred jobs were in question.

Transit strikes throughout the nation provoked emotional displays of public support, and the 1929 strike ranks among the nation's most violent. When the company attempted to run the cars on July 5 using "strike breakers" or career criminals brought from New York, jeering crowds stopped them. More than ten thousand New Orleanians gathered downtown and watched strike supporters disable and then burn the first car operated by a strike breaker. A highly sympathetic public participated in the greatest numbers by avoiding the transit system, and the streetcars remained shut down for two weeks. Former New Orleans fire department superintendent William McCrossen experienced the strike as a teenager: "Dare not—nobody, nobody would ride the streetcars. Number one, they were for the carmen. Number two, there was a danger [in riding the cars]." Brickbats greeted the few cars that ran during the first several weeks.

Small and large businesses donated various goods and services to the union local. The many support letters sent to the union included one from the Martin brothers promising, "Our meal is free to any members of Division 194." Their letter concluded: "We are with you till h—l freezes, and when it does, we will furnish blankets to keep you warm." After many weeks of irregular service, the streetcars returned in August using replacement workers recruited from rural Louisiana and Mississippi because few native New Orleanians were willing to scab on the streetcar union. The defeated men maintained efforts to win the strike, which ushered the city into the Great Depression.

The Martins had promised free meals for those who stopped by their coffee stand, but their expensive display of support seemed to have quickly changed to sandwiches strikers would pick up to share with their families.[3] "We fed those men free of charge until the strike ended. Whenever we saw one of the striking men coming, one of us would say, 'Here comes another poor boy,'" Bennie Martin recalled. The Martins maintained their support of the strikers and supplied free sandwiches for several months and perhaps longer.

Citywide knowledge of their charitable act on behalf of the transit operators contributed markedly to the Martin brothers' success. Their coffee stand and lunch-counter trade quickly transformed into a full-service restaurant as word spread about their extremely large sandwiches made with exceedingly long loaves of bread. By 1934, the Martins built an even larger restaurant featuring a bar and billiards hall on the same Touro Street and St. Claude Avenue corner. John Gendusa Bakery continued to supply the special loaves throughout the day and night. "You could go there at 3 o'clock in the a.m. and 3 o'clock in the evening—you couldn't tell the difference. . . . When we first opened up, that was the only customer we had. Of course, it was a big customer. And we served them around the clock—whenever they wanted anything there was always someone here to bring them bread," Gendusa recalled. The restaurant's volume was on a stunning scale.

"Between 900 and 1,100 loaves of bread were used every 24 hours and the restaurant was open 24 hours a day," according to Martin. "On a Carnival Day over 3,000 loaves of bread were used." The standard fifteen-inch sandwiches cost ten cents in the early days and thirty cents by the late 1940s. The extremely large twenty-inch or half-loaf sandwich originally cost fifteen cents before rising to sixty cents in the 1940s. The restaurant purchased twelve to twenty-two head

---

3. The carmen's local held benefit dances and received charitable offerings well into the 1930s. The strikers maintained the union local in order to provide death benefits to its members. John Gendusa III recalls a newspaper clipping that hung in the bakery for years. The article has long since been lost, but Gendusa remembers reading numerous times a newspaper reporter's account of locals describing the strikers as poor boys. The strikers themselves apparently used the term ironically after the article appeared. That is, they said: "I'm one of those poor boys. Give me a sandwich." Thus, the media may have played a part in fixing the term to the strikers and, by extension, the sandwich.

of cattle at a time and employed their own butcher to prepare the meat. They bought their cheese in 250-pound wheels.

Local legend has suggested that the first poor boy was French-fried potatoes with brown gravy. This is akin to gilding the *fleur de lis*. The sandwich name itself denotes poverty, so one need not exaggerate by insisting that a starch sandwich was the *ur-poor boy*. The earliest sandwiches featured the same items used before the name arose. Ham, cheese, or both as a combination, and roast beef sandwiches were the most common. Oyster loaves and soft-shell crab loaves (in season) were also popular. Bennie Martin told a reporter in 1949 that he served an aberration by request: a "ten-cent fried-potato sandwich but sells it only to school kids at noon lunch hour." Students who could not afford the thirty-cent cost of a fifteen-inch standard poor boy requested French fries covered in gravy. At one point the Martins offered free "lettuce and tomatoes sandwiches," reviving the free-lunch tradition once popular in saloons. The same interview revealed that the father of the poor boy detested the customers' traditional requests for extra gravy, which he dismissed as "sloppy." Nevertheless, Martin met his customers' wishes. The strangest desire Bennie Martin ever fulfilled was one customer's request for a banana poor boy with ketchup and mayonnaise. The addition of ketchup made the order strange. Rather than the potato, the over-ripe-banana poor boy better symbolized poverty in the city whose longshoremen off-loaded thousands of tons of the fruit each year. School children who unwrapped a banana sandwich "dressed" with mayonnaise at lunchtime immediately identified themselves as poor.

The Martins capitalized on their sandwich fame and established a few more elaborate but shorter-lived restaurants in the city. After the brothers parted ways, Clovis Martin operated a few other locations as Martin and Son Poor Boy Restaurants on Decatur Street, Airline Highway, and Gentilly Highway, the route connecting New Orleans to the Mississippi Gulf Coast. The latter became their second most famous location. Ironically, after Clovis closed this restaurant, another businessman opened one nearby and "borrowed" the Martin name. The Martins neglected to trademark the poor boy name, and the sandwich and special poor boy loaves began to appear in restaurants and bakeries throughout the city and region. As early as 1932, a competitor one block from the St. Claude restaurant touted his restaurant's "Improved Poor Boy Sandwich." One suspects that Steve's Place thrived upon the Martin brothers' overflow customers. Clovis Martin retired in the 1940s, and Bennie followed in the early 1950s. Their nephew "Red" Martin kept the St. Claude Avenue restaurant running twenty-four hours a day until 1973. By then the sandwich name had spread well beyond the Gulf Coast, including reports of use in Billings, Montana, and San Diego, California, by the mid-1960s.

Despite this New Orleans evidence of the streetcar strike, some journalists argue in favor of a nineteenth-century origin for the poor boy. Common ground is established over the French Market. Almost all legends of the sandwich name attribute its origins to the city's largest market. A couple of the stories center upon the dismissive term *boy* as used to describe African American men. Some of the most offensive accounts, concocted during the Great Depression, describe poor African American youth begging in the French Market. With loaves of stale bread, they were described as moving from stall to stall, acquiring limp lettuce from one vendor and over-ripe tomatoes from another, and then the dregs of meat from another. Black and white beggars likely were common in the markets well before the 1930s. One version recorded in 1937 by writers from outside of the city states, "The story goes that Martin couldn't resist little negro boys who eyed his snacks wistfully and finally came out with, 'Mistah, could you-all spa'h a sandwich fo' a po' boy.'" This tale turns upon both the racially derisive meaning of *boy* and the surprising generosity of one of the Martins, who responds by filling a full loaf of bread with fried oysters, ham and cheese, and other meat. It ends by suggesting that, "in retelling the Martin story, all New Orleanians put a great deal of pathos and feeling into pronouncing 'po' boy,'" so the sandwich is better known that way than as a "poor boy."

One local culinary researcher refuses to use the more familiar term "po-boy" because she believes that it originated "to mock black dialect." One might argue that, given the sandwich's origins in the mixed-race working-class French Quarter neighborhood, the term mocked white as well as black speech. Nevertheless, cognizance of a shared dialect seems to have disappeared simultaneously with the movement of white residents from the downtown neighborhoods and blacks from the French Quarter. The term *poor boy* was commonly used in the city during the early twentieth century to denote schools and orphanages for children, e.g., "The instruction in said school shall be free for poor boys." The term carried at least two meanings. As *poor boy*, it spoke to the tragedy of union men who faced off against the city utility only to be reduced to the level of beggars relying upon handouts. Applying the term to men who had once been considered to be among the aristocrats of labor provided an ironic twist. As *po-boy*, it could conjure up a scene that racists might depict as comical, the sight and sound of black men or boys begging for food or ordering a sandwich. Few contemporary New Orleans diners associate the sandwich with racist origins; time also has eroded the sense of what used to be common knowledge: the sandwich's connection to a violent labor strike. For most, the sandwich name represents just one of the city's many culinary hallmarks.

Arguments favoring a nineteenth-century origin benefit from the disappearance of French-language skills and the ready belief that New Orleanians simply mangled yet another French term, *pourboire*, literally meaning "for drinking." It also means a gratuity or a tip. The connection to sandwiches is made via *pourboire* used to mean the tips of the French bread ("pourboire"). A variant to black children begging the Martins for a meal places the scene in the late 1800s and substitutes sisters from the Ursuline Order offering the tips of their loaves to beggars. This account notes that the African Americans were begging for a dime for coffee, but the Ursuline nuns responded with bread. Since the Ursuline convent is close to the French Market, this is yet another story connecting the sandwich origins to the public market. This theory does not address why the term *poor boy* or the French-language term would have disappeared from local menus for decades and not reappear again until the mid-twentieth century.

New Orleans restaurant menus and advertisements before the 1929 streetcar strike—including the Martins—listed either sandwiches or loaves, the latter indicating sandwiches served on French bread. The first use of the term *poor boy* in the city directory appeared in 1931. (The first contracted form of the name appeared in the 1932 directory as the "Po-Boi Sandwich Shop." The non-standard spelling suggests the term may still have been quite novel.) As William McCrossen noted about dining out during the early 1930s: "You could get a sandwich anywhere, but you could only get a poor boy at Martin Brothers."

A city pamphlet published in the early 1930s lists city regulations for restaurants and other businesses preparing food. The booklet includes display advertising for dozens of restaurants, many noting their sandwiches. Among the more than two dozen mentions of loaves and sandwiches, two stand out from the majority because they advertise poor boy sandwiches. These, along with the 1931 appearance of *poor boy* in the city directory, are the earliest appearances of the term *poor boy sandwich* not associated with the Martin brothers.

A few food journalists have begun to cite one of John Mariani's publications as evidence that the term was used well before the strike. After relating the Martin brothers account, Mariani writes: "Another story says the term is related to the French for a gratuity, pourboire. Nonetheless, the term 'poor boy' for a sandwich goes back to 1875." Mariani found the citation in the *Random House Unabridged Dictionary*, which reports the term first being used between 1875 and 1880. Much more detailed treatments are found in the *Oxford English Dictionary* and the *Dictionary of American Regional English*, and both cite 1931 as the first published use. The latter traces wider application of the term *poor boy* as an adjective and a verb (e.g., "to po' boy it" in oil field work and "to make or repair in a hand-to-mouth or makeshift manner"), but only after the sandwich name had been established. No other documentary evidence has yet emerged to support the *Random House* account. Certainly, sandwiches on French bread resembling poor boys existed in the 1800s. One of the earliest references to an oyster loaf is found in the 1824 *The Virginia Housewife*. The "Peacemaker," a sandwich loaf featuring fried shrimp and oysters, is described in 1901 in *The Picayune's Creole Cook Book* and is given in full in this volume's essay on Oysters Rockefeller.[4]

One commonality among the stories of a nineteenth-century origin is a desire to connect the sandwich as closely as possible to the city's French cultural traditions. But, since French is not a living tongue in New Orleans, it is more difficult to discern fact. German bakers had already assumed the leading role in French bread baking before the Civil War, and later many Italians joined them. New Orleans' culinary history exemplifies the role of immigrants altering tradition and contributing to the public culture. The Gendusa and Martin families, both recent arrivals in early 1900s New Orleans, exemplify the role of immigrants in making profound marks upon the city's culture. One need only sample a Vietnamese poor boy to understand that the tradition of innovation continues.

---

4. The sandwich tradition stretched much further back. Well before the term *sandwich* entered the French language via England, "it ha[d] long been the custom in the French countryside to give workers in the fields meat for their meal enclosed between two pieces of wholemeal or black bread." See "Sandwich" in Montagné.

SHRIMP REMOULADE

Sharon Stallworth Nossiter

Remoulade sauce as interpreted in New Orleans is the most striking example of the evolution of a distinctive Creole recipe from its European ancestor. Unrecognizable in its New Orleans guises, it has little in common with its French relative. In France, the same *rémoulade*, generally used to dress the salad of grated celery root that is found in most any *traiteur*, has been made for generations. From a 1903 recipe of Escoffier's—mayonnaise, prepared mustard, gherkins, capers, parsley, chervil, tarragon, and anchovy essence—through to the 1995 reprint of *Larousse Gastronomique*, that comprehensive encyclopedia of classic French cookery, nothing has changed, although one is sometimes allowed the omission of capers or anchovy. In New Orleans, the sauce has been the base for numerous changes. First came the addition of cayenne pepper, Creole mustard, and shallots (New Orleans' parlance for green onions), then garlic, celery, white onion, and, even further, horseradish, Tabasco sauce, and Worcestershire sauce. It reached its ultimate American transformation when ketchup was added by some, at least by the 1940s.

Longtime New Orleans chef Nathaniel Burton, who presided over the kitchen at Broussard's for years, provided two rémoulade recipes in his 1978 cookbook, coauthored with Rudy Lombard. Since they focused on Creole cuisine, they retained the French spelling. Both his Rémoulade Sauce Creole and the Rémoulade Sauce French call for dry mustard, green onions, parsley, and horseradish, but the Creole version is oil-and-vinegar-based, with paprika, a fair amount of ketchup, and chopped celery. The French version is mayonnaise-based, and not so highly seasoned.

In New Orleans, remoulades are either red or white. "Red" remoulade often looks brown due to the Creole mustard that is a constant in the city's version of the sauce or orangish due to paprika. One might look at red remoulade as representative of the difference between the Old World and the New, the vitality of Americans versus the formality of the French. Or one might think it blasphemy, and posit that the Creoles could certainly have come up with another name for a sauce that bears so little resemblance to its origins. "White" remoulade is a mayonnaise-based sauce, a more direct descendant of French rémoulade in that respect. It may look white, green, or even yellow, depending on whether it is garnished with parsley or hard-boiled egg yolks, and is essentially New Orleans' answer to tartar sauce. The white remoulade, according to the late Howard Mitcham, is "milder in character, but has such a delicious flavor that it's preferred by many connoisseurs."

But it is the red remoulade that, like gumbo and blackened redfish before it, has made the leap from New Orleans tables to a nationally recognized regional dish. The rest of the country is most familiar with it atop not shrimp, but slices of fried green tomatoes. This modern-day classic can be found in restaurants from Maine to California, following its 1991 inspiration in the kitchen of JoAnn Clevenger's Upperline restaurant (where shrimp remoulade is placed atop fried green tomatoes) and subsequent adoption by Anthony Uglesich, owner of the much-lamented Uglesich's, who prepared it on television eleven years later for celebrity chef Emeril Lagasse's special, "Big Easy Bash." In New Orleans, it has transcended appetizer or salad status to even be featured as a poor boy. Remoulade has also shown up on lobster, crabmeat, onion rings, fried oysters, or fish, and even stuffed eggs, a longtime favorite at Maylie's, the Poydras Street Creole restaurant that closed in the late 1980s.

Twenty-first-century New Orleans remoulades may not typify the ancestral recipe, but every version gives a slight nod to its French progenitor, with mustard and parsley appearing, in widely varying amounts, in almost all. A look at the 1961 edition of *Larousse Gastronomique* gives several recipes that the French or Creole cooks in upper-class Louisiana households from the late nineteenth century onward might have recognized. There are numerous cold sauces on the record, some intended for fish and others with a broader range. Besides the classic rémoulade, consider the Mayonnaise of Dublin Bay prawns: large shrimp, marinated in vinaigrette seasoned with parsley and chervil, bedded on lettuce, and covered in mayonnaise decorated with fillets of anchovy, olives, and capers, and surrounded with quartered hard-boiled eggs and lettuce hearts. Gribiche sauce comes very close to early New Orleans remoulades, with its base of hard-boiled egg yolks, oil, and vinegar, and seasoning of gherkins, capers, parsley, chervil, and tarragon.

The two earliest New Orleans cookbooks, the Christian Woman's Exchange's *Creole Cookery Book* and Lafcadio Hearn's *La Cuisine Creole*, both dating to 1885, do not mention a sauce remoulade by name. But the Sauce Tartar in *Creole Cookery*, made of mashed hard-boiled egg yolks, raw egg yolks, oil, and tarragon vinegar, with chopped gherkins, capers, shallots, parsley, and French mustard, has a strong similarity to succeeding recipes that were called remoulade. Likewise Hearn's Sauce Froide, with its array of herbs added to a base of oil, hard-boiled egg yolks, vinegar, and prepared mustard, is described as "a good sauce for fish." By the time the definitive second edition of *The Picayune's Creole Cook Book* was published sixteen years later, rémoulade (still spelled with the French accent) had entered the vocabulary of local cooks as a cold sauce that is "always served with cold meats" or "fish, or salads." It was an oil-and-vinegar-based sauce that was thickened with hard-boiled eggs, egg yolk, and prepared mustard. Green Rémoulade was colored with spinach or parsley juice.

The mayonnaise-based sauces in the *Picayune* cookbook did not include remoulade. Instead, there was Sauce Tartare, a mayonnaise-based sauce mixed with mustard, shallots, pickle, parsley, and garlic; and a Shrimp Mayonnaise, in which boiled shrimp were topped with minced celery and onion, then covered with a "fine mayonnaise sauce" and garnished with hard-boiled eggs, lemon, beets, and celery tops. In a further variant, there were hot remoulade sauces, to be served with calf's feet or lamb brains, a famous Creole dish, according to the *Picayune* editors, but one that is little known today. It is easy to see how these various ingredients, including the beets, which even today make an occasional appearance, could be combined and re-combined to produce a number of recipes that in New Orleans are all called remoulade. As Escoffier said of various mayonnaise sauces, "it is all a matter of taste and imagination."

In the late nineteenth century, Elizabeth Kettenring Dutrey Bégué was serving a Mayonnaise of Celery and Shrimps at her famous French Market breakfasts. The rest of the menu for one particular Monday was toast bread omelet, broiled ham, potatoes with white sauce, jambalaya of chicken and ham, roast turkey, fruit, and coffee. The shrimp dish, dressed with strips of celery and sliced pickles, came in between the turkey and the fruit as a sort of salad. Bégué's recipes were published under several titles and can still be found occasionally in slim paperbound volumes on French Quarter bookstore shelves. One such publication, Mme. Bégué Recipes of Old New Orleans Creole Cookery, includes a section, "Other Famous New Orleans Recipes," which is supposed to predate 1900, the year that Bégué certified her recipes as originals. Among these is a dish credited to Victor Bero, whose Bourbon Street premises, well-known in the mid to late 1800s as Victor's, are now even better known as Galatoire's. One of Bero's signature dishes, lamb brains à la remoulade, contains a mention of anchovies, which still appear occasionally in today's cold remoulades.

Shrimp, of course, has long been a favorite element of New Orleans cooking, boiled, stewed, fried, and baked, in salad, gumbo, or savory pie. "New Orleans is famous for the exquisite flavor of the River and Lake shrimps which abound in its markets. The river shrimp is the more delicate of the two and is always eaten broiled as a preliminary to dinner or breakfast or luncheon. The Lake shrimp of larger size and firmer qualities is used for cooking purposes." Culinary historian Jessica B. Harris, whose work has explored the connection between the African diaspora and Creole cuisines around the world, writes: "Shrimp's tendency to spoil rapidly kept its consumption to areas in which it was fished, and many of these areas were those where urban slavery allowed slaves limited liberty of movement. In cities such as Charleston, South Carolina, and New Orleans, Louisiana, African-American shrimp fishermen would hawk their wares through the streets, proclaiming their freshness. Shrimp boils are as emblematic of these areas as crab boils are of the Chesapeake and clambakes are of the Northeast. In the African-American tradition, shrimp are usually served in a salad, boiled (hot or chilled as shrimp cocktail), in the Creole styles of New Orleans, and deep-fried."

As early as 1840, Chinese immigrants were operating shrimp-drying platforms in Jefferson Parish, and thus began an export market to Asia. A legacy of this enterprise is the hard-boiled-egg and dried-shrimp gumbo that occasionally appears in Louisiana cookbooks. "My family had this at least once a month when I was growing up, and we loved it," wrote Acadian chef Paul Prudhomme. As canning techniques improved in the late nineteenth century, the market for Louisiana shrimp expanded.

"Crews of eight to twenty men manned the larger sailing luggers and rowed small skiffs to set the nets, some of which had dimensions as great as 1,800 feet," writes archaeologist Laura Landry of shrimping in the late nineteenth and early twentieth centuries. "While a crew sailed the lugger, men in the small skiffs played out the net by rowing away from the lugger, then circling back. The lead, or weighted, edge of the net dragged along the bottom, forcing the shrimp and fish to collect in the wider, pouch-like central area of the seine. The shrimp were then dipped out of the net, placed in the boat's holds and kept cool with dampened palmetto leaves." Although shrimping has been a way of life for generations, among descendants of French, Spanish, Croatian, Chinese, and Vietnamese immigrants, it is harder for today's families to pass that tradition along. More competition, more regulation, and more pollution have all contributed to the decline of an industry that built many small communities in Louisiana. "Shrimping as a way of life may live on only in the stories of the fishermen."

The turning point for New Orleans remoulade seems to have come with the opening of the still-famous Arnaud's Restaurant in 1920. It was a time of innovation among local restaurateurs, and "Count" Léon Bertrand Arnaud Cazenave collaborated with his chefs to produce original recipes that appealed to traditional tastes. His first chef was a woman, Mme. Pierre, "who was said to have been a sorceress with French and Spanish food." Among the various dishes originated by Count Arnaud was Shrimp Arnaud, which omitted the mayonnaise and pounded yolks of hard-boiled eggs that had been so popular in the previous century's sauces and added several defining ingredients: lots more Creole mustard, paprika, celery, onion, and horseradish. "For the record, the Creoles took off from the French for their sauce and Count Arnaud took off from them both," wrote John DeMers in *Arnaud's Creole Cookbook* (1988). "His recipe for the rémoulade-based Arnaud Sauce, used to dress his famous shrimp, remains a secret."

Arnaud's bottles and sells its sauce, labeled "Original Creole Remoulade." Although the restaurant keeps it secret (and the label on the bottled sauce gives few clues), many writers have described a recipe as Arnaud's. In 1932, Mary Moore Bremer, writing in *New Orleans Creole Recipes*, listed Shrimp with Remoulade Sauce and Shrimp Arnaud separately. The recipe she cites as Shrimp Arnaud contains six tablespoons of olive oil, two tablespoons of vinegar, one tablespoon of paprika, one-half teaspoon each of white pepper and salt, four tablespoons of Creole mustard, half a celery heart chopped fine, half a white onion chopped fine, and a little chopped parsley. Mix it with the shrimp; chill it well. "Enthrone on crisp, chopped lettuce," she concludes, a presentation that has endured. She omits in that recipe the horseradish that is such a noticeable part of Arnaud's remoulade sauce today, but it turns up in her Shrimp with Remoulade Sauce.

The following year, Caroline Merrick Jones and Natalie Scott published *The Gourmet's Guide to New Orleans*, and their Sauce Arnaud does contain horseradish. In 1937, local writer Ella Bentley Arthur noted that "shrimp remoulade" was a "favorite way of serving cold boiled shrimp in New Orleans." Her recipe, appended to a later edition of Madame Bégué's 1906 recipe booklet, is the first sighting of a dish called Shrimp Remoulade.

Shrimp remoulade did not appear on the menu of Antoine's until the 1940s, more than one hundred years after its founding. The recipe given by the great-great-grandson of the restaurant's founder in his 1980 cookbook, *Antoine's Restaurant since 1840 Cookbook*, includes ketchup, powdered mustard, horseradish, Worcestershire sauce, Tabasco, green onions, celery, and parsley. The remoulade on the menu at Galatoire's, another flagship restaurant, also contains ketchup. The earliest reference to ketchup in remoulade was found in *Maylie's Table d'Hote Recipes* (1941), which calls for two tablespoons of "catsup," a measurement that frequently recurred in subsequent cookbooks. Twentieth-century chef Austin Leslie had an easy take on a remoulade with ketchup: "Use a mayonnaise jar, the quart size, and put mayonnaise in it until it's half full and add ketchup until it's three-fourths full. Then add yellow mustard and Worcestershire sauce. Shake all of that up and you'll be surprised. Add it to the shrimp and you are a chef."

The Creole mustard that is an essential element of most red remoulades is often thought to be a contribution to New Orleans tastes courtesy of the German and Alsatian butchers, some of whom worked in the meat markets. Schott's, for example, in the Poydras Market, was run by Germans. Zatarain's, which has manufactured a distinctive local brand since 1889, is the quintessential Creole mustard: yellowish-brown, with visible coarsely ground mustard seeds (although the family was Basque, not German or Alsatian). "It is distinguished not only by its coarse, grainy texture but also by the light tang it derives from the addition of prepared horseradish," writes Galatoire's general manager, Melvin Rodrigue. Its appearance and taste is closer to the French Pommery Moutarde de Meaux (the recipe for which dates to 1632) than to the milder, brown "Bordeaux" type mustard, flavored with sugar and herbs, that British food historian Alan Davidson claims is the German preference. The hard-boiled egg that was such a fundamental part of nineteenth-century recipes still appears today as a garnish on red remoulade, most often quartered and served on the side, sometimes transformed into a stuffed egg, or chopped and sprinkled across the top.

At a 2006 tasting of shrimp remoulades, local cooks prepared recipes from five cookbooks: *The Picayune's Creole Cook Book* (1901), *New Orleans Cook Book* (1940) by Lena Richard, *The Plantation Cookbook* by the Junior League of New Orleans (1972), *Creole Feast* by Nathaniel Burton and Rudy Lombard (1978, the entry from Charles Kirkland), and *Galatoire's Cookbook* by Leon Galatoire (1994). Appearance and taste ranged widely. Richard's mayonnaise-based recipe, for example, was heavy with chopped egg and bright with parsley. Tasters said it resembled a shrimp salad more than remoulade. Kirkland's sauce, also mayonnaise-based, was sharper due to horseradish, but found little favor. The spicier brown and red sauces still were more to the crowd's taste, and the overall favorite was in *The Plantation Cookbook*. It has the advantage of being emulsified in the blender. (That is how you know it was written in 1972.)

SHRIMP REMOULADE

½ cup chopped onions

2 teaspoons salt

¼ cup oil

2 medium cloves garlic, pressed

½ cup tarragon vinegar

½ cup chopped green onion

½ cup brown creole mustard

2 pounds boiled, peeled shrimp

2 teaspoons paprika

5 cups shredded lettuce

¼ teaspoons cayenne pepper

In a blender, place onions, oil, vinegar, mustard, paprika, pepper, salt, and garlic. Blend 5 or 6 seconds, turn off, stir, blend another 5 or 6 seconds. Add green onions and blend for 2 seconds. Do not blend longer or you will have purée. Chill sauce overnight. Arrange beds of lettuce on salad plates, top with shrimp and cover with chilled sauce.

Contrast this to the ingredients in a 1903 recipe given by Escoffier, whose cooking career covered the latter part of the nineteenth century and on into the twentieth: capers, gherkins, parsley, chervil, tarragon, anchovy essence, mayonnaise, and mustard.

And finally, the Culinary History Group also prefers a recipe they derived from Austin Leslie's *Chez Helene House of Good Food Cookbook* and their own tastings:

WHITE REMOULADE IN THE STYLE OF CHEZ HELENE

2 cups homemade or better store-bought mayonnaise

1 ½ cup chopped dill pickles

1 teaspoon prepared mustard

½ cup horseradish

1 teaspoon parsley, finely chopped

½ teaspoon garlic, finely chopped

Cayenne pepper to taste

½ gallon boiling water

1 teaspoon salt

2 teaspoons liquid crab boil

1 ½ pounds peeled shrimp

1 head shredded lettuce

For your remoulade sauce, mix mayonnaise, pickles, mustard, horseradish, parsley, garlic, and cayenne in bowl. Refrigerate. Add salt and crab boil to the boiling water. Add shrimp. When water returns to a boil and shrimp turn pink, remove and put shrimp directly into ice water to stop the cooking. Drain. Divide the lettuce on six plates, top with shrimp and a generous amount of remoulade sauce.

OYSTERS ROCKEFELLER

Cynthia LeJeune Nobles

N ew Orleanians are likely to describe their raw "ersters" as salty, sweet, slippery, briny, and creamy. Some call them metallic, coppery, and even tinny (and those are the positive adjectives). But regardless of these not-so-flattering descriptions, a peek inside restaurants such as Casamento's (not in the summer, of course), Acme, Felix's, or Pascal's Manale will reveal happy eaters downing freshly shucked bivalves as is or topping them with a quick splash of hot sauce, horseradish, or lemon. No doubt about it, local connoisseurs are addicted to oysters in the buff.

However, over the years, creative area cooks have looked past the chilled half-shell, experimenting with sauces, dressings, sandwiches, and grills. As a result, New Orleans has spectacularly refined and accented the mundane. Many of these concoctions are even legendary. *The Picayune's Creole Cook Book* (1901) takes this accolade one step further and gives New Orleans sole credit for "open[ing] the eyes of the United States to the possibilities of the oyster in every variety and form of cooking."

Of the area's fantastic array of oyster dishes, none is more revered or written about than Oysters Rockefeller. This classic was created during an 1899 European snail shortage that prompted Jules Alciatore, owner of Antoine's, to grind together a hodgepodge of local greens and to smother native oysters with the resulting sauce. The elegant broiled dish ended up tasting so rich that Alciatore named it after one of the wealthiest men in the country, John D. Rockefeller. Oysters á la Rockefeller was an immediate sensation and a must-have for visitors. One notable out-of-towner who tried Antoine's marquee dish was President Franklin Roosevelt, who, in 1937, was famously asked by New Orleans mayor Robert Maestri in his gnarly voice and working-class dialect (one that New Orleanians call a "yat" accent), "How ya like dem erstas, Mr. President?"

Today, Oysters Rockefeller is arguably the world's best-loved cooked oyster dish and is thought to be the single greatest contribution of the United States to haute cuisine. That is quite a phenomenon considering that, although chefs and home cooks have stirred up close copies, Antoine's original recipe is locked away from the public. Jules Alciatore, on his deathbed, reportedly demanded eternal secrecy from all who knew just exactly what went into that shell. This aura of mystery consequently leaves the living yearning to find the answers: Were the ingredients originally found on a relish tray? And do they include spinach? Olives? Vermouth? New Orleans food critic Tom Fitzmorris writes in his *New Orleans Food* (2006) that he received a request for his version of Oysters Rockefeller from, of all people, Bernard Guste, the fifth-generation owner of Antoine's. Seems the restaurant needed a recipe to give the many folks who ask for it, and Guste felt that Fitzmorris's adaptation was mortifyingly close to the real thing. The greens in this virtual copy include celery, parsley, green onion, fennel, and watercress. Fitzmorris adds green food coloring, an addition he says is authentic, and is quick to point out that the original recipe did not include either spinach or Mornay (white cheese) sauce.

Some twenty years after the invention of Oysters Rockefeller, Arnaud's Restaurant's colorful "Count" Arnaud popularized the now classic Oysters Bienville. Named after either New Orleans' founder or Bienville Street, where Arnaud's sits, this savory dish is a baked oyster in its half-shell topped with a creamy, sometimes cheesy, and usually shrimp-laced sauce. Interestingly, some say that Emile Commander, the original owner of Commander's Palace, should take credit for inventing the dish, while Roy Guste Jr. writes in his *Antoine's* cookbook (1979) that Oysters Bienville was actually invented around 1939 by their restaurant's chef Pete Michel and Antoine's then-owner Roy Alciatore.

Bienville and Rockefeller, in particular, receive the most press. Yet among the hundreds of oyster dishes originating from New Orleans, many old-timers swear that Corinne Dunbar's 1930s-era Oysters Dunbar, a savory casserole of oysters and artichokes, was the best dish ever invented. Contemporary diners vote for Clancy's irresistible Oysters with Brie. New Orleanians also flock to the venerable Mosca's for Oysters Italian or drive to nearby Metairie for Drago's Charbroiled Oysters. With all the hullabaloo surrounding these famed oyster specialties, it should not be surprising that, with the possible exception of crawfish, oysters are more closely associated with southern Louisiana than any other product. Louisiana's crop of *Crassostrea virginica*, also known as the American oyster, is sought after for its relative large size and sweet meat, not pearls, although the occasional small, brown pearl does form. Members of this genus are intersexual; they are hatched as males, but over their lifetimes their gender changes back and forth. The oyster's entire weight is four-fifths shell. This hard armor is salvaged and has, for centuries around the world, been used for roads, ship ballast, and raw material for lime.

Oysters have been consumed since prehistoric times and were especially popular with the Celts, Romans, and Greeks. Aristotle left scientific records about early efforts to cultivate oysters, while Pliny fancied the shellfish as the "palm and pleasure of the table." Native Americans generated large mounds of oyster and clam shells all along North America's shores, and these hills were so noted by the first Europeans settlers. Throughout the state's modern history, oysters have appeared in numerous Louisiana writings. In February 1699, Iberville (Bienville's brother and, like him, Louisiana's French Canadian founder) landed on the Chandeleur Islands and haughtily chronicled that he "found a great quantity of oysters, which are not of so good a quality as those of Europe." But the majority of historical entries are much kinder. In 1730, the Ursuline nun Sister Madeleine Hachard wrote to her father in Rouen, France, about the bounty of New Orleans, and that oysters were plentiful even in summer. In 1734, an anonymous writer who was traveling through Louisiana ate some Lake Pontchartrain oysters and pronounced them "very well tasted." Antoine Le Page du Pratz, colonial planter and friend to the Natchez, wrote in his 1743 history of Louisiana about the abundance and fine taste of the oysters in Louisiana's bayous, and also that, in the early 1700s, when new arrivals from France had tried settling at Nouveau Biloxy (Biloxi) in the Louisiana Colony, that the abundance of coastal oysters saved lives.

Although they were obviously consumed in the region in the 1700s, popular Louisiana chef John Folse writes in his *Encyclopedia of Cajun and Creole Cuisine* (2004) that most local French of that period did not consider *huîtres* edible. It seems the bivalve did not pass the snuff test until the Native Americans introduced them to the French Acadians around 1764, just one year after a primitive New York City saloon served the first colonial oysters to the public. Perhaps New Orleans' fussy French majority would not have been so particular had they known that back in Europe, Casanova was downing plates of oysters before his amorous adventures and bolstering the legend that oysters are an aphrodisiac.

Apparently, the French colonials quickly got over their aversion. At the beginning of the 1800s, Dr. John Sibley of Natchitoches visited the city and wrote, "New Orleans I am informed is plentifully supplied with Oysters in the Season of them from the Bays on Each side of the Town within 3 or 4 miles, said to be large and well flavour'd the price is fixed by Government at 4 bits or half a dollar." Around the same time, C. C. Robin, a widower from France and a reported Bonapartist, wrote about broad banks of big, quality oysters. Pierre-Clément de Laussat visited New Orleans in 1803 to reclaim Louisiana for Napoleon and then turn it over to the United States. During his year in the region, he tagged along on a hunting party that dined on, among other delicacies, oysters. Attesting even more to the oyster's foothold during this time, in 1805, "An Amateur" wrote a letter to the editor of the *Louisiana Gazette* complaining that oystermen on the street corners and their "noise and bawling" from the "konk shell" bothered the citizenry from "morning to night."

These oystermen procured their goods from the wild—from lakes and coastal waters outside the city. Here fresh water from the Mississippi, Atchafalaya, and Pearl rivers still mixes with the saltwater of the Gulf of Mexico and, along with a fairly constant water temperature, forms the ideal brackish soup. Early oyster harvesters included French, Acadian, Spanish, and Sicilian immigrants. Oyster cultivation did not begin until after 1840 with the arrival of waves of seasoned fishermen from Croatia. Writer Milos M. Vujnovich compiled an excellent history of these pioneers in his *Yugoslavs in Louisiana* (1973). Vujnovich explains that these Croatians came from the Dalmatian coast. They were sometimes called Dalmatians. More playfully, a Dalmatian might be called a "tako" (a word meaning "so-so" in various Slavic languages and the usual reply to the question "how are you?"). These former sailors from the Adriatic Sea shunned city life and rigged together one-room raised cabins on Louisiana's coast in lower Plaquemines Parish, some eighty miles south of New Orleans. During the mid-1850s, the Slavic transplants started methodical cultivation, and soon they had developed a dual method of oyster fishing: natural reef oysters for cooking and canning; cultivated oysters for raw half-shell consumption in homes, restaurants, oyster bars (then called saloons), and hotels.

Oystering is backbreaking work and was particularly so during harvest when, in the beginning, commercial fishermen picked mature oysters out of the water with their bare hands, and oftentimes ended up with bloody palms. Eventually, they advanced to using tongs. Vujnovich notes that a major breakthrough came in 1905 when Croatian Leopold Taliancich installed on his boat the first pair of oyster dredges, V-shaped iron frames with ring-mesh sac-like enclosures that scour the oyster reef bottom. In 1913, John and Anthony Zegura installed the first power-operated oyster dredges on the lugger *Venus*, and Taliancich's dredge and Zeguras' motor are still used today.

Aside from battling primitive technology, transportation from coastal oyster reefs into New Orleans was cumbersome and occupied most of the oyster fishermen's time. The first boats were nothing more than fishing skiffs and were later followed by low-decked, shallow draught, one-masted, lateen-rigged sailboats, usually some thirty or forty feet long. According to Vujnovich, these vessels were propelled by sails, oars, and push poles and were usually owned and manned by two men. By the late 1800s, two-masted schooners were used, but the upriver trip still took two days or more, particularly when the wind died down and the fisherman, or a hired mule, had to walk along the levee and pull the boat. Some resorted to paying "luggermen," experienced sailors in luggers (freight boats) and schooners, men who exclusively transported seed and marketable oysters for profit. Motorized boats arrived in the early 1900s, increasing oyster production tremendously, and the last quaint sailing "smack" disappeared in 1920.

In the mid-1800s, oyster consumption was all the rage worldwide, and New Orleans certainly had its share of oyster saloons. A sample of a common meal in 1851 was recorded by an English Mormon named Jonathan Grimshaw, who spent a few nights in New Orleans where he and his family "called at an oyster saloon and got some oyster soup and wine." During the same year a "Manhattaner" named A. Oakey Hall visited New Orleans' palatial St. Charles Hotel, finding it "garnished with oyster saloons." So popular were oysters that the accoutrement-loving Victorians had even created lavishly designed porcelain, majolica, glass, silver, and pewter "oyster plates" that featured wells to hold shucked oysters and sauce. Along with plates, special silverware was produced for both serving and eating oysters, including the oyster fork, a diminutive utensil with two or three curved or straight tines. Surveys of New Orleans city directories show that oyster hysteria peaked in 1917, the year the city housed eighty-three oyster saloons and twenty-nine wholesalers. During this time, raw oysters in New Orleans were typically served with "Maunsell White," a then-popular commercial hot sauce that was sold in most all New Orleans oyster saloons. Other accompaniments were usually lemon, Worcestershire sauce, cayenne pepper, and a plate of "hard-tack" (oyster bread) or crackers.

Even before this period of oyster mania, demand rapidly exceeded supply. In 1870, the Louisiana legislature passed Act 18, prohibiting the sale of oysters from April 1 through September 15. Act 91 of 1871 kept the oyster season closed from May 1 to September 15. Destruction of oyster reefs forced the state to mimic legislation in Maryland, and in 1886, Act 106 divided Louisiana into three oyster districts. Politics and unmarked boundaries soon neutered the law, however, leading to Act 100, which gave parishes oyster jurisdiction. Finally, in 1902, the Louisiana Oyster Commission (the precursor to the Louisiana Department of Wildlife and Fisheries) started leasing oyster bottoms. Although imperfect, all these visionary regulations not only conserved and organized the industry, but are credited with making Louisiana the largest producer of oysters in the United States today.

Legislative Act 91 covered a time period when 89 percent of the days in question are coincidentally in months without the letter *r*. Although today oysters are consumed raw year-round, up until 1962, Antoine's would not serve Oysters Rockefeller during June, July, and August. It is true that oysters spawn during summer and can be milky. More dangerous, higher levels of the bacteria *Vibrio vulnificus* can contaminate oysters during the summer. Louisiana State University AgCenter food safety experts therefore recommend that those with weakened immune systems and others at risk should only consume oysters that have been thoroughly cooked, are pasteurized, and are treated and sold in containers so labeled to reduce *Vibrio vulnificus* to non-detectable levels.

Throughout their lives, oysters are sedentary and cling to hard surfaces while they filter water for food. Oyster producers therefore farm in near-shore estuarine areas where water quality is high and shells can easily be spread along the bottom to form reefs. Another popular method is off-bottom culture, a growing system that allows for oysters to reach marketable maturity (three inches) in one year instead of the two years it takes them to grow on the Gulf bottom. For this method, seed oysters are placed into mesh bags then strapped to rafts or lines that hold fledglings until they are fully grown. After harvest, all oysters are portioned into sacks and tagged with the fisherman's name, the date, and bed location, and then sent to market.

Today oyster farming is big business in Louisiana with 8,300 leases covering 397,000 acres that produce 40 percent of U.S. oysters. Oystermen either have their own private leases or they farm from public seed grounds managed by the state. This important industry has a $300–600 million economic impact and employs some 3,500 commercial fishermen, oyster farmers, oyster dealers, and oyster processors. The oyster profession is also one that is generally handed down through families. The P & J Oyster Company in the French Quarter is the oldest continually operating oyster dealer in the Unites States, and the current owners can trace the firm's history through a myriad of family ties that began with the company's founding in 1876. Michael Voisin, chairman of the Louisiana Oyster Task Force, can boast that his family has been oystering for as many as seven generations.

Local businessman Mike Sansovich, too, is descended from an oystering family. His clan, however, is no longer in the oyster business, but his family history research gives a glimpse into the routine of a nineteenth-century oyster processor. The Sansovichs sailed to New Orleans from Hvar, Croatia, between 1850 and 1860, and Mike nostalgically relays that the family wholesale oyster business started in 1888. As he sits in his modern office he points to a painting of the male members of his rough-clad Victorian-era ancestors and their employees at the Louisiana Oyster Depot. This family-owned "oyster house" was prominently perched at 926 Chartres Street in the heart of the French Quarter, the two-story wooden structure serving as both business and home. Like most of the close-knit Croations, the Sansovich clan members belonged to the Yugoslav Benevolent Society. And Michel Sansovich, Mike's great-great-grandfather, was a grand marshal in 1883.

The family did not own boats, and like many other processors that dotted the French Quarter, they sent wagons to purchase oysters from the luggers and two-masted schooners that docked at the Old Basin Canal. Another oyster landing site was at Bayou St. John; and yet another, the "Picayune Pier," also known as "Lugger Bay," sat at the foot of Dumaine Street. At the oyster houses, gloved shuckers were paid by volume. The day's catch was opened into barrels and then sold either to retail outlets or to anyone who wanted them. Galatoire's Restaurant was reportedly one of the Sansovichs' first customers. Eventually, the Sansovich family owned five or six French Quarter oyster houses, including one in the Pontalba Building at 629 Decatur. After World War I, the oyster boat landing at Dumaine moved to the foot of Barracks Street; and for unknown reasons, the Sansovich oyster business ended in 1925. The Old Basin Canal was filled in during the 1920s, and the Barracks Street wharf closed in the early 1950s, bringing to an end oyster delivery to New Orleans by individual oyster boats.

Recipes for oyster dishes are recorded in virtually every early American cookbook, including Williamsburg's William Parks's *Compleat Housewife* (1742), which featured a batter-based recipe named To Fry Oysters. Mary Randolph's *Virginia Housewife* (1860) included directions for Fried Oysters and Oyster Loaves. Virginia's Marion Harland's *Common Sense in the Household* (1880) gave instructions for making Oyster Catsup; and caterer and former Alabama slave Abby Fisher included a recipe for Oyster Gumbo Soup in her book *What Mrs. Fisher Knows about Old Southern Cooking* (1881). Locally, Lafcadio Hearn published thirteen recipes for oysters in his *La Cuisine Creole* (1885). Here is one of the most interesting:

OYSTER PICKLE. VERY EASY AND NICE

Wash four dozen oysters; let them be fine and large, with plenty of their own liquor. Pick them carefully, strain their liquor and to it add a dessertspoonful of pepper, two blades of mace, a tablespoonful of salt, and a cup of strong wine vinegar. Simmer the oysters in this five minutes, then put them in small jars. Boil the pickle again, and when cold add a cup of fresh vinegar; and fill up the jars, cork them, and set away for use.

Another turn-of-the-twentieth-century restaurateur, Madame Bégué, in her *Old Creole Cookery* (1900), lists Oyster Omelet on her Friday weekly menu. She also leaves us a recipe for oyster soup, where, in a departure from her or from most other earlier published recipes, she cooks flour in butter before the addition of broth. Today the flour/butter combination is called *roux*, a staple of Creole cooking. Here is the recipe, one that has been copied and modified by the best New Orleans restaurants:

MADAME BÉGUÉ'S OYSTER SOUP

Take a good piece of soup meat and boil in a quart of water; season with salt only. Make a hash of green onions, parsley and chervil. Fry this in hot butter, add flour for thickening and pour the broth on the whole. Add two dozen of oysters and more water if needed, and season with a branch of thyme, two bay leaves and a piece of strong pepper. Serve with toast bread.

The 1901 edition of *The Picayune's Creole Cook Book* printed a whopping total of thirty-four oyster recipes and left this testament to oyster's popularity: "In winter . . . exceptionally palatable oysters . . . are sold in every restaurant and by the numerous small vendors on almost every other corner or so throughout the lower section of the city. In the cafes, the hotels, the oyster saloons, they are served in every conceivable style known to epicures and caterers." Fortunately, *The Picayune* also recorded an authentic recipe for La Médiatrice, the predecessor to the poor boy and an oyster sandwich, sometimes laced with shrimp, that was wildly popular in nineteenth-century New Orleans.

OYSTER LOAF

LA MÉDIATRICE

Delicate French Loaves of Bread.

2 Dozen Oysters to a Loaf.

1 Tablespoonful of Melted Butter.

This is called the "famous peacemaker" in New Orleans. Every husband, who is detained down town, laughingly carries home an oyster loaf, or Médiatrice, to make "peace" with his anxiously waiting wife. Right justly is the Oyster Loaf called the "Peacemaker," for, well made, it is enough to bring the smiles to the face of the most disheartened wife.

Take delicate French loaves of bread and cut off, lengthwise, the upper portion. Dig the crumbs out of the center of each piece, leaving the sides and bottom like a square box. Brush each corner of the box and the bottom with melted butter, and place in a quick oven to brown. Fill with broiled or creamed oysters. Cover with each other and serve.

Célestine Eustis, in *Cooking in Old Creole Days* (1904), lists an all-purpose oyster recipe called New Orleans Veal with Oysters; the mixture is little more than seasoned, chopped veal and oysters. Eustis advises using this delicacy for pâtés or serving on pieces of toast or mixing with bread and stuffing in chickens. Natalie Scott's *Mirations and Miracles of Mandy* (1929) features at least ten recipes, including instructions for the basics of baking, frying, wrapping, and serving them on the half-shell. Scott teamed up with Caroline Merrick Jones in *Gourmet's Guide to New Orleans* (1936), and the two curiously published only two oyster recipes. A New Orleans resident for most of her life, Lena Richard, in her *Lena Richard's Cook Book* (1939), leaves this unusual oyster dish:

STEWED EGGS AND OYSTERS

6 hard-boiled eggs

2 dozen large oysters

1 tablespoon chopped onion

1 tablespoon chopped parsley

2 tablespoons butter

2 tablespoons cooking oil

1 cup water

1 cup oyster liquor

4 tablespoon[s] flour

Make a roux with flour, oil, butter and onion. Add water to oyster liquor, season with salt and pepper and cook 10 minutes. Then add oysters and eggs split lengthwise with remaining seasonings. Let simmer 10 minutes longer, then serve with rice.

Mary Land came up with some of the most innovative and enthusiastic oyster recipes of the mid-1900s. Her *Louisiana Cookery* (1954) appears to have published the first local recipe for grilled oysters. In 1969, her *New Orleans Cuisine* featured Hot Oyster Cocktail and Demoruelles Deviled Oysters. Most other mid-twentieth-century cookbooks stuck with the classics. The Women's Republican Club in their cookbook offered recipes for the ubiquitous Oysters Rockefeller and for Deviled Oysters, while the Junior League of New Orleans' *The Plantation Cookbook* (1972) printed more than a dozen time-honored recipes, including one for Oysters Bienville and another for Oyster and Pecan Stuffing.

The human craving for oysters has not gone away, although they are not consumed in the same numbers as one hundred years ago. However, the oysters themselves have been threatened. In 2005, hurricanes Katrina and Rita raked through the Louisiana coastline and abruptly shut down oyster production. Initial fears predicted years of devastation, and the industry was idle for two months. In the tragic year after the storm, oyster farmers lost $205 million, with the cash amount of oysters brought to shore dropping by 30 percent. The setbacks, however, seem temporary. By 2007, the government had provided some relief dollars. Boats were being repaired or were already running. Despite a labor shortage, processors were packaging in full force, and many oyster beds were already refurbished.

Shrugging off Mother Nature's slap, the state that wrings the most out of the oyster's potential again enjoys a safe and plentiful supply. Back in New Orleans, the faithful are again scouring restaurants for the best oyster poor boy. Purists are mixing up secret sauces for shooters, and the just-shucked bivalve is again a regular on the grill. In the city's fresh environment, this slimy jewel from the Gulf fills local chefs and home cooks with new inspiration, improving the odds that one day a new oyster classic may be born, one that might even upstage old king Rockefeller.

DAUBE GLACÉE

Susan Tucker

"**D**aube Froide à la Créole has only to be tried once to be repeated" proclaimed the authors of *The Picayune's Creole Cook Book* i 1901. The *Picayune's* boast is echoed throughout many lat New Orleans cookbooks. Some printed descriptions, however, are not so ur formly pleasing and are not, to the early twenty-first-century palate, alwa tempting. Peter Feibleman writes of the same dish, daube glacée, as "chopp sliced meats, cooked with herbs, covered with a delicate brown gelatin extract from knuckles and bones—not from a packet—and set to chill in individ molds the day before." When asked to explain it, New Orleanians often like to hogshead cheese, not a name with necessarily pleasant connotations.

Some people think daube glacée is more akin to beef aspic, albeit a dress up version.[1] Overall, New Orleanians persist in cherishing its place as one of premier dishes of private elegance and celebration, and some even take a bi pleasure in the fact that outsiders find it so unappetizing. This most iconi the meat dishes remains more private than public in its serving and consu tion, more at home on the brunch, luncheon, and cocktail table than elsewl

A good understanding of daube glacée starts with the opinion that i in New Orleans has a rich history, especially surprising since locals and vis alike think of the city as a seafood town. Historian and restaurant critic Ric Collin conceded in the 1970s that the city had "some excellent steak and restaurants," and journalist Brett Anderson pointed to a "fairly rich hamb history" in the first decade of the twenty-first century. Overall, the traditi food here is enriched by the history of the city markets' butchers. Many of

---

1. We have chosen to use this French spelling of *daube glacée*, with the feminine ending. New Orleanians use this spelli changeably with *daube glacé* and *daube glace*. *Daube glaceé* is also called *daube Creole or Daube Froide à la Créole.*

men came originally from the region of Gascony in France. These were the men who sold the veal shanks and pig's knuckles needed to create the gelatin for daube glacée. Transplanted Frenchmen and their descendants, they monopolized the butcher business of the city well into the twentieth century, though the Spanish and German butchers also added their expertise to the history of meat in the city.

Hattie Horner, who visited New Orleans during the 1884–1885 World's Cotton Exposition, was impressed with the meat vendors at the French Market: "By and by I worked my way to the first opening on the left, and going in found that I was in the first of the five great divisions—the meat-market. Around every pillar that helps to support the roof, wide stands are built. Meats of all description, fresh and nicely cut, are displayed, and here the noble butcher, to the number of hundreds, howls in his own particular language the universal virtues of his own particular meats."

Because the city's butchers continued offering a wide variety, meat dishes remain associated with some of the same traditions that greeted travelers in the 1880s. Grillades deserve mention, if only because they appear on so many brunch menus of the city. Still popular in the late twentieth and early twenty-first centuries, grillades, like much else in this book, began life as a poor family dish. For this preparation, the inferior pieces of meat could be cut into squares or strips, and a gravy could be made. Today grillades are most often made from the round steak of veal or beef, although some cooks use pork. A roux is made and the slightly pounded pieces of meat, along with seasonings of garlic and onion, are browned. In New Orleans, tomatoes and other seasonings are added next; in the countryside, tomatoes are optional. Grillades are served most often with grits, but also with rice, or even beside various bean dishes. They are hearty fare, beloved for their rich and pungent flavors and textures. And they are served in the most modest of homes and the fanciest restaurants. They are another of the city's foods that cross many boundaries.

Any discussion of Creole meats should also mention *bouilli*, for even more than daube glacée and grillades, this dish appeared on the city's early menus. Today, bouilli is a lightly flavored stewed or boiled meat, usually a simple boiled brisket. But, in the early days of New Orleans, it was the leftover piece of meat remaining after bouillon had been made. There is an entire chapter of bouilli recipes in the *Picayune's* second edition. Its presence in the cooking of Quebec is a suggestion of the connections that the French Canadian founders

of New Orleans and others brought south from the traditions of camp food easily cooked over a fire after a day or night of fur trapping. In rural Louisiana, bouilli is a more spicy soup, but in New Orleans it remains a tender piece of brisket.

Bouilli was popularized in the modest coffee and boarding houses, some of which evolved into great restaurants. In the late nineteenth century and through most of the twentieth century, one such establishment was Maylie's. The story of Maylié and Esparbé's (as it was first called, the name changing to Maylie's in the early twentieth century)—as that of Creole meats in general—begins with the sort of men Hattie Horner saw at the French meat market. Bernard Maylié and Hypolite Esparbé came from Gascony, and it was in that region, in the village of Lacave, that Marie and Anna Boussion grew up as the daughters of innkeepers. Maylié hailed from about eleven miles away, in Belbèze; Esparbé, born in 1847, grew up in the same *département* as Maylié, the Haute-Garonne. By the 1870s, the two men had made New Orleans their home. Maylié worked as a butcher; and Esparbé, as a bartender. After a short time, they opened a coffee stall at the Poydras Street Market. Around 1878, Maylié visited France with the intention of marrying Marie Boussion, but instead he married her sister, Anna. There is a happy ending, though, for when Marie later came to live with Anna in New Orleans, she met her brother-in-law's business partner and married him shortly thereafter.

Maylié and Esparbé moved their business from the Poydras Market to a building across the street around 1878. Marie Esparbé's culinary talents made her a natural for food preparation. At first, the restaurant built its business upon offering 11:00 a.m. breakfast to market workers. In those early years, the fare was simple, usually consisting of stew, a cup of coffee, and a glass of wine. In 1882 Maylié and Esparbé began a dinnertime table d'hôte service that garnered a long reputation. Its most famous dish was bouilli, served as the first course, and in this, they complied with a much older and rural French way of beginning a meal. This tradition had gone out of style in much of France even by 1825, when Jean Antheleme Brillat-Savarin published his famous treatise on food. The great man apparently hated boiled beef, and anyone looking for harsh words on the topic can easily find them in his works. Americans today, even a few New Orleanians, seem to agree with him, but Maylié and Esparbé preserved the older tradition, and bouilli with horseradish was popular for many years.

In its very plainness, bouilli conformed to the French Creole penchant for economical dishes. Writing of the recipe in 1941, Eugénie Lavedan Maylié provided advice to the homemaker: "When bouilli is cooked at our restaurant, it is cut into large pieces of about 8 to 10 lbs, but for a small family buy a piece of beef brisket about 4 lbs. Do not make the mistake of getting an inferior piece of soup meat—it must be brisket. To this amount of meat allow about 6 qts. of water and boil slowly for four hours. This meat is not seasoned. It is suggested that a good sauce can be made by the guest of Creole mustard, horseradish, catsup, and other seasonings." Although Maylie's closed in 1987, Tujague's today retains the tradition of bouilli (called brisket by them) as a house specialty between the soup and the entrée.

Unlike grillades and bouilli, daube glacée is very rarely served in restaurants. Tracing the history of daube glacée recipes brings one, once again, squarely within the tradition of the private, economical Creole kitchen, where certain recipes are reserved only for locals and where food has an assigned place, symbolically and literally, within the "culinary year." More than other dishes, this one is hidden in the home; John DeMers notes in his book *The Food of New Orleans*, "This famous Creole dish is to meats what calas are to desserts—seldom seen yet fondly remembered."

The first two New Orleans cookbooks, both published in 1885—the Christian Woman's Exchange's *The Creole Cookery Book* and Lafcadio Hearn's *La Cuisine Creole*—include daube glacée. The former, true to its efforts to present New Orleans as an American city while also marketing the quaintness of the past to tourists, gives its title in English:

COLD JELLY DAUBE

Four lbs. round of beef; season well with salt, pepper, a little garlic, 1 bay leaf, and 1 clove. Lard well through and through; sprinkle with a tablespoonful of vinegar, and let it stand for 24 hours. Put the daube in a pot with a small piece of lard; cover with heavy cover on a slow fire, and let it smother for about 4 hours, until thoroughly done; then take off the cover, let it fry a light brown, then remove from the fire. In a separate pot, have 3 pigs feet and 3 calves feet boiling steadily till they leave the bone (to be skimmed well at the first boil); add one carrot to boil about ½ hour, then slice in length and place at bottom of bowl when the daube is to be served. Break 2 eggs, whites and shells to be beaten together and boiled with jelly briskly, then strain through thick flannel or cloth. Mix the daube gravy with jelly; let it rest about ½ an hour, then pour slowly over the daube. Set it in a cold place, and when cold, take the lard from the top with a spoon, and with a round edge knife detach carefully the daube and turn into a round plate. To avoid breaking the jelly, place the plate on top of the bowl and turn it over.

With a different marketing strategy, but one also intended for tourists, Lafcadio Hearn retained the French name, accompanied by an English explanation in the recipe title. This and other recipes in Hearn's book were always rumored to have come from information provided him by Creole women, notably Adrienne Goslé Matas:

DAUBE GLACÉE OF BEEF, FOR COLD SUPPERS

Take a thick round of beef—from four to six inches is the best size—make holes in it and stuff them with salted pork or bacon; roll each piece, before it is drawn through the beef, in pepper, salt, sugar, and vinegar, with minced parsley, and a very little minced garlic. If the weather is cold it will be better to keep the meat till the next day before cooking it. Boil two calf's feet or four pig's feet until they drop to pieces; pick out the bones and strain the liquor; set it away to jelly, or put it on ice to make it jelly. The next morning, put one half the jelly in a large stew pan, then add the beef, and cover it with the remainder of the jelly. Paste the pan over very tight or cover it extremely well, so that none of the flavor can escape. Cook this about four hours; when done, take out, cover with the liquor, and set it aside till it is jellied. This is delicious to eat cold, for suppers and collations.

Several aspects of Hearn's recipe are significant, the first being that this version adds an editorial comment, telling of daube glacée's use for suppers and collations. Hearn thus shares with his readers not only the ingredients and instructions, but also something of how one might learn of the dish as a child growing up in New Orleans. Not a native himself, Hearn implies to us that daube glacée is a family dish, that is, a supper dish light enough to be used following a period of fasting and enjoyed by people still closely enough attached to the French colony to retain the correct French spelling.

Other recipes for daube glacée appeared steadily beginning in 1900, each attesting to some special quality in the dish. In almost all editions of *The Picayune Creole Cook Book*, a statement appears that advises the readers of its special place: "This is one of the most excellent dishes made by the Creoles, and is always a great standby for luncheons in winter." An increasing number of recipes appear in the following decades, with high points hit in the 1960s, the 1970s, and the early twenty-first century. When protein itself became highly touted as the center of every meal, then daube glacée regained its popularity. In choosing eighteen books that feature daube glacée, one can trace collectively no less than sixty-seven ingredients, with the only consistent materials being meat, vegetables, spices, and stock. Of the meats used, most recipes call for beef, and one of these also adds veal, while one calls for corned beef. In all the recipes, not much attention is given to the quality of the red meat used. This absence underscores the definition of the Creole as the thrifty cook, implying that, with the usual care and spicing of dishes, the quality of meat is not so important. Yet it also presents an impediment to readers who are outside the Creole community: What kind of meat should be torn up, diced, or shredded?

The recipes assume that the daube or roast, flavored and served the day before, will be ready and waiting for the cooking of the daube glacée. Care and attention are diverted to securing veal knuckles, salt pork, hog's head, or pig's feet. The leftover beef will be cooked with these fatty, boned meats, spices, and stock. After three or four hours of cooking, the meat is tenderized and spiced. When chilled, the jellied effect comes from the fats, oils, and marrow released in this process. Differences between the eighteen recipes from New Orleans cookbooks rest in the variety of other additives: the extra fats, such as the lard, oil, or bacon grease in seven of the recipes, and fermented liquids, such as vinegar or wine (most often sherry, but also red wine) that appear in all but five. Incidentally, among those cookbook writers not focusing on New Orleans cuisine, the most gracefully authoritative of all British food writers, Elizabeth David, provides one of the most elegant descriptions for daube glacée, or, as she calls it, *Boeuf à la Mode* (cold beef in jelly). To her, the finished dish has a "beautiful limpid appearance" or is, in fact, "polished."

The decoration and presentation as described in these cookbooks greatly varies; but in custom with cold dishes everywhere, directions usually urge that daube glacée be made pleasing or attractive. In this, New Orleanians again followed French tradition. *Larousse Gastronomique* translates Antonin Carême: "The basis of a cold buffet is attractive presentation. Judicious cooking and careful seasoning are also supremely important. Good jellies are essential. These must be clarified, perfectly transparent." The mold can first be decorated and set with nicely cut carrots and celery, olives, hard-boiled eggs, lemons, beets, or radishes. Other serving suggestions incorporate the use of lettuce, crackers, bread, biscuits, mayonnaise, Creole mustard, or horseradish. Molds themselves are never discussed. Today, knowledge handed down from mother to daughter relates that egg cartons might be used for small molds holding portions just the size of Ritz crackers. Other advice concerns using molds that are easily pliable, using Pyrex custard cups, and shredding versus cubing meat.

Although the writers of the *New Orleans Carnival Cookbook* (1951) believed that daube glacée could be served with "practically anything," its place today rests clearly on holiday tables. Until the mid-twentieth century, New Orleanians prepared it only in the late fall and winter, for, as *The Picayune Creole Cook Book* noted, only in colder temperatures could proper chilling be attained. These months, of course, coincided with Thanksgiving, Christmas, New Year's, and Carnival. So daube glacée became a food of celebration. In *Christmas in the South*, author Randall Bedwell takes pains to trace daube glacée back to the mid-1800s as a New Orleans holiday tradition. The 1972 cookbook by the Junior League of New Orleans offers further documentation of this tradition in the form of an 1840 Creole holiday feast that included daube glacée alongside quail on toast, roast turkey with cornbread dressing, quince jelly, soufflé potatoes, and a French burgundy. The Christmas tradition is noted more recently by daube glacée's inclusion on various holiday season *réveillon* menus, such as that of the Palace Café. (Réveillons were traditional meals eaten after Midnight Mass on Christmas Eve. Modern restaurant réveillon menus are served over a period of a few weeks.) Even today, although daube glacée is commercially prepared in one or two New Orleans grocery stores all year round, only during the period from Thanksgiving through Mardi Gras is it sold in large quantities, often by special order.

Refrigeration, however, has resulted in some changes. Beginning in the 1960s, daube glacée appeared as a summer dish. In 1967 Marie Louise Snellings, for example, defined it as especially suitable as a summertime main dish. And Feibleman, writing with Lillian Hellman about the year in special foods, added daube glacée to his chapter "Food for the Fourth of July."

Although served in all seasons today, the association of daube glacée with celebration has not changed. This link is important because New Orleans' main claims to fame, exceeding even the claim of its food, are the revelry of Carnival and the inescapable presence of music on the streets where jazz was born. Daube glacée, in some ways then, resembles other foods that are seductive in their links to family, friends, joys, and pleasures and prized for complementing these images.

The lengthy preparation time required adds another reason to proclaim this food as one reserved for special occasions. Natalie Scott, writing in 1931, realized that long hours of cooking might appear daunting to some. She therefore gives two cold daube recipes, noting that they are the "gift of champion daube glacé makers, and . . . the only two I have ever seen that do not meander though paragraphs calculated to quell the most ardent culinary enthusiasm." At the beginning of her Green Shutter Daube Glacé she adds, "Ef yo' gonna stint yo' money, bes' not set yo' min' on a gol' chain: don' sta't out for a cold daube, lessen yo' gonna pay it time en' trouble." Despite the borrowing of language style from Joel Chandler Harris and Scott's own bothersome habit of idealizing and insulting (at once) African American cooks, the message remains: the creation of daube glacée will take time.

The long lists of herbs and seasonings also add to the definition of the celebratory in daube glacée. Spiciness is an important component in this role, at least to many outsiders, since the city itself is often likened to "an aging coquette, with a spicy past" and food should reflect this past. Spiciness is important because of the cool blandness of the aspic and the need to make leftover beef special.

Finally, a part of this celebratory nature is linked to the ties of daube glacée to its French heritage. If a dish is given a special status within this older revered culinary past, it is often served for special events. Waverly Root and Richard de Rochemont chose daube glacée as one of the foods that show just how much French, the language of cooking, has remained in Louisiana. Of course, the word *daube* itself is French, but the meaning is more complicated for New Orleanians. *Larousse Gastronomique* includes the vague explanation that the term *daube* "in ancient cookery . . . was reserved almost exclusively for braised meat to be eaten cold." Over the years in France, daube came to mean a hot dish, beef cooked slowly in a *daubière* with red wine, vegetables, and seasonings, and that meaning also transferred to New Orleans. Most New Orleanians today, however, mean the cold version when they say "daube" and have retained the older serving style and meaning. This way of letting daube stand for the older meaning of a cold meat dish extends from the nineteenth century to the present. *La Petite Cuisinière Habile*, for example, a book known to have been used in New Orleans in the 1840s and 1850s, included a cold dish known as *Dindon en Daube*. This recipe added a veal knuckle to turkey meat to make the jelly. The recipe instructs, "It is customary to serve the turkey en daube the day after cooking it, cold and with its jelly."

In the twentieth century, Feibleman and others use the word *daube* to mean daube glacée as a way of heightening the Creole association, rather than a contemporary French connection. Although the index of his *American Cooking: Creole and Acadian* gives glazed beef as the parenthetical translation for daube glacée, his account of "the cooking of the daubes" shows the meticulous pains and the long hours required of someone he defines as an insider to Creole culture, whose "grandmother spoke no English at all." In the 1990s, the food writer Gene Bourg also used the word *daube* for daube glacée, musing that "daube wasn't something you ever ate in restaurants," but he also later spoke of daube served as a stew at Casamento's. And daube with spaghetti is also a hot dish in other New Orleans neighborhood restaurants.

Peter Feibleman, Gene Bourg, and John DeMers place daube glacée in the home kitchen. But who is in this kitchen? Although Feibleman was born in New Orleans, he required an interpreter of daube glacée, a white woman named Phyllis Eagen, who would distribute daube glacée to other women:

> Part of the pride that many women take in a Creole heritage is their knowledge of food, and Phyllis is no exception. Her kitchen is a large square roomy room with plenty of surfaces to work on and a table at the center to sit at. . . . Now watch: No less than a dozen beef roasts, each weighing about two and a half pounds, are lined up on the sideboard because Phyllis isn't going to make daube glace for herself alone. Two or three of the people in the kitchen will walk off with one daube apiece, and there is the woman who lives a few blocks away—she's been promised one, and so have her children—and there is the relatively new invention of the freezer, which permits Phyllis to keep a few for the future.

Earlier elite women, both white and African American, as well as their usually African American cooks, were first given control over the perpetuation of Creole identity though their connections to food, food preparation, and culinary literature. These women's prominence continued well into the twentieth century. For example, only three men's names appear as authors among forty-five books listed in a bibliography of cookbooks on Louisiana published from 1860 to 1960. In the collection of the Vorhoff Library at Tulane, of the twenty-three cookbooks published on New Orleans cuisine between 1901 and 1960, 65 percent were authored by individual white women and another seven titles were authored by groups, five of which were exclusively women's clubs. In addition, the cookbook considered the most authoritative on Creole cuisine is *The Pica-yune Creole Cook Book*, first published in 1900 as *The Picayune's Creole Cook Book*. Urban rumor has always held that the recipes in that book were contrib-uted by readers of the newspaper's women's pages and are attributed to women's oral traditions. This legendary attribution seems to hold some truth when one digs deeper and finds numerous articles on food by journalist Catharine Cole in the pages of the newspaper, the *Daily Picayune*. Also, if one looks at a 1933 cookbook by Natalie Scott and Caroline Merrick Jones, one finds that they du-plicate some of the *Picayune* recipes, sometimes noting the names of various cooks (most often women) and reproducing the two-column arrangement of all editions of the *Picayune* cookbooks. Other twentieth-century experts on Creole cookery were Lena Richard, Mary Land (whom James Beard credited as start-ing the national interest in the cuisine of the region), and Deirdre Stanforth.

Most of these writers gave considerable attention to the influence of Africa on Creole cuisine—and, indeed, the Creole kitchen as defined in edition after edition of *The Picayune Creole Cook Book* features prominent allusions to Afri-can American women: the "negro cooks," the "mammies," "Aunt Chloe," and "Ma-tilda." In the first edition (1900), this "cook of cooks" is visually presented on the cover complete with kerchief and wooden spoon; and in the sixth edition (1922), a similar representation places her seated at an open hearth, with the caption, "A Creole Kitchen of Sixty Years Ago." Despite this prominence, it is important to remember that not until the twentieth century would African Americans be encouraged to write down their recipes for publication. The first of these was Lena Richard, who interestingly dedicates her book to her former employer, an elite white woman. In this Richard inverts the tradition of white women who thanked African American women, while also cementing the role of both races of women as purveyors of Creole cooking traditions. This dedication is to Mrs. Nugent B. Vairin. Though probably not intentionally, the white woman's name is hidden behind that of her husband in much the same way that the African American's first name is the only name given by white authors.

Most in New Orleans today report that there is very little difference be-tween the cuisines of the white and black Creole communities, but they believe that daube glacée is more often chosen by women than by men. Scholars such as Josephine A. Beoku-Betts have argued that cooking forms an integral part of fe-male traditions. Scholars see cooking and its attendant duties as at once oppres-sive and empowering to women: "Even though food preparation perpetuates relations of gender inequality . . . it can provide a valued identity, a source of empowerment for women, and a means to perpetuate group survival." Arjun Appadurai similarly shows how women are given control over the perpetuation of a national identity through their connections to food, food preparation, and culinary literature.

Though not credited with achieving a national identity, women in New Orleans are often recognized as saving Creole culture and, certainly, Creole cooking. Today this Creole heritage reflects the French origins of food in the names given various dishes, the Creole reconfiguration of this legacy, and the place of New Orleans cuisine in a tourism economy that requires its practitioners to share—or sell—their traditions. Those both empowered and disempowered by Creole traditions "sell" many of their recipes but maintain some control by retaining, at least in spirit, other recipes within their private domain. Daube glacée is one such food, perhaps the last one, retained in spirit and often in actuality as a part of a world closed to outsiders.

For the most part, television chefs have taken over promoting the city's cuisine to a national audience. Gumbo and jambalaya are served in cities from coast to coast, the result of decades-long familiarity; yet only infrequently, and indeed not at all until the 1970s, did daube glacée appear in cookbooks outside of Louisiana. In a search of some one hundred cookbooks, we only found one recipe in *Colorado Cache Cookbook*, put out by the Junior League of Denver in 1978. Daube glacée also took the place of honor as one of John Folse's television show's recipes of the week in 1997. In late 1999, daube glacée recipes also began appearing on the Internet and in the nationally marketed *Every Day's a Party: Louisiana Recipes for Celebrating with Family and Friends* by Emeril Lagasse.

Yet daube glacée remains a private food. Recall that from Lafcadio Hearn onward we see daube glacée as a homey dish—perfect for a cold supper in the kitchen or a ladies' lunch in the dining room. But the private nature also has to do with the use of leftover meat, something usually associated with home, and the lengthy process of boiling down bones for jelly, a time during which women could work alone or together at other chores.

The number of ingredients also reflects a degree of secrecy, and the long instructions were necessary before the invention of gelatin itself or before recipes added consommé, which already either contained the boiled down shanks or added gelatin. Although the first gelatin patent was awarded in 1845 and the plain Knox brand gelatin reached popularity by 1908, Creole women remained loyal to the boiling down of bones at least until the 1930s. This reluctance to move toward the use of commercial gelatin is consistent with one of the Creole cooking prerequisites to make economical use of all materials. Not until Metairie Garden Club's *Favorite Recipes from Old Metairie* (1938) and Saint Matthew's Guild's *De Bonnes Choses à Manger* (1939) do we find recipes that list commercial gelatin. Even today, recipes with canned soup or commercial soup mixes or other prepared ingredients are handed around with some secrecy; only two published recipes with any time-saving features are said to be favorites. Some of the recipes of the late twentieth century completely transform the Creole specialty by calling for corned beef instead of fresh meat; Lipton onion soup mix instead of fresh vegetables; garlic powder and Tabasco for spices; and beef or chicken consommé for stock. Yet a 1962 recipe, still favored by many New Orleanians, without either gelatin or consommé, is found in William Kaufman and Sister Mary Ursula Cooper's *Art of Creole Cookery*.

Privacy is also retained since there is so much variation in published forms, particularly with regard to the many inconsistencies in how to handle the cooked meat. Both Hearn's and *The Picayune's* recipes call for the daube to be cooked tender, until the meat falls apart. In *De Bonnes Choses à Manger* the author says to pull and shred the meat with a fork. The Women's Republican Club's *New Orleans Carnival Cookbook* includes the instruction that the meat must be sliced, and in the Junior League of New Orleans' *Plantation Cookbook* it must be diced. When queried, noted food writer Marcelle Bienvenu recalled that her aunts—classic daube makers who took over whole refrigerators each Christmas for the molds to be given as gifts—were a bit shocked to learn that some cooks shredded their meat even before cooking.

Spicing in the dish might also contribute to the realm of the private. Most recipes conform to the use of fresh garlic, salt, black pepper, cayenne, bay leaves, thyme, and parsley. But over the years, the delicate act of spicing the dish has been challenged by recipes using garlic powder, Worcestershire sauce, or Tabasco. The popularity of these ingredients coincided with the rise of Cajun and Creole cuisine in the United States in the 1970s. Traditional methods, however, still involve mixing original spices to taste. The use of Tabasco (considered local since the McIlhenny family has homes in New Orleans, even though Tabasco is made 130 miles away, in New Iberia) is never hidden, though many cooks will not tell you they use Worcestershire sauce, and many will apologize even for the use of green onions. Most New Orleans cooks are surprised to learn that local restaurateur Christopher Blake advised the use of canned onions and carrots in his recipe; these New Orleanians attribute this "failing" to the times in which he wrote. In the late 1970s and early 1980s, New Orleans cookbooks caught up with the rest of the nation's habit of turning to prepared foods. From the restaurant he ran in his home, Blake was locally, as James Beard was nationally, intent on telling New Orleanians how to eat better on less money.

Blake calls daube glacée the "poor man's elegant dish." In his 1986 *Patout's Cajun Home Cooking*, Alex Patout writes that daube glacée was traditionally served at Cajun weddings and receptions because it could stretch a small amount of meat for a large group and it did not waste the pan drippings. But daube glacée is very infrequently, some say never, urged upon the visitor. Even in the tourist literature, daube glacée is rarely mentioned. The exceptions are to be found in the 1938 WPA guidebook to the city and Carolyn Kolb's *Dolphin Guide to New Orleans*, both of which discuss Creole home cuisine. Indeed, daube glacée is only listed on the menus of two well-known restaurants throughout the twentieth century. The first was the restaurant called Corinne Dunbar's, which operated from 1935 to 1987 in a private home. More recently, daube glacée has appeared on the menu at Broussard's since 1998 and the previously mentioned réveillon menu at the Palace Café at Christmas time in 2006. Finally, privacy is also maintained because outsiders, those from "away," are not so fond of daube glacée.

Daube glacée thus has become a mark of a certain type of home, a certain type of resident, who defines himself or herself as a New Orleanian. Overall, as is the case with much else that is both modern and traditional in cooking, daube glacée remains symbolic of a number of varying traditions. Daube glacée uses leftover ingredients or replicates a time when they were used; and once made, it reposes on a table designed to celebrate traditional ties to the past.

The favorite recipe of the New Orleans Culinary History Group is from *The Plantation Cookbook*:

DAUBE GLACÉ

2 ½ pounds boneless beef chuck

1 ½ pounds boneless pork

Salt

Pepper

3 tablespoons bacon grease

2 veal knuckles (broken in 3 pieces)

3 onions, sliced

3 carrots, sliced

12 cloves, sliced

5 cloves garlic

8 sprigs parsley

5 bay leaves

1 teaspoon thyme

1 cup chopped celery

1 teaspoon allspice

½ teaspoon cayenne

3 cups beef bouillon

1 cup white wine

2 cups water

½ cup brandy

4 tablespoons gelatin

1 cup water

5 tablespoons lemon juice

3 tablespoons Worcestershire

2 tablespoons salt

½ teaspoon Tabasco

2 teaspoons white pepper

½ cup finely chopped pimento

Garnish: finely chopped parsley, lemon slices

Remove fat from meat; dry well. Salt and pepper meat. In a 6 ½ quart Dutch oven, sear meat in very hot bacon grease. Replace bones and seared meat in Dutch oven; add onions, carrots, cloves, garlic, parsley, bay leaf, thyme, celery, allspice, and cayenne. Pour in beef bouillon, wine, water, and brandy. Cover and simmer 3 hours. Remove meat, cool and dice. Strain stock through cheesecloth with several ice cubes to congeal grease. Soften gelatin in 1 cup water and heat to dissolve. To stock add lemon juice, Worcestershire sauce, salt, Tabasco, white pepper, pimento, and dissolved gelatin. Stir well. The stock should have a very salty and peppery taste as meat absorbs seasoning while jelling. Place diced meat in 2 oiled 1 ½-quart loaf type Pyrex dishes. Slowly add seasoned stock. Chill. When jelled remove grease from top, unmold and slice with very sharp knife. Decorate with finely chopped parsley and lemon slices.

Alternate: To serve as hors d'oeuvres mold in a 3-quart rectangular Pyrex dish. Unmold; cut in small squares to fit on top of crackers.

TURTLE SOUP

Sharon Stallworth Nossiter

Soup is a significant cultural element of New Orleans tables, be it a delicate but flavorful opening course or a thick and filling main dish. Gumbo takes its place as a soup so special that it creates its own category. Creole vegetable "soup bunches," composed of slices of cabbage, a turnip or two, carrots, parsley, and green onion, are as popular today in the city's grocery stores as they were one hundred years ago at the local butcher shop. Adler's, the century-old Canal Street jewelry store and purveyor of the accoutrements of traditional New Orleans entertaining (café brûlot bowls, oyster plates, and silver-plated hot-sauce holders), sells a set of soup bowls picturing indigenous New Orleans soups and inscribed with recipes from the city's well-known restaurants: Antoine's Creole Gumbo, Bon Ton Crawfish Bisque, Commander's Palace Oyster and Artichoke Soup, and Galatoire's Turtle Soup.

The leading society hostesses of the Garden District, composing their ideal menus for the February 16, 1890, edition of the *Daily Picayune*, tended largely in the direction of asparagus soup; although one, Mrs. Samuel Delgado, suggested turtle soup as an admirable element of a cold-weather menu. The editors of *The Picayune's Creole Cookbook* second edition of 1901, always eager to pontificate on the glories of New Orleans tables and their ancient ties to France (although culinary historian Jessica Harris deems the book "rooted in the creolized African-American tradition of New Orleans"), note that the Creole population, while dispensing with the morning cup of bouillon typical of a well-regulated French household, continued with the practice of a daily serving of soup at dinner, a happy custom which spread even into the other side of town, the much-despised American sector. This custom continues: Galatoire's general manager Melvin Rodrigue noted in 2005 that "many of the restaurant's patrons do not consider dinner to be a complete meal without a soup course." Longtime local food writer Tom Fitzmorris recently identified no fewer than twenty restaurants serving his favorite soups, among them two turtle soups and five gumbos. Other recommendations range from crab-and-corn to Vietnamese pho, Catalan zarzuela, oyster, lentil, and roasted garlic. The popularity of a range of soups, the newer offerings of creative chefs and immigrant populations combined with the traditional mainstays of Creole cuisine, reflects New Orleanians' open-mindedness toward new foods and loyalty to traditional favorites.

The most unusual of local favorites remains turtle soup—unusual if only because New Orleans is the only remaining outpost of a European-style turtle soup, once the darling of epicures and aristocracy, now fallen prey to changing tastes and dwindling supplies. Originally and most characteristically made with sea turtle, it is now dependent on fresh-water turtles as the marine turtle has been hunted to the point of endangerment. Its harvest, illegal in the United States since 1971, is tightly controlled around the world. Alligator snapping turtles and common snapping turtles from the eastern half of the United States now provide much of the meat for the commercial market in Louisiana.

Earlier indigenous people of the Gulf Coast and the Caribbean islands, through which many Louisiana colonists passed, ate turtle, either its eggs or its meat or both. Noted food historian Waverly Root claims that the sea turtle "was so important for Gulf Coast Indians that it has been called the 'buffalo of the Caribbean.'" Some thought that eating turtle meat before battle would protect them from injury, he wrote. Turtle broth was supposed to cure sore throats and was fed to babies. In the Caribbean, turtle soup was the staple of many ordinary eaters. But the English, with their West Indian plantations, brought enormous sea turtles to London in the mid-eighteenth century, live in tubs of seawater. Steaks of turtle meat and fins were at first exotic and then became a part of English and American cookery just as some of the first American cookbooks were being published.

"To Dress a Turtle" appeared in Amelia Simmons's influential *American Cookery*, the first cookbook written by an American, published in Hartford, Connecticut, in 1796. She also provided a recipe for mock turtle soup, calling it "To Dress a Calve's Head. Turtle fashion." Simmons lifted the instructions for turtle soup from Englishwoman Susannah Carter and her *Frugal Housewife*, but Simmons's inclusion of them and the subsequent copying of her own work by other cookbook writers provided specific information for the housewife who wanted to prepare the easily found "shellfish." Such it was considered by many, to the point that some Catholics could eat turtle meat during Lent, and Jews couldn't eat it at all. Simmons's or, rather, Carter's recipe called for baking in casseroles, much in the manner of what came to be called Calapash in the Low Country of South Carolina, where the turtle was stewed, then packed back into its own shell and baked. *Calapash* is the word for the turtle's upper shell, and it is also the gelatinous green substance found next to the upper shell. (Calabash, on the other hand, is a hard vegetable shell, like a gourd, which can be used as a vessel—an interesting similarity to note.)

The *Creole Cookery Book* of the Christian Woman's Exchange also packs the shell with its Terrapin Pie, a casserole of well-chopped turtle meat mixed with butter, eggs, allspice, mace, shallot, and soaked, mashed bread, and additionally gives a recipe for turtle steaks. Carter's recipe called for Madeira; Calapash, for wine or whiskey, cloves, mace, and lemon; and Turtle Steaks, for a squeeze of lemon before serving. Prosper Montagné's *Larousse Gastronomique* (1961) notes that the aromatic mixture of basil, thyme, bay, and marjoram, called "turtle herbs," was used to flavor soups or sauces called *à la tortue.*

The *Picayune's Creole Cook Book* brings together the most characteristic flavorings of turtle soup in its recipes. Green Turtle Soup is made with the calapash, or *calipee* (gelatinous and yellow, found adjoining the lower shell), of a sea turtle. It is spiced with cloves and allspice; a quarter of a small lemon is chopped and added near the end, and a glass of sherry is added just before serving. Turtle Soup No. 2 also calls for cloves and allspice; the sherry is added before serving, and the lemon is sliced thin and added to the soup. Turtle Soup No. 2, however, differs in one major way from all preceding recipes in that it calls for tomatoes. Sometime in the seventeen years between the 1885 publications of *The Creole Cookery Book* and Lafcadio Hearn's *La Cuisine Creole* and the 1901 edition of the *Picayune* book, tomatoes had become a recognized ingredient of Creole turtle soup. Local food writer Marcelle Bienvenu, who edited a 1987 version of the *Picayune* book, identified Turtle Soup No. 2 as the version most featured in New Orleans restaurants and most popular among the city's residents. Its garnishes are most often chopped hard-boiled egg or lemon slices, and sherry is offered to taste.

In *Creole Feast*, Chef Nathaniel Burton provided recipes from the Creole chefs of thirteen well-known restaurants of the 1970s and gave sometimes as many as five versions of a dish. It is an interesting way to compare the permutations of recipes, all of which differ, but each of which is identifiable as an icon of New Orleans tables. It is no wonder that New Orleanians can spend hours disputing the fine points of preferred versions of a favorite when so many are offered. But Burton's late 1970s book, co-written by civil rights activist Rudy Lombard and edited by acclaimed author Toni Morrison, also provides an interesting contrast to the celebrity chef culture of 2008. Until fairly recently, the renown of a restaurant rarely extended to the men and women who worked in the kitchen. The cooks of restaurants such as Broussard's, Galatoire's, the Caribbean Room at the Hotel Pontchartrain, and Corinne Dunbar's were anonymous except to those who worked and trained there. "I knew black people were cooking in homes and restaurants like Broussard's and Galatoire's," said Lombard, whose mother cooked for the president of the Cotton Exchange. "I couldn't name names, so I set out to discover who they were." He discovered a group of people, self-taught, most of whom began as dishwashers. Not all were even from New Orleans. But they were all black cooks, who learned from other black cooks. "French, Spanish, Cajun, Italian—all these ethnic groups live in New Orleans, but they are not running the kitchens of the best restaurants in the city," Lombard wrote. "The single, lasting characteristic of Creole cuisine is the Black element."

In the years since then, the culture of professional kitchens has changed, to some degree. There are chefs who bring along their untrained employees and promote them to the line, but there are fewer black executive chefs in New Orleans restaurants, more culinary school graduates in the top kitchens, and much more emphasis on celebrity. Chef Paul Prudhomme was one of the first celebrity chefs, and under his lengthy tenure, New Orleans turtle soup underwent another historic mutation. Prudhomme, who grew up in the Acadian countryside of Louisiana, began his New Orleans career at Commander's Palace in 1975. Turtle soup had been on the menu at Commander's for years, as had a unique soft-shell turtle stew. But Prudhomme revised the soup by, among other things, adding finely chopped spinach to the characteristic flavors. "I understand turtle soup," Prudhomme said recently in an interview with the author. "I've done it for the last 50 years. . . . Spinach will give a nice tartness to it. People don't think of spinach as being tart, but I always have. It has a unique tartness. And one of the things about turtle soup, it was sort of too reddish, so that was one of the reasons for the spinach. It gave it a bump in color as well as the taste."

Prudhomme left Commander's, which is owned by the Brennan family, in 1979 to open his own K-Paul's Louisiana Kitchen, but spinach stayed in the soup at both places. Given the number of chefs who have moved through the kitchens at Commander's and at K-Paul's in the last twenty-eight years and then gone into other kitchens or opened their own restaurants, it is not surprising that Prudhomme's turtle soup is most familiar now to New Orleans diners. Another familiar style is that of Galatoire's, which has served the same turtle soup since it opened in 1905.

Historically, turtle soup gained popularity with the European explorations of the West Indies, where turtles became an important food resource for sailors and pirates and a luxury item on English tables. As exploration continued westward, the popularity of this easily found and exploited meat grew. Almost three hundred years ago, Bienville, the founder of New Orleans, enjoyed a soft-shell turtle soup here in which the shell was eaten as well as the meat, and Commander's Palace was still serving a soft-shell turtle stew in 1973. In 1803, Pierre Laussat, the last French colonial administrator of New Orleans, wrote: "The Mississippi furnished the soft-shell turtle (*testudo ferox*) which connoisseurs prefer. It is irascible and mean and has a head like a serpent. From under its carapace a long, pointed snout and a pair of beady eyes project. It lifts its head boldly. Cooks in these regions prepare these animals perfectly." He served twenty-four gumbos as his final official entertainment, "six or eight of which were sea turtle," which were preferred to the freshwater turtle.

Turtle soup was a gift to those who indulged in the lavish banquets of the eighteenth and nineteenth centuries. "The special quality of turtle soup was said to be that it did not 'cloy.' In other words, one could eat almost any quantity without ill effects. . . . When banquets started with this soup, the diner was considered best able to enjoy the numerous rich dishes to follow." According to the anonymous writers of *The Picayune's Creole Cook Book*, land terrapin was "unfit to eat," although freshwater terrapin, which is the sort used today, could be "a most relishable article of food if cooked according to Creole methods." They recommended the female diamondback terrapin, in season from November to March, adding that the males were of far less delicate flavor. This book contains more instructions for butchering and dressing the turtle. The whole business sounds far too visceral for most of today's cooks, accustomed to buying their meat pre-cut and packaged. To wit: "Often . . . after this operation [the beheading] is performed the turtle will exhibit extraordinary signs of life, the flesh quivering constantly." And the writers caution against a second boiling or re-warming of the soup, which they warn will deprive it of much of its delicious flavor.

Writing in the mid-twentieth century, Mary Land noted the presence of the following types in Louisiana: alligator snapping turtles and the common snapping turtle, green sea turtles and the sea loggerhead turtle, the land gopher, and "the famous diamond back terrapin." The fat female turtle was highly prized, Land wrote. She recommended feeding an alligator snapping turtle— which eats frogs, snails, worms, and other turtles as well as aquatic plants—on milk for several days before killing it. Sea turtle meat had to be boiled for several hours and then simmered until it fell apart. Her recipes for alligator snapper, diamondback terrapin, and green (sea turtle) soup all call for Madeira or sherry and chopped hard-boiled eggs. Land also gives recipes for turtle eggs in uses other than soup, either boiled for half an hour or in a "puff": boiled yolks mashed, mixed with hen egg whites, rolled into a ball, floured, and fried. Eggs have always been a component of the soup, whether hard-boiled chicken eggs or the turtle eggs found within the female's sac in the spring. Leah Chase writes in *The Dooky Chase Cookbook* of her Uncle Charlie going out into the swamp with a long iron rod to prod for snapper, or cowan, turtles. "He had to do this carefully because they were always snapping at him." Easter dinner was the traditional time for this dish in her rural Creole household.

In 1971, lovers of turtle soup retrenched when the sea turtle trade ended with the passage of the Endangered Species Act. The venerable Antoine's (c. 1840) began serving potage alligator au sherry in the mid-1970s, when turtle meat became scarce, and neither the alligator soup nor turtle soup remained on the menu in 2008. The turtles that replaced the sea turtle include the alligator and common snapping turtles, diamondback terrapins, red ears, and soft shells from all around: Oklahoma, Kansas, Georgia, Arkansas, and the lakes and rivers of the East Coast, especially Maryland. Very little comes from Louisiana, said Harlon Pearce, owner of Harlon's LA Fish, which supplies seafood to many New Orleans restaurants. All of the meat he buys is wild caught, as turtle farms exist mostly to stock pet stores and for the Chinese market, which prefers to buy its turtles live.

The price of turtle meat has tripled in recent years, Pearce said, due largely to the Chinese market, where turtle meat is still a fashionable delicacy and is also thought to have medicinal qualities. Outside of New Orleans and the Brennan's restaurant in Houston, the biggest North American markets for turtle meat are Asian populations in California, New York, and Canada, he said. A few states, worried that the huge Chinese demand could threaten the animals with extinction, have passed laws banning commercial harvesting of wild turtles. Louisiana has banned the harvesting of alligator snapping turtles and put a size limit on diamondback terrapins.

Philadelphia, ancestral home of Old Original Bookbinder's Restaurant, progenitor of Bookbinder's Snapper Soup, available by the can today at select grocery stores, still serves up turtle soup. But as can be seen by the name of the Bookbinder's specialty, menus sometimes deceive the unwary by calling it "snapper soup," snapper in this case being the traditional turtle used, not the fish. Philadelphia, along with Baltimore and Washington, was once a stronghold of turtle soup, with commercial preparations available for the unwilling turtle-soup cook. "We omit a receipt for real turtle soup, as when that very expensive, complicated, and difficult dish is prepared in a private family, it is advisable to hire a first-rate cook for the express purpose," wrote Philadelphian Eliza Leslie, author of the immensely popular *Directions for Cookery in Its Various Branches* (1840). "An easy way is to get it ready-made, in any quantity you please, from a turtle-soup house."

"Turtle barbecues were popular in New York in the eighteenth and nineteenth centuries," wrote Root. "However, when turtle became rare as these singularly defenseless animals were gradually killed off, Americans do not seem to have felt the disappearance keenly; turtle had always remained a little foreign to the spirit of Anglo-American cooking." This is a curious conclusion, since the French, who influenced so much of New Orleans' Creole cuisine, apparently had little appetite for turtle soup, while the English were quite fond of it. "Turtle soup is seldom appreciated in France and therefore rarely figures on the menu," wrote the famed French chef Escoffier. "In England, where turtle soup is often served, an excellent one can be bought in cans. It is also available in America."

In New Orleans, we tend to call a turtle a turtle, not a snapper, although some restaurateurs are suspected of supplementing or replacing the turtle with veal or beef trimmings and depending on the essence of the dish—its flavoring of lemon, cloves, and sherry—to carry off the illusion of turtle soup. Natalie Scott offers a strange but economical substitute for Turtle Soup de Famille, with boiled, sieved red beans taking the place of any meat at all. This particular recipe, a child of Prohibition, calls for adding sherry flavoring, grape juice, or cooking wine, "if you are lucky enough to have some."

Mock turtle soups have been a feature of recipe books as long as real turtle soup, for cooks unwilling to wrestle with the reality or price of a turtle going into soup. These call for anything from calf's head and liver to legs or knuckles of veal and calf's feet, which would give the traditional gelatinous texture to the soup. Célestine Eustis (1904) gives the rather unlikely "Baltimore Style of Making Terrapin Stew Without Terrapin," featuring a rabbit, a calf's head, and left-over chicken livers, gizzards, fried ham, or bacon, the dish to be cooked for two hours each of two days. A further substitute, known to many cooks, was mock turtle eggs, to garnish one's mock turtle soup, or even real turtle soup should your turtle not be of the egg-bearing sex or inclination. Scott's recipe for them called for hard-boiled hen's egg yolks mashed with butter and a beaten raw egg to form "a material which as clever cook you sculpt to the shape of turtle eggs," and she made the dubious claim that "not even a turtle could distinguish them from her bona fide eggs."

In the 1973 revision of his wide-ranging look at New Orleans restaurants, from neighborhood and working-class restaurants to the grandest of all, Richard Collin identifies a dozen or so establishments serving good turtle soup, most of them long gone in 2008: the restaurant at D. H. Holmes, Kolb's German Restaurant, Etienne Restaurant, and Jaeger's Seafood Tavern on Elysian Fields. Even cheaper eating places often had turtle soup, he noted in his chapter "Poor Boys, Workingmen's Restaurants, New Orleans Lunch and the Great Center City Disaster Area." "There is a pleasant regularity in this class of restaurant. Each day there are from one to four plate specials at or close to $1. For most of them, Monday is red beans and rice day. . . . [A] favorite Tuesday lunch is lima beans or butter beans, again with sausage or another meat. Meatballs and spaghetti is a favorite Wednesday lunch while corned beef and cabbage often appears on Thursday. Friday is gumbo, turtle soup or fried oysters day."

Turtle soup is not so ubiquitous, or cheap, these days. An informal survey in the summer of 2007 found at least two dozen restaurants that serve turtle soup, some on the daily menu and some as a special, but they were all on the upper end of the catering scale. Pearce, the seafood dealer, sees it as a personal mission to make sure that turtle soup never vanishes from New Orleans tables. "We do things different than other people here, and that's what I'm worried about losing," he said.

PAUL PRUDHOMME'S TURTLE SOUP

Makes 8 to 10 main-course or 16 to 20 appetizer servings. This is a dish for a special occasion.

3 tablespoons plus 2 teaspoons Chef Paul Prudhomme's Meat Magic® OR

Vegetable Magic® OR Magic Seasoning Salt™

1 teaspoon dry mustard

3 pounds boneless fresh turtle meat (see note) or beef stew meat

4 tablespoons unsalted butter

4 tablespoons margarine

½ pound spinach, very finely chopped

2 cups very finely chopped onions

1 cup very finely chopped celery

[3 bay leaves]

3½ cups canned tomato sauce

⅔ cup all-purpose flour

1 teaspoon minced garlic

11 cups (2 quarts plus 3 cups, in all) Rich Turtle or Beef Stock

1 cup, lightly packed, fresh parsley

¼ lemon, seeded

6 hard-boiled eggs, cut in quarters

⅓ cup sherry wine plus sherry to add at the table

Note: In Louisiana, fresh turtle meat is available in the better grocery stores and seafood markets. It's scarce, but before you give up looking for it, try Chinatown markets. It is also marketed frozen and the frozen is fine for turtle soup.

Combine the seasoning mix and dry mustard in a small bowl and set aside. Finely chop the turtle meat in a food processor or with a knife. In a 5-quart saucepan or large Dutch oven melt the butter and margarine over high heat. Add the turtle meat and cook until browned, about 6 to 8 minutes, stirring occasionally. Stir in the seasoning mix, spinach, onions, and celery [and bay leaves]; cook for about 15 minutes, stirring occasionally. Stir in the tomato sauce and cook 10 minutes, stirring frequently toward the end of cooking time. Add the flour and garlic, stirring well; cook 5 minutes, stirring almost constantly and scraping the pan bottom well. Add 2 cups of the stock, stirring well to dissolve any mixture from the pan bottom. Then stir in 7 cups more stock, scraping pan bottom well. Bring soup to a boil, stirring occasionally and

scraping pan bottom as needed. Continue boiling and stirring 5 minutes. Reduce heat to maintain a simmer and cook about 45 minutes, stirring fairly often and scraping pan bottom well.
(While stirring and scraping the bottom, if the mixture sticking to the spoon looks scorched,
quit stirring and pour the soup into a clean pot, leaving the scorched mixture behind.)

Meanwhile, in a food processor or blender, process the parsley and lemon until both are
minced; add the eggs and process a few seconds, just until eggs are coarsely chopped.

When the soup has cooked 45 minutes, add the egg mixture to the soup, stirring well.
Stir in the remaining 2 cups stock and the sherry. Cook 20 minutes more, stirring and scraping
pan bottom occasionally. Remove from heat and discard bay leaves. Salt to taste and serve
immediately.

To serve, allow about 1 ½ cups in each bowl for a main course, or ¾ cup as an appetizer.
Pass additional sherry at the table (allow 1 to 3 teaspoons per 1 cup serving).

The following recipe is one favored by the author, and it borrows from
Galatoire's recipe and those of other cookbooks.

TURTLE SOUP AU SHERRY IN THE STYLE OF GALATOIRE'S

1 large onion, coarsely chopped

2 celery stalks, coarsely chopped

3 green bell peppers, seeded and roughly chopped

1½ pounds ground turtle meat

1 gallon veal stock

1 8-ounce can crushed tomatoes

¼ cup hot paprika

3 tablespoons salt

1½ teaspoons chopped fresh thyme

1 lemon, seeded and sliced into 8 pieces

2 hard-boiled eggs, coarsely chopped

1 cup dry sherry

½ cup minced parsley

2 cups vegetable oil

2 cups flour

Mince the onion, celery, and bell pepper in a food processor. Sauté the turtle meat and minced
vegetables in a little oil until all of the turtle meat is browned, about 5 to 7 minutes. Add the

stock, tomatoes, paprika, salt, and thyme. Bring to a boil, then reduce heat and simmer on medium for 40 minutes. Add lemons, eggs, sherry, and parsley; simmer for another 30 minutes, skimming off any foam from the top of the soup.

While the soup simmers, make a roux. Put the 2 cups oil in a heavy pan and heat on medium. Whisk in the flour, and cook, stirring continuously until the roux is light brown. Add the roux to the soup slowly. Don't let it boil over. Simmer another 5 minutes. Serve with a cruet of sherry, letting people serve themselves to taste.

GUMBO

Cynthia LeJeune Nobles

G umbo is the star of New Orleans gastronomy. Savory, dark, piquant, complex, and downright mysterious, this soup is the one New Orleans dish that first-time visitors think they have to have. More than a tourist "to do," however, gumbo is a staple menu item found in many Louisiana homes, especially in the southern parishes. It is such an important thread in the state's overall culinary fabric that the legislature adopted it as Louisiana's official cuisine. But gumbo's significance goes beyond its appeal at the dining table. Besides satisfying taste buds, this dish personifies the word "Creole"; like its human counterparts, gumbo was born in the New World and took cues from the old but adapted to the new. Remarkably, gumbo has been simmering on local stoves for almost three hundred years. And even with a few modern deviations, each pot is tied to those early roots, and each bowlful is an edible mosaic of the history of the varied cultures that colonized New Orleans.

While the English word for okra developed from *"nkruman"* or *"nkruma"* in the Gold Coast Twi language, the Creole/Louisiana word "gumbo" is derived from the word for okra in the Central Bantu dialect of West Africa, the region that was also the home of many of the first Louisiana African slaves. Most of these slaves came to the colony after 1719. They brought with them a love for spices, smothered greens, and stews. A favorite vegetable of the slaves was okra, known to these particular Africans as *"ki ngombo."* The word may also have evolved into *"quingombo,"* and was later shortened to *"gombo,"* then "gumbo."

The Oxford Encyclopedia of Food and Drink in America takes a different approach and gives attention to a derivation from the Choctaw word *kombo*, for "sassafras," the leaf that is powdered to make the thickening ingredient filé. Okra and filé are said to have first been used by the colonial French in 1722 after a much written about, but never documented, culinary uprising called the Frying Pan Revolt, or the Petticoat Insurrection. The quaint story goes that a group of frustrated housewives banged on pots in front of Governor Bienville's home, protesting their bland diet of cornmeal mush and the lack of familiar ingredients. Bienville reportedly pawned the ladies off to his housekeeper, Madame Langlois, who knew the way of the Choctaw and taught the French women how to cook rice, crabs, shrimp, crawfish, and wild game. Langlois also introduced them to filé, and supposedly the ladies threw the aromatic powder into gumbo, a dish that, by then, they'd already learned to cook from African slaves. If this legend has any truth, then we can surmise that gumbo, in some form, had become part of the diet by the time the French moved camp from the Gulf Coast in 1718, and that filé, although an important ingredient, lent only its thickening power and flavor to the cooking, and not its Native American name.

Aside from the name debate, other battles persist over the dish's evolution. Mary Barton Reed's 1931 graduate thesis refers to Célestine Eustis's *Cooking in Old Creole Days* (1904), and these two early culinary sleuths buy the school of thought that gumbo was a Native American dish that was served only on special occasions. Similarly, respected food writer Waverly Root opines that gumbo meant the vegetable okra, but the word somehow attached itself to the name of a hodgepodge stew originally enjoyed by Native Americans. Another more celebrated argument of gumbo's genesis centers around the possibility that the dish started out as bouillabaisse. In the nineteenth century, French bouillabaisse was one of New Orleans' favorite dishes, as evidenced by the famous English author William Thackeray, who recalls in his *Roundabout Papers* (1891) that he had dined on Lake Pontchartrain and eaten bouillabaisse that was better than what was served at Marseilles. This dish may well have also been popular in colonial times. A quick glance at traditional recipes, however, shows that a typical Marseilles version consists of several types of fish, including rascasse, a bony rock fish, poached in a broth heavily laden with olive oil and saffron, with nary a mention of okra, ham, rice, or even roux, the three latter ingredients all mainstays of the French cooking that certainly existed at the time.

Peter Feibleman, however, consulting with Louisiana food experts in *American Cooking: Creole and Acadian* (1971), thinks that gumbo did start out as bouillabaisse. He believes that after a century of cooking with non-traditional ingredients, the stew was no longer recognizable and had turned into a new dish known as gumbo. Echoing this school of thought, Chef John Folse says that history proves that bouillabaisse evolved into gumbo as a central part of Cajun and

Creole cuisine. Judy Rose, from the *Detroit Free Press*, also writes that French bouillabaisse turned into gumbo, and *New York Times'* food writer and New Orleans resident Julia Reed mirrors that notion. But, New Orleans *Times-Picayune* columnist and acclaimed food expert Lolis Eric Elie disagrees. In a sharp reply to the *New York Times* he says, "As for the relationship between gumbo and bouillabaisse, I can find very little." Elie bolsters his position by referencing a passage from a 1764 court document uncovered by historian Gwendolyn Midlo Hall, author of *Africans in Colonial Louisiana* (1995). Hall's research reveals testimony that two escaped slaves sold goods along New Orleans' streets and "cooked gumbo filé and rice." From this finding, Elie hypothesizes that African maroons, or escaped slaves, not French immigrants, were gumbo's originators.

Of particular interest, Hall's findings point out that the slaves of that period ate their okra with rice, the African *ya ya*, an important gumbo component. Rice was grown in the United States since 1685, when a British ship put into the harbor at Charleston, South Carolina, and left behind a small quantity of Golde Seede Rice that the captain had brought from Madagascar in East Africa. It was another thirty-five years before French colonists began importing slaves especially to grow rice, but by the 1720s, the grain grew along the Mississippi River.

Gumbo's historic pairing with rice is one of two convincing reasons why neither Native Americans' stews nor French bouillabaisse morphed into today's soupy gumbo. Native American stews were centered around corn, an ingredient rarely found in gumbo. It *is* true that nineteenth-century Acadians universally ate their gumbo with corn grits, not rice, as documented by French visitor C. C. Robin in his 1803–05 trip to the Acadian parishes. At the time of Robin's writing, mechanization and artificial irrigation had not yet arrived in the western part of the state. Although some Acadians did own slaves, milling rice by hand with a mortar and pestle made rice a luxury. But, although corn grits served as a base starch, corn in its kernel form was not typically added to gumbo. During this same time period in New Orleans, however, slaves and indentured servants did the bulk of the manual labor, including milling grain. And in the city where gumbo was born, the dish was served with rice, the starch that not so coincidentally came across the Atlantic Ocean with the slaves, their okra, and their familiarity with eating stew with rice. Secondly, the French are experts at technique, not experimentation. In Louisiana's colonial days, cooks brought from France certainly could have substituted local redfish for bouillabaisse's rascasse and found acceptable ingredients to fill in for the rest. But although French cooks were, and still are, masters of measuring, kneading, mixing, and seasoning, they would rather serve a fallen soufflé than completely overhaul a traditional recipe. The gumbo we enjoy today is the child of grand experiments, and it is unlikely that French cooks would have sullied their time-honored bouillabaisse with okra or filé.

A lack of foodstuffs certainly forced the slaves to try out new things at the stove. Likewise, the common French colonial housewife, like the slave, did not have much in her kitchen. Aside from having to stretch sparse pantries, these two groups of cooks had to tenderize tough roosters, hens, and beef. The author of *Lost New Orleans* (1980), Mary Cable, mentions the cheap, leathery fowl and trail-worn cuts used in the nineteenth century, and she explains that New Orleans cooks boiled them in kettles for hours. This long simmering process inadvertently produced a hearty stock that could have easily been thickened with okra, roux, or filé. No doubt, bouillabaisse broth would certainly taste fine in gumbo. But the modern dish more likely sprung from the custom and needs of the African slave and lowly immigrant who combined everything in one pot and extended whatever was at hand.

Other influences quickly presented themselves. During the 1700s and 1800s, several diverse ethnic groups trickled into the Louisiana territory, and with them came the individual ingredients that add interest to modern gumbo. In 1721, over 125 Germans settled forty miles upriver and west from New Orleans, bringing with them knowledge of sausage-making and agriculture. As noted elsewhere in this volume, these hardworking and wildly successful farmers and residents of the "German Coast" rowed down the river to New Orleans and sold fresh vegetables, corn, rice, and indigo and are credited with saving the French colony, more than once, in times of famine. Their produce undoubtedly found its way into gumbo. But it is their *andouille*, a heavily smoked and seasoned French-named German pork sausage, which is a mainstay of rustic country gumbos.

The German impact combined with the influences of Africa and France. These three distinctive cuisines had another jolt in 1762 when Spain took over the colony. Along with stylish architecture and more efficient government, the Spanish brought along *their* cooks and their version of *jamon*, "ham." Virginia hams date back to the mid-seventeenth century, and the French had introduced their jambon earlier to then-isolated Louisiana. And although some speculate that the French jambon sparked the name, the Spanish are credited with combining their ham with rice, *ya ya*, to produce the spicy Creole favorite jambalaya, the New World version of paella.

The Spanish also brought *chaurice*, a "spicy smoked sausage," and they were prolific users of onions, garlic, and parsley. The aromatics were a hit in gumbo, but a quick glance at 1885's *La Cuisine Creole*, the second Louisiana cookbook, shows that ham, and not sausage, was popular in New Orleans gumbo at the time. Lafcadio Hearn, a New Orleans newspaperman and food connoisseur, is credited with compiling the recipes for this book, and ham is present in almost every one of his eight gumbo recipes. Even his seafood gumbos contain ham, and this trend continues in various cookbooks published through the 1950s.

The Spanish government saw a need to strengthen defenses and to build up troop numbers, and so they recruited a group of fishermen from the Canary Islands. These people and their families, who came to be known as the Islenos, settled south of the city in Louisiana's marshes and along the coast. With the Islenos came a love for well-seasoned food. Besides guarding the city, the energetic outdoorsmen also supplied locals with enormous amounts of shrimp, crab, and oysters. Their efforts may be a key reason why seafood gumbo grew so popular.

Fate influenced gumbo again when in 1755 the British military triggered *Le Grand Derangement* (the Great Expulsion). That year the redcoats banished approximately eighteen thousand Acadians from Nova Scotia, then called Acadie, the home to a group of French colonial farmers, fishermen, and trappers. They were later coined *Cajuns*, the word a corruption of the word *Acadian*. During the expulsion, over half died from disease and starvation. Six thousand sailed to disparate places like France, England, the American colonies, Saint-Domingue, and even the Falklands. From these locales, almost three thousand re-congregated in Spanish-owned and French-speaking Louisiana. Eager to start new homes, they settled in the twenty-two parishes south and west of New Orleans, their influx starting in the year 1785 and mostly ending by 1795.

The New Orleans Creoles were cordial to the new provincials and would let them recuperate in the city for about a month, then always nudged them south to the lands around Bayou Lafourche and west to the uncultivated prairies, marshes, and wooded lakes inhabited by the Attakapas. Isolated in their new home, the Acadians foraged for squirrel, duck, goose, turtle, rabbit, deer, raccoon, opossum, snipe, grouse, and wild turkey and caught shrimp, crab, and crawfish. Many of these foods didn't even have a name in their dialect. But over the years, this group of hearty peasants threw their catches into their cast-iron cauldrons. They seasoned and added ingredients with a comparative heavy hand and ended up with their own hearty version of gumbo, a dish similar to what is served in New Orleans, but one that typically lacked seafood before the introduction of refrigeration.

Historian Carl Brasseaux has done extensive research on the Acadians, and writer Jim Bradshaw references him in an article in the *Lafayette Daily Advertiser* (April 27, 1999) as saying that the introduction of gumbo to the Acadian kitchen drastically changed their view of cuisine and was an amalgamation of different cooking techniques. For example, the slaves likely introduced the Acadians to okra. They also gave them hot spices, while the Native Americans introduced them to filé and herbs. The Germans of Louisiana's German Coast are generally credited with teaching the Acadians how to make sausage, especially andouille. The Native Americans taught their new neighbors how to make *tasso* (dried strips of pork or beef). Another wave of immigrants arrived during and after the Haitain slave revolutions (1791–1804), bringing white French planters and their families, free people of color, and slaves—and their preferences for slow cooking and more spicy food. In the 1800s, pepper bushes traced back to Saint-Dominque (now Haiti) grew in Creole gardens, and a bottle of *vinaigre pimente* was usually found on every Creole table and was considered a necessary addition to a bowl of gumbo.

Proper seasoning of gumbo is essential, and in Louisiana adding just the right zing is considered an art. Salt, of course, is universal, and the French, Spanish, Africans, and Native Americans were certainly all familiar with its use. But even though local Native Americans had, for centuries, been evaporating seawater to make salt, the first French imported theirs from France. Commercial salt production in the state started in 1790. Today Louisiana's salt mines provide nearly a quarter of all domestic production. Avery Island is the site of one of five salt islands along the Gulf Coast and home to Louisiana's most famous manufactured product, Tabasco hot sauce, a regular favorite in gumbo. First compounded in 1868, Tabasco sauce takes as its base Tabasco peppers, a special variety of red capsicum peppers from Mexico. Edmund McIlhenny had been given seeds of *Capsicum frutescens* peppers that had come from Mexico or Central America in the mid-nineteenth century. To make their sauce, the peppers are crushed, aged with vinegar and salt, strained, bottled, and sold around the world by the McIlhenny family.

Black pepper, a staple in south Louisiana cooking, originated from Madagascar, an island just east of Africa, a continent that apparently always appreciated highly seasoned food. Ground cayenne pepper, also called "red pepper," is not traditionally found in French cooking but is almost always included in gumbo. Cayenne found its way to Louisiana through the Spanish and was eagerly adopted by the slaves.

Although no early nineteenth-century New Orleans recipes exist, documentation of gumbo can be found from the early 1800s. Rumor had it that Dr. John Sibley, formerly of North Carolina, was running away from his second wife when he moved to Natchitoches. He was appointed by President Thomas Jefferson as a U.S. Indian agent for the Orleans territory in 1805, but before that, in 1802, he visited New Orleans and wrote about "the dish they call gumbo which is made principally of the ochre into a thick kind of soop [sic] & eat with rice, it is the food of every body for dinner and supper." A year later, Pierre-Clément de Laussat, the last French colonial prefect, hosted a twelve-hour soiree in honor of the Spanish Marquis de Casacalvo. The guests were served twenty-four gumbos. Besides chronicling the use of the word, Sibley and Laussat give clues to gumbo's Spanish colonial popularity and illustrate that the dish could be both humble and refined. They also prove that, back then, this gumbo existed in various forms, already a New Orleans staple.

The U.S. flag was raised over New Orleans during the last days of 1803, and soon U.S. citizens from far and wide poured into the city by the thousands. In no time, they became the majority. And, to the shock of a culture that fancied itself sophisticated, these "foreigners" brought Protestantism; a crude language and manners (at least to the French); and pork, corn and more corn, with an outright boring outlook on food. American architect Benjamin Henry Latrobe wrote in his account of travel to the city in the early nineteenth century that unfamiliar foods like crawfish, then an upscale gumbo and bisque ingredient, are "disgusting." Another American, Reuben Thwaite, dined "a la Francaise" around 1807 at a Baton Rouge boardinghouse and shared Latrobe's culinary timidity: "It [gumbo] then becomes so ropy and slimy as to make it difficult with either knife, spoon or fork, to carry it to the mouth, without the plate and mouth being connected by a long string, so that it is a most awkward dish to a stranger, who besides, seldom relishes it, but it is a standing dish among the French Creoles, as much as soup and bouilli is in France." With these accounts in mind, it is easy to assume that the Americans, as the newcomers were called, contributed to the evolution of gumbo only by assuring a strong economy and, therefore, guaranteeing a supply line for ingredients. But they also owned or hired African American cooks who, in turn, eventually taught those in the American sector—the other side of Canal Street—how to appreciate gumbo.

In 1812, the same year Louisiana became a state, the adventurous Creoles of New Orleans were among the first to embrace tomatoes, and they started enhancing gumbo and jambalaya with this vegetable/fruit. By this time, all the essential ingredients for gumbo had arrived. A later influx of Irish and, especially, Italians certainly added new and impressive ingredients to the food stalls. But despite an enthusiastic acceptance of pasta and olives, later immigrants do not seem to have significantly affected the preparation of Creole gumbo.

One of the hallmarks of gumbo is that, with a big enough pot, it can easily be doubled or tripled and is always a good choice to feed a crowd. During C. C. Robin's 1803–05 visit, he recalled that gumbo was served at local dances. Kate Chopin, in her late 1880s "At the Cadian Ball," wrote about the well-to-do rice planter Alcée Laballière, who, looking for a little action, left his fields behind and reached the Cajun ball too late for the midnight chicken gumbo. Apparently, the practice of serving gumbo to the crowd at a *fais-do-do*, a country community dance, has a long tradition in Acadian Louisiana. The *réveillon*, another midnight gathering, was popular with the Creoles until the Civil War. Good Catholics, they fasted Christmas Eve and New Year's Eve, so after midnight mass, appetites were large. On the cusp of Christmas Day, the reveillon (as now written), and especially the more elaborate and heavily attended New Year's midnight meal, would have likely offered gumbo.

In New Orleans, Mardi Gras, yet another institutional party, is associated with floats, champagne toasts, and royalty. But during Acadiana's Mardi Gras, gumbo reigns king. Dating back to medieval and even Roman times, today's version of Mardi Gras involves masked men and women, concealing their identity and parodying authority. On Fat Tuesday in rural Louisiana, thousands ride the countryside, originally on horses, but now in pickup trucks, and beg for gumbo ingredients. *Le Capitaine* leads his group to farms where the owners throw chickens in the air. Housewives offer sausage and onions, and some even donate money. After much singing and dancing and quenching of thirsts, the triumphant beggars return to town, where the community gathers to share in a *gros gumbo* and a dance that ends promptly at midnight, signaling the beginning of Lent.

The first known published recipe that mentions gumbo appears as Gumbo—A West India Dish in *The Virginia House-Wife*, an 1824 cookbook by Mary Randolph, who gives directions for little more than boiling okra in salted, buttered water. Many of the Caribbean slaves that originated from West Africa used the word *gumbo* for okra, and it is easy to deduce that Randolph's recipe is meant to describe the vegetable preparation. Randolph's book does also includes Ochra Soup, an amalgamation of okra, onions, fowl or veal, lima beans, a bit of bacon or pork, and tomatoes, all thickened with flour and butter—the concoction still not the typical Creole gumbo, but much closer to it than her West India Dish. Randolph's Ochra Soup is also similar to *callaloo*, a one-pot spicy stew that was popular in the Caribbean at the time. Callaloo is a close cousin to gumbo and centers around greens or seafood, and sometimes okra, and is still a favorite dish in the islands.

Mrs. Lettice Bryan's 1839 *The Kentucky Housewife* features a recipe similar to Randolph's Gumbo, called West India Gumbo. But another more familiar version appears in Marion Cabell Tyree's *Housekeeping in Old Virginia* (1879). Tyree's Gumbo Filit A La Creole calls for chicken, allspice, cloves, red and black pepper, parsley, thyme, oysters, and *filit* made from pulverized sassafras leaves, the inclusion of filé hinting that New Orleans cooking habits were making their way up through the United States.

Abby Fisher, a southern slave who relocated to San Francisco after the Civil War, could not read or write, yet she dictated recipes to her husband and published one of the first African American cookbooks in the United States. Her 1881 *What Mrs. Fisher Knows about Old Southern Cooking* includes simple recipes for Oyster Gumbo Soup, Ochra Gumbo, and Chicken Gumbo. Her oyster gumbo includes filé and chicken, and the latter two are made with okra. Fisher had cooked in Mobile, a coastal city that has its own strong seafood gumbo tradition. From New Orleans, Hearn's 1885 *La Cuisine Creole* lists eight gumbos, along with general remarks on the dish.

The word "gumbo" appeared in print often in the mid-nineteenth century, a time when travelers often wrote diaries. A. Oakey Hall, a Manhattan journalist, visited the city in 1840, and through his whimsical writing he describes a scene at the elegant St. Charles Hotel, where diners who had just enjoyed a bowl of gumbo were anguished by merely looking at the pots of the stuff on the buffet, and so rushed back for seconds. Gumbo's magnetic reputation is later confirmed by Thackeray, who, after dining on it at a dinner party before the Civil War, pronounced that it was the best soup he'd ever tasted.

Paige Gutierrez's *Cajun Foodways* cites an anonymous manuscript, attributed to Louisiana Justice Joseph A. Breaux, that includes a colorful and unpalatable yet informative passage describing a gumbo served some time at the end of the nineteenth century:

> *Gumbo* is the national dish of Louisianans. . . . It is made from all sorts of meats, fowl, birds, game, fish, etc. cooked on a slow fire in their own juices, with salt, red pepper, and black pepper. The whole is sprinkled with a large amount of dried and powdered sassafras leaves which give an aroma and a certain viscosity to the sauce, much like water in which linseed or macaroni has been steeped. It is hard for a housewife serving *gumbo* to choose pieces swimming in a blackish sauce that leaves them unrecognizable. Her only recourse is to plunge her spoon haphazardly into the homogenous substance and pour its contents into her guest's plate. The guest then fills the remaining space with a quantity of rice.

This "homogenous substance" appears to be a filé gumbo. And although Breaux's mythical housewife uses a barnyard full of ingredients, she does obey gumbo's golden rule—never add okra and filé in the same pot. Although this decree has been known to be broken, today's purists still insist that there are only two types of gumbo, okra and filé—period. Those desiring more nuances classify it into three broad categories, Creole Gumbo, Cajun Gumbo, and Gumbo Z'Herbes, then sub-categorize it into Gumbo Fevis (okra gumbo), Gumbo Filé, or plain roux gumbo, and then break it down at least a dozen times more according to the main ingredients. This mind-boggling number of gumbos represents different taste and regional preferences. Creole Gumbo is usually associated with seafood and tomatoes, along with one or two of the thickeners: okra, roux, and filé. And although chicken is a family favorite, and hunters are partial to wild-game gumbo with sausage, the typical tourist is likely to be served the familiar gumbo of shrimp, crab, and oysters.

African Americans in New Orleans follow the traditional okra/roux Creole template but are more likely to enhance theirs with several kinds of meat and seafood. A prime example is Leah Chase's version. Chef extraordinaire and co-owner of New Orleans' Dooky Chase (the restaurant ravaged by Hurricane Katrina, but spruced up and re-opened September 2007), Leah Chase still whips up the recipe she has used for a half a century. Hers is a glistening, brown mélange of seafood, ham, smoked sausage, crab, shrimp, *chaurice*, and whatever else looks good that day.

Despite these modern preferences, New Orleans cookbooks from the late 1800s and early 1900s feature just as many unsmoked meat-based gumbos as seafood ones and almost always include basic filé and okra gumbos, recipes that call for chicken and, as mentioned earlier, ham. One peculiar cabbage gumbo recipe in the ninth edition of *The Picayune Creole Cook Book* (1938) even calls for steak, ham sausage, and milk, with no roux, okra, or filé. Herbert Asbury declares in his book *The French Quarter* (1936) that some brilliant chef worked the kitchens of La Bourse de Maspero's City Exchange Hotel (a combination inn, ballroom, bar, restaurant, real estate office, and slave auction) and in 1838 introduced gumbo to the New Orleans restaurant scene. We are sure that in 1840 Antoine Alciatore founded Antoine's, the country's oldest family-run restaurant, and from the beginning featured Gombo Creole on its menu. The Junior League of New Orleans *Plantation Cookbook* offers a recipe that is typical of what was served both at home and in early restaurants:

SEAFOOD GUMBO

STOCK:

5 quarts water

2 dozen boiled crabs

3 pounds raw shrimp (heads and shells on)

1 carrot

1 onion, quartered

½ cup coarsely chopped celery

Fill a 6-quart stock pot with 5 quarts of water. Pull off back shells of crabs, adding shells to stock pot. Discard inedible spongy fingers, break crabs in half, and set aside. Peel shrimp, adding heads and shells to pot. Set shrimp aside. To stock pot, add carrot, onion, celery, and cover, simmering for two hours. Strain stock, and return to pot.

GUMBO:

3 cups finely chopped onions

1½ cups finely chopped celery

1 cup finely chopped green peppers

3 cloves garlic, finely chopped

3 pounds okra, cut into ¼-inch pieces

1 cup and 1 tablespoon cooking oil

2 tablespoons flour

1 16-ounce can tomatoes, drained

½ cup diced ham or sausage

1 teaspoon basil

3 bay leaves

¼ cup parsley, chopped

Salt

Pepper

Tabasco

Worcestershire Sauce

2 cups cooked rice

Sauté onions, celery, green pepper, and garlic in ½ cup oil until soft. Fry okra separately in ¾ cup of oil over medium flame, about 45 minutes or until soft and ropy texture is gone. Stir often. More oil can be added if okra sticks. In separate frying pan, make brown roux with 1 tablespoon oil and 2 tablespoons flour. Add tomato pulp and cook into a paste. Add ham, thyme, basil, and bay leaves. Cook for 5 minutes. Add sautéed seasoning and okra to stock and, while stirring, slowly add the roux mixture. Simmer for 1 hour. Add peeled shrimp, crab halves, parsley, and cook an additional ½ hour. Season with salt, pepper, Tabasco, and Worcestershire sauce to taste. Freezes beautifully. Serve in gumbo bowls over rice.

The second wide-ranging gumbo category is dedicated to Gumbo Z'Herbes, (corruption of the original French name for the dish: Gombo aux Herbes), which is the lesser-known and sometimes meatless (*maigre*) green vegetable gumbo. Although the French *potage aux herbes* is similar, some believe that this gumbo form may have originated with the African slaves, who brought their knowledge of stewing a dish of greens, creating an adaptation of the aforementioned Caribbean-inspired callaloo. The Germans, too, could have originated the dish.

The Catholic Germans had a tradition of serving a stew containing seven different greens on Maundy Thursday or Green Thursday in Holy Week. Another version of the custom says that they cooked it on Holy Thursday and served it Good Friday. But, regardless of when it was served, if you ate seven greens and met seven people during the day, you had good luck. The green gumbo tradition survives (though typically with meat) in New Orleans with Leah Chase, who whips up a hearty pot every Holy Thursday at Dooky's. Aside from her masterful offering, Gumbo Z'Herbes is typically absent from restaurant menus, though in the first decade of the twenty-first century it is beginning to be served at the Gumbo Shop and is sometimes served at the Praline Connection. Here is a recipe from a manuscript collection:

GUMBO AUX HERBS

1 lb. veal, or pickle pork or ham

1 bunch of greens, mustard or turnip greens (rough greens)

1 bunch of spinach, or beet greens (soft greens)

Add celery tops, the outside leaves of cabbage (not too much), some lettuce leaves, a small handful of parsley and green onions

1 cup oatmeal

1 large onion

Put about 3 tablespoons of oil (Wesson oil or lard) in an iron skillet to heat, slowly, while you cut up the veal and pork into small pieces (the size of the last joint of your little finger). Also cut very fine the large onion and smother this in the grease while you salt and pepper the meat and dust it with a little flour. Now brown the meat, stirring so the onions will not burn. This can be slowly cooking while you prepare the greens, which should be washed carefully before starting.

Grind the greens through a meat grinder, or boil them and chop them very fine, saving the water to add to the gumbo.

Put the meat and the greens into a large pot. Add about 2 quarts of hot water (or the juice of the boiled vegetables). Add two bay leaves and a few garlic cloves. After this gets to a good rolling boil, add the raw oatmeal and let cook slowly for about two hours, stirring often, to keep the oatmeal from going to the bottom and sticking.

Serve with fluffy rice and French bread. (We usually have ham and potato chips on the table for anyone who did not fill up on gumbo, but that is all.)

Cajun Gumbo, the third category, is Creole gumbo's country kin. This rustic gumbo often contains okra or filé and is almost always thickened with a generous amount of dark roux. Unlike professional chefs in New Orleans, Acadians do not strain out aromatics or de-bone fowl or meats. The first Acadians, especially, would not have considered wasting onions or bell peppers. To this day, they leave in seasoning vegetables as part of the finished dish. Cayenne pepper, although not used in great quantity—not so as to make the gumbo searingly hot—is used more liberally in Acadiana than in New Orleans. Seafood is also popular among the Acadians, especially around the coastal areas and down Bayou Lafourche, but the western parishes are more likely to use chicken, wild duck, and sausage. The Junior League of Lafayette's *Talk About Good* (1969) is a perennial favorite of Louisiana food lovers. Mr. and Mrs. James Gauthier's recipe from this book is typical of gumbo that was served in 1900. The oysters would have been added by those who lived along the coast. Still the type served in Acadiana homes, this version is always topped with chopped parsley and green onions, "onion tops," and oftentimes served with a side of potato salad. Here is one interpretation of that Acadiana gumbo, as served in the author's home:

CHICKEN, ANDOUILLE, AND OYSTER GUMBO

½ cup cooking oil

½ cup flour

1 whole chicken, cut up

1 large onion, minced

1 large green bell pepper, minced

3 cloves of garlic, chopped

2 stalks of celery, chopped

1 quart cold water

3 quarts boiling water

1 pound andouille sausage, cut in ½-inch slices

salt and pepper to taste

1 pint oysters and their liquor

1 tablespoon minced parsley

2 tablespoons minced green onion tops

1 heaping teaspoon filé

hot, cooked rice

Heat oil in 2-gallon pot. Add flour to make a dark-brown roux, stirring constantly. Add chicken and stir constantly about 10 minutes. Add onion, bell pepper, garlic, and celery, and work it under the chicken; cook about 2 minutes and add cold water. When it boils, add the hot water, sausage, salt, and pepper.

Simmer until chicken is tender, about an hour. Add oysters and bring to a boil. Shut off the fire and sprinkle the parsley, onion tops, and filé over the gumbo, stirring continuously. Never let gumbo boil after adding filé. Serve over rice.

Old Creole establishments served gumbo made from fresh ingredients. As stated earlier, their hired cooks usually had access to the best of everything. But early New Orleans accounts lead us to believe that the dish, like so many New Orleans specialties, was also a good way for the average housewife to use leftovers. Gumbo was especially useful for stretching a single chicken or a pint of oysters that might otherwise inadequately fill the plates of the whole table. Hearn references gumbo's economy, as does the Christian Woman's Exchange's *Creole Cookery Book* of the same year, 1885. Gumbo is still considered a good use for odds and ends that are past their prime. A Thanksgiving turkey carcass, barnyard hens, or forgotten wild ducks in the freezer, for example, often end up in the gumbo pot.

Aside from ingredient contrasts, other variations are noticeable in the way gumbo is served. Elizabeth Kettenring Bégué, restaurateur and mother of the brunch, published *Mme. Bégué and Her Recipes* in 1900, and in this ground-breaking little volume advocates serving gumbo in a tureen, the vessel used by wealthier New Orleans hostesses. Yet, since this book was marketed for tourists, it is safe to assume that most people, then as today, served gumbo straight from the pot on the stove. Only for company, and usually in the more wealthy homes, would a porcelain dish be dedicated to gumbo or soup.

As stated earlier, Cajun gumbo receives heft from a relatively large amount of roux. The thickener, however, was optional in many early Creole gumbo versions, and gumbo z'herbes typically contains little, if any at all. The term *roux* in French means russet brown and refers generally to the mixture's color. The fourteenth-century chef Pierre de Lune, cook to the French monarchy, is generally cited as its inventor, although the Medicis of Florence stake an earlier claim. Scholars tell how this royal family brought it to France in 1553. By 1651 France's culinary guru François Pierre La Varenne described a thickener made by cooking flour in lard, and by the end of the century, cooks referred to this mixture

either as *farine frit* or roux. By the mid-eighteenth century the French were using butter for roux fat. Roux first entered gumbo in the early nineteenth century
in New Orleans. The Acadians, with limited access to expensive flour, did not
use it until the late nineteenth or early twentieth centuries.

Louisiana's colonial cooks used hog lard and bear fat for roux. Whenever
Hearn's recipes call for a flour-based thickening agent (he never uses the word
"roux"), he uses lard, as do Bégué in her 1900 Creole Gumbo recipe and Natalie
Scott in her 1931 book, *200 Years of New Orleans Cooking*. Célestine Eustis's *Cooking in Old Créole Days* (1904), too, sometimes uses lard and flour as a thickener
and, like, Hearn, never actually calls it roux. Until the 1950s, Acadians used hog
lard exclusively for fat. Now dietary habits, availability of commercial vegetable
oils, and the decline of *la boucherie de cochon*, "the communal hog slaughter," have
made lard a memory in most Acadian cooking.

In 1955, I-Ron Pot Roux Company, based in the Ville Platte, Louisiana,
became one of the first companies to successfully package and market roux. Today several brands are commercially available. This convenience is a huge break
from tradition, but one that does make it faster to cobble together a pot of
gumbo. Some hurried cooks now even microwave roux, a practice that Chef
Kenny Gautreau told the *Atlanta Journal-Constitution* is "a sacrilege."

Although roux is universally made from flour and fat and traditionally
stirred over a medium fire, regional differences exist in the finished product's
color. New Orleans Creoles darken their roux a shade beyond the almond-
colored thickener used in France, while the typical Acadian home cook stirs
roux until it is a few shades from burning. Surprisingly, darker roux makes thinner gumbo, but, to Acadians, the intense flavor produced by dark roux is more
important than heft.

As soon as it is the proper color, a typical New Orleans Creole (or any cook
wanting a New Orleans–style gumbo) adds onions, parsley, thyme, and bay leaf
to the roux. This is the technique repeatedly described in all the editions of *The
Picayune Creole Cook Book*. Tomatoes, too, are commonly added at this stage.
Acadians, at that point, stir in the "trinity" of onions, bell pepper, and celery, and
then add garlic (and usually no tomatoes). Celery, first recorded in France in
1623, does not appear in early New Orleans Creole gumbo recipes, but in the last
fifty years it has become standard. The technique of adding aromatic vegetables
to cooked roux after removing the pot from the flame stops roux from browning
further. It is safer, also, to add stock before the too-hot roux could splatter.

Roux's mystique and fame grew gradually, beginning with Natalie Scott's 1931 proclamation that "a roux of flour and lard is the initial step." These words evolved into "but first make a roux," by Mary Land in 1954. That same year Louisiana's Les Vingt Quatre Club tried to initiate the commercialization of Cajun cuisine and published *First—You Make a Roux*. Now, the ubiquitous "first, you make a roux" seems to begin every newspaper, magazine, and online gumbo recipe. Aside from Scott's early mention of the word, "roux" appeared in Florence Roberts's 1934 *Dixie Meals* in a recipe called Shrimp Gumbo, and in 1940 in Lena Richard's *New Orleans Cookbook* in a recipe named Okra Gumbo Filé. Richard was the first African American in New Orleans to publish a cookbook, and her recipe, like the recipes of Scott and Roberts, along with most early New Orleans recipes, only calls for a tablespoon of flour and a tablespoon of lard or butter.

Roux remains a mystery to most Americans, and until the 1970s gumbo itself was still relatively unknown outside Louisiana and the Gulf Coast. Even in New Orleans, where it has always been enjoyed at home, menus from the early 1900s through the 1950s reveal it was served in startlingly few restaurants. But this period of virtual anonymity ended when Senator Allen J. Ellender from Terrebonne Parish posthumously threw gumbo into the limelight. During the thirty-five years Ellender served in Washington, five U.S. presidents had sampled Creole dishes cooked by the "Chef Supreme." Ellender died while in office in 1972, and as an edible memorial to their deceased colleague, the Senate added to its cafeteria menu Louisiana Creole Gumbo (made with seafood). A recent look at a weekly menu showed that gumbo, this one chicken, is still served at the Senate cafeteria. Although it can be said that Ellender formally introduced gumbo to the nation, Chef Paul Prudhomme and his Blackened Redfish in the early 1980s vaulted Louisiana cuisine to celebrity status. Riding on that one faux Cajun dish's coattails, anything with too much pepper, including gumbo, grew to be the rage.

In a 2005 oral history with Brett Anderson of the *Times-Picayune*, Prudhomme, originally a country cook from the Cajun town of Opelousas, recalls that he was the first executive chef from the United States that Commander's Palace hired. Before 1975, Commander's Palace chefs had always been European. Naturally, Prudhomme reworked the menu to his liking. And one of the items he radically changed was gumbo: "The gumbo I did at Commander's was a roux gumbo. To my knowledge, it never had been before. . . . I put it in and it became a staple. It was chicken and andouille gumbo. It was down-and-dirty Cajun. It was what Mama used to do. I'd go into the country and buy the andouille from the guy I'd known since I was a kid. We didn't have andouille in New Orleans until later." In that era, the Creole and Acadian styles of cooking were still miles apart. Ella Brennan, from the famed restaurant dynasty, was Prudhomme's boss, and apparently there was a tug-of-war over the menu; Prudhomme was obviously trying to cook Cajun, and the Brennans were trying to convert him into a Creole. They reached a compromise. But, as noted by Anderson, ever since Prudhomme and Brennan found common ground, gumbo in New Orleans has not been the same: "It has changed . . . as chefs from all over Louisiana and the nation at large have descended on New Orleans and thrown countless influences into the pot. In some cases, the resulting gumbos are virtually indistinguishable from what older locals may remember from growing up. In others, they couldn't be more different."

A quick glance at recently published New Orleans recipes show that, indeed, gumbo now contains more roux, sausage, and hot pepper, while in southwest Louisiana some adventurous cooks are adding thyme, bay leaf, and separately made stocks. For better or worse, restaurant chefs are adding wild mushrooms, paprika, cumin, beans, and all manner of vegetables, validating the saying that gumbo includes whatever you can find. Certainly these experiments pique interest. But in a state where mosquitoes are more welcome than change, "nouvelle" gumbo has yet to pass the test of time.

Regardless of outside innovation, in Louisiana inherited gumbo techniques are sacred. Mothers still whisper to their offspring that they must first sauté okra to prevent slime. Don't boil the pot after you add filé; it will be stringy. And okra is best in summer when it is fresh. Gumbo pots are handed down in wills. Gumbo even merits its own festival and, in 1973, the governor of Louisiana issued a proclamation naming Bridge City "The Gumbo Capital of the World." Legitimizing all the hoopla, historians give recognition to gumbo's niche in regional food preparation and categorize this now-classic dish as a unique example of original American gastronomy. That is quite an honor for something that sprang from the sassafras of the Native American, the one-pot cooking tradition of the African, and the needs of the thrifty French housewife. And although we never will definitively know its beginnings, we do know that gumbo is a satisfying meal in a bowl and is unquestionably a positive legacy of Louisiana's chaotic history.

✒

TROUT AMANDINE

Patricia Kennedy Livingston

When *GQ Magazine* food writer Alan Richman sniffed that the trout *meunière* amandine he had for lunch at Galatoire's in 2006 "looked and tasted fried rather than sautéed," the ensuing storm in a sauté pan may have been his intention. If so, he surely achieved his goal, for his review was promptly answered by Brett Anderson, restaurant critic for the New Orleans *Times-Picayune*, who pointed out, "Although the traditional French preparation of meunière calls for the fish to be sautéed, it is still a little like dissing tuna sashimi for being raw, as Galatoire's has been serving trout amandine meunière fried for better than a century." Indeed, the beloved restaurant's cookbook uses both *sauté* and *fry* when describing the recipe, whereas the version from Arnaud's, another respected Creole restaurant, uses only *fry* in the instructions for preparing both trout amandine and trout meunière. French dictionaries list both verbs *frire* and *sauter* (of which the past participle is sauté) for the English word *fry*. And English dictionaries generally define *fry* as cooking over direct heat in hot oil or fat, and *sauté* as frying lightly in fat in a shallow open pan. So much for semantics.

Even Kim Severson, writing for the *New York Times*, got into the act, although her concern centered on Richman's incredible statement that there are no Creole persons living in New Orleans, in spite of having interviewed Leah Chase, whom she calls "the city's most revered Creole cook, and food writer Marcelle Bienvenu, described as one of Louisiana's longtime culinary authorities." Severson blames Richman's vitriol on the fact that he "never liked New Orleans."

As it turns out, Galatoire's does fry their trout meunière (the word is French for "miller's wife," a reference to the flour) amandine, according to David Gooch, a descendant of founder Jean Galatoire and one of the managers. Gooch noted in an interview, "We fry it or sauté it, either way, whichever way the customer wants it." This venerable New Orleans restaurant—it was established in 1905—is well known for the close relationships that frequent customers develop with their waiters; one doesn't ask for a table, but inquires whether a particular waiter is available. So the waiter knows the preferences of his regular customers, whether for fried or sautéed trout. And besides, as food critic Tom Fitzmorris pointed out as recently as 2006, even though food might be "much better grilled, seared, or broiled," deep-frying "is still the default technique in most New Orleans restaurants."

Gooch explains that there is a difference, for in his kitchen *sauté* means just a little butter in the bottom of the pan, whereas *fry* means deep fry, for which the batter is a bit thicker. Galatoire's classic trout meunière amandine is deep-fried, which is why the recipe calls for a gallon of oil, seemingly a huge quantity for only six servings, but the appropriate amount to submerge a plump fillet of fish.[1] The dish has been on the menu continuously as long as Galatoire's has had a menu, and it has always been made the same way. It is the restaurant's most popular dish, with fifty to one hundred portions served each day.

The recipe in the cookbook specifies (and the preference in the restaurant kitchen is for) speckled trout from the Gulf of Mexico, as long as they are available, but cooks can use other firm white species, including drum, sheepshead, or redfish—local fish that have a similar texture. White trout from the Atlantic is suitable if it is fresh, but Gooch said it doesn't have a good shelf life and tends to get mushy if it is not perfectly fresh. Gooch said the current menu lists the dish as "Poisson Amandine," rather than trout, and if the customer asks for trout and it is unavailable, the waiter will identify the species to be served. Actually, when serving regular customers at Galatoire's, waiters rattle off the list of species that look especially fine—generally puppy drum, pompano, redfish, red snapper, and sometimes sheepshead in addition to the favored speckled trout—and the diner then decides on the fish and the method of preparation. Only neophytes peruse the menu.

Writing in his 1970 *The New Orleans Underground Gourmet*, Richard Collin declared Galatoire's trout meunière amandine to be "a platonic dish," which he says means it is "the best imaginable realization of a particular dish. If you

---

1. Most recipe writers and cookbook editors now use *filet* to refer to steak and *fillet* for fish; they are pronounced the same. Among the sources quoted here, the writers have used the terms interchangeably, and we have left them as published.

prefer, perfect is a good translation." Collin goes on to say that although Galatoire's version of the dish "is the most consistently perfect I have tasted ... many
newcomers find it difficult to take trout seriously as a worthy dish. The trout
as prepared in Galatoire's kitchen and in many of the other grand New Orleans
restaurants bears no relationship to any other trout in the land. Trout is one
of the most serious staples of the New Orleans French cuisine and in New Orleans it is raised to extraordinary heights." This is the Culinary History Group's
modification of Galatoire's recipe:

TROUT MEUNIÈRE AMANDINE IN THE STYLE OF GALATOIRE'S

3 cups sliced almonds, toasted

2 eggs

2 cups whole milk

salt and pepper to taste

6 speckled trout fillets, 7 to 8 ounces each

2 cups flour

1 gallon vegetable oil

1 serving meunière sauce

Lemon wedges for garnish

Toast the almonds in a 300°F oven for 15 to 20 minutes, stirring every 5 minutes. When they are
light brown, remove from oven and set aside.

Whisk together the eggs, milk, salt, and pepper. Salt and pepper the trout fillets and flour
lightly. Dip each in the egg wash, making sure to coat both sides. Let excess egg wash drip off.
Dredge the fillets in flour again, gently shaking off excess.

In a large, heavy skillet, heat the oil to 350°F. The oil is ready when a pinch of flour
sprinkled over it browns instantly. Add the trout, fry for 4 to 5 minutes. Remove when the crust
is golden brown.

Top each fillet with almonds and warm meunière sauce. Garnish with lemon, and serve
it up.

MEUNIÈRE SAUCE IN THE STYLE OF GALATOIRE'S

4 sticks salted butter (1 pound)

1 tablespoon freshly squeezed lemon juice

1 tablespoon red wine vinegar

Melt the butter in a medium saucepan, over medium heat. Whisk it constantly for 8-10 minutes, until the butter has separated with the sediments being dark brown but not burned, and
the liquid a deep golden color. Remove from heat, and add the lemon juice and vinegar while
continuing to whisk slowly. The browned butter sauce will froth until the acids evaporate.
When the frothing stops, the sauce is ready.

Fitzmorris's assessment of Galatoire's dish is less enthusiastic; to him the
trout is second to their pompano. The latter, to him, is a superlative fish, and
he praises the restaurant for serving it in a "distinctive toasty brown-butter meunière sauce . . . as good a seafood dish as you can eat." David Gooch said his
restaurant serves pompano either grilled or sautéed, whereas perhaps the most
famous version in New Orleans is Antoine's pompano en papillote, cooked and
served in a waxed paper bag with a rich sauce. "New Orleans considers pompano its best fish," wrote Mary Moore Bremer in 1932, and she "also believes
there is none better. Since it is rarely found except in the waters of the Gulf of
Mexico Mississippi Sound and the Louisiana Grand Isle shore, we feel proud
and proprietary." A salt-water species usually weighing under three pounds,
pompano must be taken in depths of at least seven feet and beyond 2,500 feet
from shore. Strike nets may be used legally between August 1 and October 31
of each year.

Fitzmorris's accounts are excellent, in general, in valuing the haute cuisine
restaurants and their great expertise with seafood. At Galatoire's, the trout there
is "similarly good, fried to an incomparable lightness." He admits that the classic dish at that restaurant, with its simple lemon-butter sauce, is "the definitive version" and is also done well at Christian's (which has not reopened after
sustaining damage from Hurricane Katrina), Clancy's, and Delmonico's. Fitzmorris says he prefers the fish with a different sauce, though, the "other style of
meunière sauce, uniquely New Orleans and generally credited to Arnaud's," one
of butter, lemon, and enough veal stock to turn it brown, plus onions, garlic,
parsley, bell pepper, red wine, and various seasonings.

A version popular with home cooks is found in the New Orleans Junior
League's *The Plantation Cookbook*. There are significant differences between this

recipe and that of Galatoire's, both in the preparation of the fish before cooking and the cooking method itself. Note that although *The Plantation Cookbook* instructions use the word *fry*, the method is what most people think of when they say *sauté*.

TROUT MEUNIÈRE OR AMANDINE

8–12 trout fillets (allow ⅓ pound per person)

Milk to cover

2 teaspoons salt

4 drops Tabasco

1½ cups flour

1 teaspoon white pepper

1 stick butter

2 tablespoons oil

SAUCE:

2 sticks butter

½ cup sliced almonds (optional)

2 tablespoons lemon juice

2 teaspoons Worcestershire sauce

1 teaspoon salt

¼ cup chopped parsley

Soak fillets in a mixture of milk, 1 teaspoon salt, and Tabasco for at least 30 minutes. Season flour with 1 teaspoon salt and white pepper. Remove fillets from milk, pat dry, coat lightly with seasoned flour, shaking off excess. In a saucepan, melt 1 stick butter and add oil. In a large skillet, pour butter mixture to a depth of ⅛ inch. When grease is very hot, fry fillets, a few at a time, turning once. Cooking time will depend on size of fillets. Do not crowd fillets. Keep grease very hot and at proper depth by adding more from saucepan as necessary. Place cooked fillets on a warm platter and keep hot. When all are cooked, empty skillet and wipe out any burned flour.

    Prepare sauce in same skillet by melting 2 sticks butter and lightly browning almonds. Add lemon juice, Worcestershire, salt, and parsley. Mix and heat well. Just before serving, pour some sauce over fillets and serve remaining portion in sauceboat.

Another variation of trout amandine dispenses with a wash or soaking entirely but uses heavy cream in the sauce. It is from a cookbook assembled by the Baton Rouge Junior League and is attributed to Mrs. Frank Rieger Jr.

TRUITES AUX AMANDES (TROUT WITH ALMONDS)

4 medium-sized trout, 1–1½ pounds

¾ cup flour (or less)

⅔ cup butter

½ cup heavy cream

⅔ cup toasted, slivered almonds

Salt and pepper to taste

1 thinly sliced lemon

Clean, wash and scale trout. Dry thoroughly and roll lightly in flour. Melt the butter in a frying pan. When it is hot, but not brown, put in trout. Cook over low heat 5 to 7 minutes; turn carefully, and cook on other side for the same length of time. When golden brown, salt and pepper them and lay them carefully on a heated serving platter. Add cream to the butter remaining in pan; mix rapidly; add almonds and stir carefully so that the almonds will not be broken and heat again just to the boiling point. Do not boil sauce. Spoon sauce over trout; add thin rounds of lemon and serve immediately. Serves 4.

Mary Land not only cooked and wrote about New Orleans cooking in the 1940s and 1950s, but also hunted her own game and caught her own fish. Her version of trout amandine is brief and no-nonsense:

TROUT AMANDINE

6 fillets of trout [which she says is really spotted weakfish]

½ teaspoon salt

½ teaspoon white pepper

1 cup sifted flour

Enough cream to cover

2 cups slivered almonds

½ cup butter

Salt and pepper fish and soak in cream several hours. Drain and roll in sifted flour. Fry fish in
butter. Sauté almonds in a small skillet and sprinkle over fish when ready to serve.

Such variations in local cookbooks are perfectly understandable, for as
former Antoine's proprietor Roy F. Guste Jr. pointed out, "The most important
key to Louisiana cookery is that no two cooks prepare any single dish exactly the
same way. We all have our own palates and our cooking will eventually reflect
that individuality." Food writer Peter Feibleman took the notion a step further:
"No two Creole chefs ever cook alike, or want to. If you have the same dish in
five different places you will probably have five different eating experiences, all
on a par with the best food in other cities. When the old Creoles passed recipes
on to their children they didn't say them aloud, let alone write them down, but
merely whispered them, and this very secretiveness is what has produced the
marvelous individuality of Creole dishes."

Although typical Creole dishes, using indigenous foodstuffs, were prepared
regularly in home kitchens at every social and economic level, it wasn't until
after World War II that such favorites became common on restaurant menus,
according to Pamela D. Arceneaux of the Historic New Orleans Collection.
She noted in an interview, "Before that time, restaurants tended to present classic European dishes, without regard to what people were eating at home. The
idea was that when you went out to eat, you wanted something special, something different from what the housewife or cook prepared. Unfortunately, most
early restaurant menus were for special occasion dinner parties or luncheons,"
not necessarily indicative of what was available on a regular basis. And even
these menus don't shed much light on the preparation. For example, when the
members of the Young Men's Gymnastics Club gathered in 1897 to celebrate
the organization's twenty-fifth anniversary, the fish course was "filets of speckled
trout a la maitre d'hotel." We know the species, but cannot ascertain how it was
cooked and sauced. Interestingly, many of these early fish courses were served
with French-fried parsley, an accompaniment that was still served in the late
twentieth century by the Bitoun brothers, who ran a number of small restaurants. Maurice Bitoun called it "French popcorn." Tom Fitzmorris advises the
use of curly-leaf parsley fried in oil retained after frying chicken.

Lafcadio Hearn's *La Cuisine Creole*, originally published in April 1885, contains recipes for a number of fish dishes, including fillets that are marinated,
dredged in flour, then fried in lard, as well as a number of different sauces. Hearn

wrote, "Send it to the table with sauce to suit the taste." One can almost hear the pride in his voice in the boast that this book, comprised as it is of recipes contributed by many New Orleans friends, "is the only one in print containing dishes peculiar to 'la Cuisine Créole.'" Hearn also mentions codfish, to be baked, stewed, served with a butter roux, or made into cakes; croakers and mullets, to be fried; broiled flounder; broiled Spanish mackerel; redfish or snapper, which he suggests boiling; and baked stuffed trout. He gives several recipes for appropriate sauces, including à la Provençale and à la Venitienne.

Creole Cookery, published in 1885 by the thirty-two members of the Christian Woman's Exchange and written for home cooks, suggested boiling or stewing fish as well as sautéing or frying, flaking to form cakes, baking, and roasting. Specifically mentioned were redfish, red snapper, trout, mackerel, codfish, salmon, flounder, sheephead, halibut, and perch as well as the popular "any fish." Another early cookbook for home use was The Picayune Creole Cook Book, published by one of the newspapers. It first appeared in 1900, and although copies of that first edition are rare, later versions are readily available. It contains recipes for sheepshead, redfish, red snapper, grouper, flounder, pompano, Spanish mackerel, bluefish, speckled trout, green trout, perch, croakers, and several small fish grouped together. The book gives sauces, too, such as Hollandaise, Creole, à la Tartare, à la Maître d'Hotel, drawn butter, and Genois, and mentions, without instructions, à la Chambord and à l'Orly. If a sauce does not accompany the fish, the cook is urged to add at least a simple garnish, such as fresh parsley or lemon slices. It should also be remembered that until well into the twentieth century, fish comprised merely one in a series of courses, hardly the main course and center of attention that trout amandine has become.

Speckled trout from the nearby Gulf of Mexico is the preferred fish for trout amandine, and another complaint Richman made was that he was reasonably sure the fillet of fish wasn't trout, for it was obvious to him that it had been filleted from a fish much larger than the average speckled trout, perhaps a fifteen-pounder of some other species. Well, Gooch has already mentioned that the dish is listed as "fish amandine," and the waiter will happily divulge the species to the customer, but, according to the Web site of a commercial fisherman, although the average size of a speckled trout is about one pound, they can grow up to sixteen pounds.

"Specks," as they are affectionately called by game fishermen, are a saltwater species of the Louisiana coast, thriving in areas of brackish water as far out as the closest petroleum drilling rigs. They swim in schools, and as they mature and grow in size, they move farther out into deeper water. They can be caught year-round. The species is also known as spotted sea trout, yellow-mouth, and paper-mouth. Similar species live in the freshwater Great Lakes and streams of the American Northwest. Henry Poynot, a former sports fisherman who now operates Big Fisherman seafood market on New Orleans' Magazine Street, said speckled trout are the best for eating. In an interview in 2007, he described them as "a mild fish, firm and flaky. I caught more speckled trout in my childhood than most people do in a lifetime. They're fun to catch, but I ate so much as a child that now I'd rather have anything else—salmon is my favorite. Anyway, now there's a season on specks in Louisiana, and it's closed one week out of every month. There had been about 1,200 gillnet fishermen in Louisiana, but only twenty-five of them bought a license to catch them one by one with a pole. You can't make a living with a fishing pole." Louisiana's law states quite clearly that specks may not be caught with nets or even be on a boat that has such a net: "Possession of red drum or spotted sea trout [speckled trout] on board any vessel on which there is a gill net, strike net, hoop net, trammel net or seine is prohibited." However the regulations also say, "Any commercial species for which there is no specified size or take limit may be taken in any size or quantity." And fishermen may have only two pounds of finfish per person for their own consumption on board, and then only if the vessel is equipped to cook such fish.

So these days specks are still easy for the recreational angler to catch, but hard to purchase. Restaurateurs are cagey about their sources, preferring not to give away classified information to the competition. Poynot said he buys his from wholesalers, "from Mississippi and Carolina." Even so, he can't always get them, and he won't buy fish imported from Mexico. "We turn down about one-third of all they send because they're not fresh enough. They aren't bad, but sometimes the quality isn't what we expect, and what our customers expect. And you really can't farm-raise trout because they're very hard to keep alive," he said. He added that although he can tell the difference between shrimp from Louisiana and those from Mississippi, he can't tell if the trout he accepts come from Gulf or Atlantic states. The difference is more about texture than taste, Poynot explained. "Shrimp are bottom feeders. In Mississippi, they usually come from the Gulf, which has a sandy bottom, so sometimes sand and grit get into them, whereas in Louisiana shrimp are usually caught in mud-bottomed waters. So there's almost never any sand."

At Langenstein's Supermarket Uptown, speckled trout sell for two dollars more a pound than rainbow trout, but seafood manager Steve Brantley explained in an interview that specks are what people want. He too said they are sometimes hard to get because "there's a tag limit even for commercial fishermen," but cooks can substitute tilapia with good results. "Also, restaurants sometimes pass off drum for speckled trout," he said.

Fitzmorris scoffs at the idea of eating or serving tilapia. He first noticed it about 1996, but recently wrote in an e-mail, "Tilapia, which is without question the worst commonly-served fish here, . . . [is] found mostly in second-rate restaurants. A few serious chefs use it as a fallback, but any restaurant that features it as the fish of the day is doing very little for its customers." Gooch was adamant that Galatoire's never offers tilapia, but that is to be expected, as that venerable restaurant is noted for its adherence to classic New Orleans dishes and ingredients. He said drum is their first choice if specks are unavailable, but as mentioned, waiters don't hesitate to tell customers if that substitution is necessary.

Apparently the species has always been popular, for an illustration that dates from the 1580s in a book about Louisiana's history and recipes shows a Native American couple sitting on the ground surrounded by corn, berries, a squid, and what looks very much like a speckled trout: a long body, spots most numerous on the back, and a lower jaw larger than the upper jaw, which has two prominent canine teeth. If the depicted fish was a speckled trout, it should come as no surprise, for it would simply have been among nature's bounty available to residents of south Louisiana, surrounded as they are by lakes, estuaries, the Mississippi River, and the nearby Gulf of Mexico.

Early fishing, trapping, and trading were surely beneficial and necessary to natives and settlers, especially during the French period and into the first decade of Spanish rule. According to historians Gilbert C. Din and John E. Harkins, "vendors plied their edibles throughout the city." But the second Spanish governor, Alejandro O'Reilly, arrived in 1769 to find the "provincial food supply in disarray." He then fixed prices and set up penalties for those who violated the newly established tariffs. Din and Harkins quote a translation of the Spanish laws that governed all colonies, noting that prices were to be "determined on the basis of the cost of the article or commodity, plus a reasonable gain for the producer or retailer, and on the wealth of the community."

The Cabildo, or the city government, also oversaw the building of public markets. Thus in 1780 the first market was opened, and two years later a new structure was erected, this time with "plastered walls, a paved brick floor and sidewalks, a gallery and a loft with a staircase." This first market was only for the sale of meat, but in 1784 another public market was built to handle other food. Peddlers, fish sellers, and hunters were still operating independently, but that fall the government ordered them to sell only in the markets. "Fishermen, who often left putrid fish and entrails on the ground, could no longer sell their catch throughout the city. They now had to go to a designated place and sell by the pound using honest weights." Exempted were city truck-garden owners, slaves sent by masters from nearby plantations to sell, and those who brought products—such as salt, meat, oil, suet, and pork lard—by boat to sell on the levees.

By the mid-1780s, the public markets were becoming congested, and the fire of 1788 destroyed them, so the Cabildo opened a new market in 1790. Then in 1798 the government voted to build a public fish market, which was completed the following year. In 1840, another fish market and wild-game market were built next to the vegetable market in the French Market. More and more markets followed, such that every neighborhood in the city had a public market by the early twentieth century. The city regulated sales for safety purposes and to provide revenue for itself. But in the 1860s, laws restricting the establishment of private markets began to be eased, and small grocery stores also came to supply perishables. For example, in 1869, Schwegmann's Grocery and Bar was opened at the corner of Burgundy and Piety Streets.

The 1900 city directory, while not indicating fish markets as a separate category other than mentioning that the French Market included one, listed sixteen public markets, most of which surely sold fish and crustaceans. By the 1930 edition, however, the same directory included four fish wholesalers and twenty-two columns of retail grocers, including four national chains. That same volume contained four columns of restaurant listings. The first national self-serve grocery store chain, Piggly Wiggly, opened seven stores in New Orleans in 1919. Although there are no records of what foods were offered in these stores, it is probably not a stretch of the imagination to assume that the popular and generally plentiful speckled trout were among the fresh fish sold.

The species' popularity has made it sometimes scarce, but the waters around New Orleans, both fresh and salt, teem with so many other fish and crustaceans that no one need fear a lack of something to put on the dinner table, even during meatless Lent. As Chef John Folse points out, from our early history "fish and shellfish were abundant. Native Americans enjoyed freshwater finfish, including gar, choupique (or grindle), catfish, paddlefish, sunfish, bass, eel, pike, soc-a-lait (or white crappie), sturgeon, sardine, gizzard shad and buffalofish. . . . Shallow coastal waters and bays provided drum, croaker, speckled trout, redfish, flounder and mullet." Folse also notes that the coastal state "is sixteen percent water, with miles of streams, rivers, and bayous from which to draw substance." Shellfish have always been tremendously popular, and many people recall eating tiny Mississippi River shrimp at the tables of grandparents in the mid-twentieth century. But the trout has always been a staple of our tables.

And the almonds? They are not grown anywhere near New Orleans but were part of the dish in France, and thus have remained married to trout meunière from the beginning. Fitzmorris relates how Ella Brennan, a proprietor of Commander's Palace, suggested her chef try using pecans, which are grown in Louisiana, but trout with buttery pecans never caught on, although pecans remain a popular addition to desserts and side dishes, such as sweet potato casserole for holiday meals, and are often toasted and seasoned to be served as an hors d'oeuvre.

Home and restaurant cooks from all regions boast a wide variety of ingredients and cooking methods in their repertories, so Louisiana cannot claim a unique position here, but the richness of its natural resources and the influence of diverse cultures from Europe, Africa, and the Caribbean have created a cuisine that is, indeed, different from that of its neighbors—Creole.

RED BEANS AND RICE

Karen Trahan Leathem and Sharon Stallworth Nossiter

For many years, Louis Armstrong, arguably New Orleans' most famous native son, signed his letters, "Am red beans and ricely yours, Louis." Armstrong loved red beans, which he learned to cook at an early age. When he was released from his year-and-a-half stay at the Colored Waif's Home, where he was sent for shooting a gun in the air on New Year's in 1913, the young teenager took over the household cooking for his father and stepmother, keeping his voracious young stepbrothers fed with red beans and rice. In his autobiography, he reels off a list of favorite dishes from his sister Mama Lucy's repertoire: courtbouillon, gumbo, and cabbage and rice. He added, "As for red beans and rice, well, I don't have to say anything about that. It is my birth mark." He mentions red beans more than any other food in his autobiography, *Satchmo*, and he ate it everywhere, from New Orleans' tiny Chinatown to Harlem soul food joints. When he was getting acquainted with his fourth wife, Lucille, he asked her, "'Can you cook red beans and rice?' which amused her very much. Then it dawned on her that I was very serious." For the rest of his life, Armstrong took red beans, the ultimate comfort food of New Orleans, with him everywhere.

Armstrong is not the only one who equates the dish with home. Less than a month after Hurricane Katrina, Mayor Ray Nagin confidently predicted New Orleanians would return to the city. In making this assertion, he turned to the language of food, which stood both metaphorically and literally for the ties to home. He told reporter Anderson Cooper, "I know New Orleanians. Once the beignets start cooking up again and, you know, the gumbos in the pots and the red beans and rice are being served on Monday in New Orleans and not where they are, they're going to be back." It would not be the last time Nagin invoked red beans and rice; he has mentioned the dish as either a way to lure people back home or else as a proxy for community and family. Just over three months after Katrina, he told a crowd of evacuees in Atlanta, "What's up, New Orleans! I miss y'all! The red beans and rice just ain't the same without ya'll! So we need y'all back quickly."

Although many New Orleanians remained skeptical of Nagin's rhetoric, post-Katrina statements reveal that the mayor was not off base in this emotional linking of red beans and rice with home. New Orleans writer Randy Fertel tells of a trip back to the city five months after the storm: "Like many in the New Orleans diaspora, I longed for the proper ingredients to recreate our food. Five weeks after the storm, I returned to New York from New Orleans with my suitcase filled with Camellia Brand red beans, green baby lima beans, crawfish tails, ham seasonings, and smoked sausage (or, as we say, 'smoke sausage')." Wayne Baquet, whose family has operated various Crescent City restaurants over the years, including the defunct Eddie's and the current Lil' Dizzy's, recalled cooking for sixteen evacuated relatives in suburban Atlanta in the days after Katrina: "You couldn't find the things you wanted to cook with. You couldn't find the kidney beans, red beans, you couldn't find pickled meat. We had to make our own hot sausage. We were missing so many things that we had to improvise and make happen."

Even as red beans and rice represent the heart, home, and family, they also stand as a symbol of New Orleans itself. In the spring of 2007, capitalizing on the ubiquitous symbol of New Orleans' rebirth after Hurricane Katrina, forty or so fiberglass fleur-de-lis sculptures graced city streets in a public art display sponsored by the Fore!Kids Foundation. One featured red beans nestled among black and gold strokes, colors undoubtedly referencing another prominent symbol of a reborn city—the Saints football team. But the sculpture's creator, French-born artist and restaurateur Jacques Soulas, was hardly the first artist to take advantage of the symbolic value of red beans. In 1973, jewelry designer Mignon Faget came out with one of her first lines, which featured the red bean. Throughout New Orleans, red beans crop up everywhere, replacing stars as quality indicators in the *Times-Picayune*'s restaurant reviews, on official BayouWear at the New Orleans Jazz and Heritage Festival, and even—years ago—as names for gorillas at the Audubon Zoo. Chef Paul Prudhomme, who grew up in Cajun country about 150 miles from New Orleans, was familiar with red beans from his childhood, but they were "just another dried bean, like pinto beans and lima beans." When he moved to New Orleans in the 1970s, he "discovered that red beans were a cultural phenomenon, a tradition dating back for hundreds of years."

How did red beans and rice become so associated with the city? While there will never be a definitive answer to that question, this emblematic food shares qualities with other dishes discussed in this volume. Like gumbo and bread pudding, red beans suggest frugality, scraping together a meal out of leftovers and common staples. New Orleans jazz musician Bob French says: "Here's the thing: I live alone. I can cook a pot of red beans and eat off of it for three days. How much is that? Eight dollars?" Like many of our other iconic dishes, red beans and rice is an easy and cheap way to feed a crowd. And it is this communal aspect to red beans that is in large part responsible for its popularity. Although you can order a single serving at a restaurant, when people cook it at home, they rarely cook less than a pound, which is how the beans are most commonly sold. Generally, people are cooking for family, or a crowd—it is a dish to be shared. Amy Sins, in her poignant yet celebratory cookbook, *The Ruby Slippers Cookbook: Life, Culture, Family, and Food after Katrina,* pointed out how her family shared red beans in a modern way—not over a common table, but doled out as loving gifts. Sins recounts, "In fact, my great grandmother made such a large pot of beans on Monday, all of her eight grown children would show up with an empty pot to get some for their families. This tradition still continues. My mom makes a big pot of beans and freezes them in plastic containers. When my sister moved into her first apartment, she was given several containers to reheat for dinner. Funny enough, she called my mom the first night and asked for a recipe for rice!"

The first recipe we offer is the earliest we could find, one that dates back to about the time of Louis Armstrong's birth. The first New Orleans cookbooks, from the 1880s—Lafcadio Hearn's *La Cuisine Creole* and the Christian Woman's Exchange's *The Creole Cookery Book*—don't include red beans. But surely they were being cooked in local households at that time, for the dish was firmly established by 1901, when *The Picayune's Creole Cook Book* recognized its nutritional value and connected it to communal living:

> Beans, whether white or red, are among the most nutritious of food substances. In all the ancient homes in New Orleans, and in the colleges and convents, where large numbers of children are sent to be reared to be strong and useful men and women, several times a week appear on the table either the nicely cooked dish of

Red Beans, which are eaten with rice, or the equally wholesome White Beans à la Créme [sic], or Red or White Beans boiled with a piece of salt pork or ham. . . . The Creoles hold that the boys and girls who are raised on beans and rice and beef will be among the strongest and sturdiest of people.

The recipe that appeared on the next page is one that New Orleanians would recognize today, with the exception of one ingredient:

RED BEANS AND RICE
HARICOTS ROUGE AU RIZ

1 Quart of Dried Red Beans.

1 Carrot. 1 Onion. 1 Bay Leaf.

1 Tablespoonful of Butter.

1 Pound of Ham or Salt Meat.

Salt and Pepper to Taste.

Wash the beans and soak them over night, or at least five or six hours, in fresh, cold water. When ready to cook, drain off this water and put the beans in a pot of cold water, covering with at least two quarts, for beans must cook thoroughly. Let the water heat slowly. Then add the ham or salt pork and the herbs and onion and carrot, minced fine. Boil the beans at least two hours, or until tender enough to mash easily under pressure. When tender, remove from the pot, put the salt meat or ham on top of the dish, and serve hot as a vegetable, with boiled rice as an entrée, with Veal Sauté, Daube à la Mode, Grillades à la Sauce, etc.

The ending of this recipe points to another characteristic of red beans and rice in New Orleans. Although the dish—with or without sausage—served alone is more than filling, many restaurants, especially modest neighborhood lunch spots, have traditionally offered not the turn-of-the-century favorites mentioned above but, instead, more modern equivalents—most often fried chicken or pork chops.

While other Crescent City foods have their place in rituals—king cake during the Carnival season, fig and sesame cookies for the St. Joseph's Day altars, gumbo z'herbes for Holy Thursday—red beans and rice claims its place in the New Orleans pantheon of food due, in part, to its status as a *weekly* ritual. As every New Orleanian and many a visitor know, red beans and rice is a Monday dish. This place on the Monday menu comes with its own tale of origin. The most common version says that since Monday was washday, an activity that required continuous labor, common sense dictated that the dish of the day should be something that required little attention. Leon Soniat, in his story-filled cookbook of New Orleans dishes, wrote: "Monday was always washday for Memere [his grandmother] and Mamete [his mother]. . . . The procedure usually involved three large tubs—the tub in which the clothes had been soaking and in which they would be scrubbed on a washboard, another tub filled with water in which the clothes were rinsed, and the third tub filled with water to which a few spoonfuls of bluing had been added. . . . After being washed, some of the clothes were dipped into the starch and then hung out to dry. . . . Being involved in such an all day operation left very little time for cooking. Thus, the custom developed of cooking red beans and rice on Mondays, a custom which holds even today."

But there is another part to this Monday tale, and that is the Sunday ham bone. Since ham was a common Sunday dish, slow-cooked beans the next day made good use of the ham bone. "In New Orleans," explained Peter Feibleman in *American Cooking: Creole and Acadian*, "a ham bone is considered the whole point of the ham. Without it, you could hardly live through Monday, for on that day, as everyone knows, you need it to get a lyrical taste into what sounds at first like the drabbest of all local recipes—the classic Monday dish of red beans and rice. . . . [E]very Tuesday morning, even though I have not lived in New Orleans for 20 years, I still find myself wondering just what I missed in my meals the day before."

Red beans made sense in the weekly household schedule and made use of the previous day's ham bone, but that doesn't really explain the tradition. After all, laundry day was not unique to New Orleans, and neither were Sunday hams. But only New Orleans has red beans and rice as a Monday dish. Like many creation tales, the Sunday hambone–Monday washday theory makes a believable package, but it doesn't tell the full story. Like other famous dishes of the Crescent City, such as gumbo and jambalaya, it is difficult to trace the origins of red beans and rice, and just like these other creations, it seems to be the happy product of a number of influences. Like gumbo, it borrows from a number of ethnic and racial groups that make up the people of Louisiana.

Some of the inspiration for red beans and rice likely came from New Orleans' French culinary heritage. *The Picayune's Creole Cook Book* includes a recipe for "Red Beans, Burgundy Style/Haricots Rouges à la Bourguignonne," which involves the classic French steps of an onion stuck with cloves and the addition of a glass of red wine. The Red Beans and Rice/Haricots Rouges au Riz recipe itself is closer to the typical modern recipe, save for the use of a carrot. *Glandoulat*, a traditional red bean dish from southwestern France, an area from which a number of French immigrants to New Orleans came, bears a strong resemblance to New Orleans red beans, without rice, and again, with the addition of carrots and red wine. A similar dish, red beans cooked with red wine and prosciutto, exists in the Italian Piedmont, bordering France; some of New Orleans' early Italian immigrants came from this region. *Potée alsacienne* from Alsace-Lorraine is yet another dish featuring red kidney beans, pork, and sausages.

But French bean dishes are served on their own, without rice. For that ingredient, we turn first to Africa, then to the developing rice culture of Louisiana. Chateaugué, one of Bienville's thirteen brothers and sisters, is rumored to have brought two casks of rice from Saint-Domingue for sowing along the Gulf Coast in 1716. Although we don't know if this seed shipment produced a crop, we can see it as an early attempt to establish a dietary staple. It is likely that the colonists, who had few slaves at that point, realized the need for experienced rice farmers. In West Africa, rice is a critical staple and an integral part of the cuisine. Anthropologist Judith Carney writes, "In much of West Africa to this day, a meal is not considered complete unless served with rice." The majority of Louisiana's early slaves came from Senegambia, the major rice-producing region, known to early European explorers as the Rice Coast.

The slave trade itself was intimately tied to rice. For starters, slave traders needed grain to feed the slaves during the Middle Passage. And plantation owners in parts of the New World who sought to exploit agricultural possibilities requested slaves who knew how to grow rice. The story of this transferal of grain, knowledge, and culinary culture is best known for playing out in South Carolina, but it also occurred in Louisiana. In 1719, along with the first slave ships to arrive directly in Louisiana, came more rice. The Company of the West, which held the royal charter to Louisiana before being absorbed into the better-known Company of the Indies, gave specific instructions to the captains of *L'Aurore* and *le Duc du Maine* upon their departure for the West African coast. "The captains were instructed to try to purchase several blacks who knew how to cultivate rice and three or four barrels of rice for seeding, which they were to give to the directors of the company upon their arrival in Louisiana," writes historian Gwendolyn Midlo Hall, citing French government documents. Rice was an immediate success. Thanks to the labor of forty-six black and two Indian slaves, "the Kolly concession on the Chapitoulas coast just north of New Orleans produced six hundred quarters of rice from fourteen quarters that had been sown" by 1721, Hall informs us. From that point, rice production increased, with "settlers near New Orleans contract[ing] to furnish one hundred barrels of rice in straw to the king's warehouse for four francs two sous a barrel."

Rice quickly became an important part of the diet for settlers and slaves, and so was only occasionally exported to the French islands or Spanish Pensacola. As Hall writes, "In French Louisiana, there was always rice. It was cultivated in and around the capital. Heavy rains and floods that destroyed corn and other crops often spared the rice. When Indian warfare forced settlers to flee the countryside, when maritime shipping was cut off, when flour did not arrive from the Illinois country because of ice blockages or warfare along the Mississippi River, there was rice." Antoine Simon Le Page du Pratz, who arrived in New Orleans about the same time that rice did and spent the next fifteen years in Louisiana, wrote, "They eat their rice as they do in France, but boiled much thicker, and with much less cookery, although it is not inferior in goodness to ours.... They make bread of it that is very white and of a good relish; but they have tried in vain to make any that will soak in soup." Slaves soaked the rice and pounded it into a batter, much as the Native Americans did with cornmeal. As Daniel Usner points out, "Slaves were able to use rice and corn interchangeably to make, among other dishes, what Le Page du Pratz heard some call 'couscou.'"

The colonial governments of Louisiana continued to keep rice in their warehouses for times of low supply, which sometimes led to speculation on the part of the directors and disagreements over what amount of rice had been contracted for and how much delivered. By 1803, when Frenchman C. C. Robin was traveling throughout Louisiana, he observed, "Its consumption in the country is tremendous and one sees it on all tables adapted to creole customs. It is eaten in place of bread, and on many plantations, with paps and corn bread, it replaces bread entirely."

The early New Orleans Creole cookbooks do not make a fetish of rice. The Creole Cookery Book of the Christian Woman's Exchange (1885) has recipes for "callers," a colloquial spelling of calas, the folkloric but today mostly unavailable rice fritters that were traditionally sold by female African American street vendors, both enslaved and free. "The Cala women have almost all passed away, for, as remarked at the beginning of this book, there is a 'new colored woman' in

New Orleans, and she disdains all the pretty olden industries and occupations which were a constant and genteel source of revenue to the old negro mothers and grandmothers," the editors of the *Picayune* book wrote regretfully in their turn-of-the-twentieth-century cookbook.

The *Picayune* book notes that a true cala is not made with self-rising flour, as had become popular in families who still made them at home, but entirely with rice and only a little pounded rice flour to bind it. This is different from a recipe called Rice Fritters, or Beignets de Riz, which does call for wheat flour. *The Creole Cookery Book* also includes recipes for several breakfast-type rice breads, rice pudding, and *riz au lait* and notes that curries and gumbos should be served with rice. It also has instructions for "Carolina boiled rice," "Rice as cooked in Japan," and "To prepare and boil rice." Lafcadio Hearn, oddly enough, in his book of the same year, calls for Patna rice for his baked soup. But these books were published as a transformation in rice cultivation was taking place.

Before the Civil War, South Carolina had occupied the apex of that world, producing the famous "Carolina Gold" that was exported by the ton through the port of Charleston. Even as South Carolina dominated rice production, though, Louisiana began growing more rice, mostly along the Mississippi River, but also in the southwest part of the state for home consumption. In the 1840s Louisiana rice emerged as a commercial crop, grown by smaller farmers looking for crops requiring less capital investment than sugarcane. After the Civil War, developments in heavy mechanized equipment that couldn't be used in the swampy rice fields of Carolina and the lack of an enslaved workforce in traditional rice-growing areas left an opening for Louisiana. In the 1870s, Louisiana rice crops grew by leaps and bounds, from 16,701 barrels in 1870–1871 (about a quarter of what South Carolina and Georgia combined produced) to 62,000 in 1878–1879 (about half of the South Carolina and Georgia total). This increase occurred in part because New Orleans had crucial support services, from transportation by water and rail to financial resources both from banks and agricultural brokers, and, finally, a quickly developing milling industry. A number of mills occupied "rice row" between Decatur and Chartres streets, from the Custom-house to the French Market. Some of these mills abandoned the methods of the South Carolina processors and introduced modern techniques borrowed from the flour mills of the Midwest, allowing them to reduce the amount of broken rice. But the New Orleans rice industry reached its zenith in 1900, when the new mills of the coastal prairies of southwestern Louisiana and southeastern

Texas challenged the New Orleans system. Land developers and railroad companies lured farmers from the Midwest during a late 1880s drought, and a host of entrepreneurs ranging from Midwestern agricultural researchers to Polish Jewish immigrants helped develop the techniques and infrastructure of the burgeoning industry. Irrigation improvements in the form of canals and new pump systems, along with adapted Midwestern farm machinery, sealed the deal. By the early twentieth century, Louisiana rice researchers from private industry and the Louisiana State University rice experiment station (established in 1909) were busily striving to find newer, more productive varieties. Today, Louisiana ranks third behind Arkansas and California in rice production, growing about 15 percent of the U.S. crop.

Sixteen years after Hearn's book and *Creole Cookery* were published, out came the *Picayune* book, with a nine-page chapter on rice comprising twenty-nine recipes for rice, including four jambalayas. The same year as the *Picayune's* now famous second edition, 1901, saw the publication of the *Carolina Rice Cook Book*, containing 237 historic rice recipes compiled by Louisa Cheves Smythe Stoney, wife of the chairman of the Carolina Rice Kitchen Association. The most important source for Stoney's book was *The Carolina Housewife*, "the first edition of which appeared in 1847, at the apogee of Low Country cooking." Despite South Carolina's head start, the *Picayune* editors were happy to lay claim to a profound knowledge of rice cookery, predicting that rice would become more and more popular "when the people of the great North and West learn how to cook it as well as the Creoles of Louisiana."

The *Picayune* book refers to jambalaya as a Spanish-Creole dish, and many have embraced that idea, noting that the frequent combination of seafood and pork in jambalaya resembles that of paella. On the other hand, "it is said to be an Indian dish, and very wholesome as well as palatable," wrote Hearn. "It can be made of many things." Others have pronounced the word a combination of the French *jambon*, for "ham," a common ingredient; the Acadian *à la*; and the African *ya*, meaning "rice." Karen Hess makes a case for the similarity of jambalaya to a Provençal dish of *jambalaia*, unknown in that region today, but with historic ties to ancient Islamic pilaus.

A further connection between Africa and the spread of rice cultivation here is noted by Carney, who points to the method of rice cooking used in the New World. Rice cooked by the absorption method produces separate grains, and that is how West Africans cook their rice. Both Italians and Spaniards begin with cooking the rice in animal fat or olive oil. Even in areas settled and influenced by the Spanish, the rice cooking method follows the one used in Africa.

The Spanish affinity for rice, of course, brings to mind the variety of dishes in Spain and the Caribbean that combine rice and beans. The Valencian *moros y christianos* (Moors and Christians) of black beans and rice became a classic Cuban dish. Moreover, Spain can lay claim to bean and sausage dishes (similar to France's cassoulet), particularly from Catalonia. This latter connection may be significant for New Orleans, which had a substantial number of Catalan grocers and wine sellers during the territorial period, so much so that *marchand catalan* (Catalan merchant) was used to refer to all grocers in the city. Finally, while most beans and rice (also known as peas and rice) dishes in the Caribbean consist of beans and rice cooked together and thus differ substantially in technique from the New Orleans version, a few—such as Nicaragua's *gallo pinto*—are cooked separately. Although the *congri oriental* of Cuba's Oriente Province consists of rice and beans cooked together, it presents two factors of interest: it uses red kidney beans and that is the region settled by Saint-Domingue exiles who eventually relocated to New Orleans. This trail from Saint-Domingue to Cuba to New Orleans illustrates the strong ties that New Orleans had to the Caribbean and points south during this period, through shared colonial administrators, trade, and migrations. As writer John Thorne says in his marvelous essay "Rice and Beans: The Itinerary of a Dish," "the logical point for any investigation of the roots of this dish should start in the Caribbean, not the American South."

No matter how one spins the tale of the origin and evolution of New Orleans–style red beans and rice, what is certain is that Crescent City cooks have a lot to say about how to cook the dish properly. "The secret is known to you, though," confides Peter Feibleman, "if you've sat as a child in a New Orleans kitchen on a Monday and seen the cook either crack the ham bone or make sure that one end of it is open. . . . [I]f it is, the thick marrow from the bone leaks into the simmering beans, coats them, cooks slowly with them, seems to drain them of starch and produces a silky food that is more like incredibly tender meat than like a vegetable." Although the marrow from ham bones or ham hocks produces creamy beans, many recipes advise smashing some of the beans against the side of the pot. That technique, Leon Soniat assured his readers, "will produce a creamy smoothness." Once one gets past the issue of creaminess, unanimity about what is necessary to make red beans ends. Recipe variations are endless, as are the ingredients and cooking methods considered crucial.

The beans used for red beans and rice are a variety of *Phaseolus vulgaris* and originated in Central America. Dark red kidney beans (not the same as those used in New Orleans red beans and rice, which are light) were the first of the New World beans to reach Europe in the sixteenth century; they subsequently became very popular in France, particularly in regions that favored pork or goosefat, such as Languedoc and Alsace-Lorraine. Today, the light red kidney beans sold in New Orleans are grown elsewhere, mostly in New York, Michigan, and Colorado. New Orleanians remain devoted to the Camellia brand of red beans (with a reported 90 percent market share), although a few other brands can be found in local stores. Camellia dates back to 1947, when L. H. Hayward and Company of New Orleans transformed its wholesale produce business to packaging dried beans, peas, and lentils. In the 1970s, the company moved its operation to Harahan, a New Orleans suburb.

While many insist on the necessity of the ham bone, others hone in on pickled meat. Austin Leslie summed it up this way: "Pickled pork is hard to get anywhere other than New Orleans. It's just fresh pork pickled the same way you do a cucumber. If you can't buy pickled pork tips, just get some fresh pork, cut it up, put it in a jar of vinegar and let it soak for about two or three days. Then put it in the refrigerator. Pickled pork gives red beans a special taste." Red beans and rice recipes are fairly consistent when it comes to herbs and spices. As Leah Chase, the reigning doyenne of Creole cookery, says, "I don't think anybody is really cooking red beans, for instance, unless they put a little thyme in them, and some bay leaf." Other spices and condiments sometimes include dried basil and hot sauce. The traditional final touch for red beans is added at the table, with either plain vinegar or else the liquid from peppers bottled in vinegar, either homemade or manufactured.

While red beans have remained popular as a "made from scratch" dish (in part because it is easy to cook), New Orleanians haven't turned their backs on canned red beans. In the 1950s, Pierre Chauvin, the founder of Gonzales Products, used his grandmother's recipe to produce canned Blue Runner Creole Cream Style Red Beans; the company was purchased by Richard Thomas in 1993 and renamed Blue Runner Foods. The Blue Runner beans are also sold in institutional quantities and used in some restaurants. Trappey's also offers New Orleans–style red beans in a can, formerly manufactured in New Iberia in southwest Louisiana, but now made elsewhere since purchased by B&G Foods of New Jersey. Still, slow-cooked beans, simmered over the burner for several hours, remain the norm; and most cooks who used canned beans treat this as a second-best option that comes into play when time is a factor. Those who resort to it often improve it with a few home-cooked elements, such as sautéed onions, bell pepper, celery, and garlic. And, of course, the rice has to be made. All in all, beans from a can make a quick, utilitarian meal, usually just enough to feed one or two, or perhaps stretched to satisfy a small family.

But it is not this quick, "modern" version of making do that we wish to leave with you, but the "way red beans and rice were cooked in the old days—loaded with meat and steeped in a rich, natural gravy." It is the modification of the careful recipe of Rima and Richard Collin, two New Orleans academics who made significant side careers out of their passion for Creole cuisine. The Collins' recipe, combined with changes by the Culinary History Group, eschews sausage—these days a common addition—in favor of the traditional ham bone and pickled meat.

RED BEANS AND RICE FOR EIGHT PERSONS

2 pounds dried red (kidney) beans

First cover the beans in cold water (there should be 3 inches above the beans); let stand overnight; then drain.

Have ready the following:

½ cup thinly sliced green onion tops

two chopped onions

½ cup chopped green pepper

1½ tablespoons finely minced garlic

3 tablespoons finely minced fresh parsley

1 pound baked ham, cut into 1-inch cubes

1 pound pickled pork, cut into large chunks

1 large ham bone (ask the butcher to leave some meat on it and saw it into 4-inch lengths)

1 teaspoon freshly ground black pepper

¼ teaspoon cayenne pepper

2 bay leaves

½ teaspoon dried thyme

1 tablespoon salt

Heat the beans in about 2 quarts of water, add all ingredients except salt, bring to a boil, and simmer for at least 2 hours. When beans are tender, mash some against the side of the pot. Add salt and then serve with rice.

MIRLITON AND SHRIMP

Susan Tucker and Sara Roahen

STUFFED MIRLITON

2 [to 8] medium mirlitons

1½ lbs. shrimp, peeled, deveined, and diced

⅓ lb. ham, diced

½ lb. crabmeat

2 cups onions, finely chopped

⅓ cup parsley, finely chopped

⅓ cup green peppers, finely chopped

3 toes garlic, finely chopped

1 tsp. thyme

2 bay leaves

2 eggs, beaten

2 sticks butter

2 cups bread crumbs

Salt, pepper, and hot sauce to taste

Preheat oven to 350 degrees. Boil mirliton for 15 minutes. [The authors suggest using about 8 mirlitons.] Halve, remove pit and scoop out all of the mirliton meat. Dice mirliton meat and set aside. Sauté onions, parsley, green pepper, garlic, thyme, and bay leaves in butter for 10 minutes. Next, add shrimp, ham, [crabmeat], salt, pepper, hot sauce, and mirliton meat. Mix and sauté gently for 30 minutes. Remove from heat and vigorously stir in beaten eggs. Add enough bread crumbs to bind. Divide stuffing between mirliton halves, sprinkle [remaining] bread crumbs on top, and dot with butter. Bake in 350 degree oven, until crust is golden brown. Serves 4.

The late Creole chef Austin Leslie included the above recipe in his cookbook published in 2000 with the note, "Here's what happens when Caribbean squash meets with pure Creole-Soul!" In many ways, his description is an apt one. Historically, mirlitons have a strong connection to the Caribbean, and emotionally, they evoke the memory of countless simple home gardens in New Orleans neighborhoods. This history, and especially this evocation, make the mirliton a sort of enchanted vegetable, ready in the minds of so many, passionately recalled for its pairing with shellfish, its usually pale green color, its darker green leaves, and its effusive growth. Almost any New Orleanian born before 1960 will tell you about mirliton vines in yards of mothers and fathers, aunts and uncles, grandmothers and grandfathers, and neighbors. As Sylvia Cureau wrote to us in a 2007 e-mail after Hurricane Katrina, "We lived in the Upper Ninth Ward off St. Claude and Gallier and my grandfather would have a mirliton bush that we children could get lost in." Such memories serve as a small but important buffer against all the sadness that grew from the levee failure in that area.

Known most often in other parts of the United States by its Spanish name, *chayote*, or by those more inclined to choose an English name, *vegetable pear*, the mirliton has graced the tables of this city since the 1870s or 1880s. In this chronological placement, it arrived later than other vegetables. Even from the early 1900s, there are no memories of the mirliton in the calls of the vegetable vendors—I got your Creole tomatoes; I got turnip greens picked yesterday. There are no songs to the mirliton in blues or jazz. Still, alongside red beans and rice, New Orleans French bread, and bread pudding, stuffed mirliton is a favored dish of the family table. Only in the very late twentieth century did it become occasionally visible in the high cuisine of the city.

In 1718, when Jean-Baptiste Le Moyne, sieur de Bienville, established New Orleans as the capital of Louisiana and somehow convinced a few others that this place might become a fortress from which to control the wealth of the North American interior, richness of any kind was relative. Most critically, food was hard to come by and the soil of the new capital was, for the most part, muck. What could grow here and who would have the stamina to try? Bienville found his little band of French and French Canadian men not so industrious when it came to farming, and Native Americans of the area proved not subservient or plentiful enough. The first African slaves were captured in battle with the Spanish in 1710; importation by the French began in 1719, with some one thousand slaves arriving before 1720. The slave traders were instructed to bring slaves with experience in rice growing, and rice was grown here shortly after that. But problems persisted. Neither did the importation of France's undesirables—many from debtors' prisons—help the food crisis much.

Thus, when John Law sought to protect this French investment in the New World in 1720, one of his first acts was to sponsor the arrival of two thousand Rhinelanders. These colonists eventually settled above New Orleans in present-day St. James and St. Charles parishes, on land granted to them by Bienville. Known even today as the German Coast or the Côte des Allemands, this settlement is the fourth oldest of all German ones in the United States. It grew quickly when, in 1721, more Germans arrived under the leadership of the Swede Karl Friedrich D'Arensbourg. Still more came in 1722 after a disappointing residency in Arkansas; on their way back to Europe by way of New Orleans, they were persuaded to stay. By the time of the Louisiana Purchase in 1803, the reputation, indeed, the near mythologizing, of these industrious Germans as the saviors of the city's markets was known far and wide. The last French colonial prefect, Pierre-Clément de Laussat, recalled the German immigrants' importance when he scrambled to make one final effort to increase the population of Louisiana. In 1803 he extolled "this class of peasants, especially of this nationality . . . the most industrious, the most populous, the most prosperous, the most upright, the most valuable population segment of this colony." His solution to the need for hard workers: "Bring every year 1,000 to 1,200 families from the border states of Switzerland, the Rhine and Bavaria."

Well into the nineteenth century, New Orleans citizens continued to depend on the rural German American farmers. Sugarcane and rice were the main food crops, but the farmers also raised and sold in the city okra, turnips, spinach, cauliflower, artichokes, onions, garlic, cabbage, sweet potatoes, and Irish (or what today is called white) potatoes. Root vegetables were particularly important. The farmers also made butter, sold their extra eggs and poultry, and harvested many different kinds of fruit—all of which enriched the New Orleans table.

Among these, okra remains the vegetable most important to the city. Several aspects make this so: its use in most gumbos, its distinction as the best known of all crops brought from Africa, and the ease of cultivation, even in the hot summer. Yet, cooked alone, okra is "fastidious," as Natalie Scott once wrote, and this may explain why it is not so popular outside the South. Okra must be sautéed or baked for a few minutes before being added to dishes such as gumbo. Otherwise, okra gets too slimy. Some cooks in the city also advise that okra should be cooked in a porcelain-lined, agate, or at least a dark-colored, pot. Plain stewed okra and tomatoes, common all over the South, is a favored dish in New Orleans; but more New Orleanian, and also a favorite in community cookbooks, is shrimp smothered in okra and tomatoes.

Among the various other vegetable dishes beloved by New Orleanians today is the breadcrumb-and-garlic-stuffed whole artichoke, a preparation that is inextricably linked to the city's still-strong Sicilian population. Sicilians began to arrive in this port city around 1880, a time of economic hardship and social unrest in their homeland. Accustomed to working the land at home, they took to truck-farming almost immediately and soon controlled the produce section of the French Market. Parts of the French Quarter came to be called Little Palermo due to the concentration of Sicilian immigrants living there.

As noted, artichokes were grown in the eighteenth century along the German Coast, and artichoke recipes appear in early New Orleans cookbooks, some of which contain recipes for artichokes stuffed with ham and other meats. The Christian Woman's Exchange book (1885), for example, contains a recipe called Fonds L'Artichoux—Stuffed. But the currently popular method of paving every leaf of the artichoke with a garlicky breadcrumb and olive oil mixture (which might also include herbs, cheeses, anchovies, lemon, and other ingredients of the cook's choosing), and then baking or steaming it whole, only begins to appear in cookbooks published in the latter half of the twentieth century, such as in Mary Land's *Louisiana Cookery*. Still, in *Jesse's Book of Creole and Deep South Recipes*, authors Edith and John Watts conclude their recipe for this dish with the comment, "Artichokes prepared in this manner are served as a vegetable or appetizer course; but they are also frequently used by the Creoles as a Sunday-night snack or luncheon dainty." Here, as in the neighborhood restaurant tradition, where spaghetti is often served alongside Creole dishes, you have the mingling of the Italian and the French, the new and old traditions existing side by side.

The evolution of the New Orleans breadcrumb-stuffed artichoke is unclear, but seems to point always to this complexity of more than one culture. New Orleanians in general do not like plain vegetables, so the addition of breadcrumbs and olive oil is consistent with other prepared dishes. One doesn't find the stuffed artichoke in Sicily today or earlier. But in New Orleans the stuffed artichoke is widely available in restaurants and stores run by those of Italian heritage as well as in specialty groceries and delis. Too, stuffed artichokes are always part of Saint Joseph's Day feasts and altars.

This saint day and these altars are important to the city, so much so that it is hard to meet a New Orleanian of any background who does not know that Saint Joseph is mythologized to have saved Sicily from famine in the Middle Ages. Not to be forgotten is that he is the patron saint of families, immigrants, happy death, and pregnant women. This hagiographic tendency among the general population has to do with food: on the days leading up to Saint Joseph's Day, altars with decorative, lavish displays of food occupy homes, churches, and even offices. These are generally open to the public, and one will be given a lucky fava bean upon visiting, and more elaborate treats if one is present for the blessing. In recent times, Super Sunday, that day closest to St. Joseph's Day, also involves another multicultural celebration, that of the African American Mardi Gras Indians parade.

Artichokes are usually a surprise to visitors to New Orleans tables, probably because for most of the twentieth century U.S. artichokes grew in quantity only in California. They require moist, rather cool mornings and sunny afternoons. New Orleans does have these conditions in fall and winter, but humidity here makes moistness even an understatement. Still, according to a number of New Orleanians, artichokes have grown here for centuries. Researchers at the Hermann-Grima House, for example, speak of the Chevalier Jean de Pradel growing artichokes in the 1750s at his plantation across the river. Food writer Pableaux Johnson mentions an artichoke plantation where today's Warehouse District stands. Artichokes also appear in hotel menus of the mid-nineteenth century. Undoubtedly, the Italian farmers who came in the late nineteenth century added more to the availability of artichokes, but they were probably always here. A later urban myth was that Newcomb College, the coordinate college for women within Tulane University, was left one such artichoke farm in the 1930s. The dining hall there served steamed artichokes so often that some explanation was needed. New Orleans gardeners of today often grow artichoke plants, which, when their purple flowers emerge, remain a favorite at the Saturday and Tuesday Green Markets.

Pommes de terre soufflées, perhaps the most prominent of New Orleans vegetable preparations because of its place on the menus of haute Creole restaurants, offers another rich story of origin. This account revolves around the creation of a dish by Collinet, chef of King Louis-Philippe. The king was said to be a passenger on a train as it made its inaugural run from Paris to St. Germain-en-Laye in 1837. Knowing that the king loved fried potatoes and insisted on having them at every meal, the chef charged a messenger with alerting him when the train could be seen approaching. The potatoes could then be plunged into hot grease and served to the king steaming hot as soon as he debarked. The plan went smoothly, until it became known that the king wasn't on the train after all. His advisers had insisted that he make the trip in a carriage instead, for safety's sake. Hearing this, the chef removed the potatoes from the hot grease and, having no extra potatoes with which to start the process over, re-submerged them some time later, when the king actually arrived. This double-frying technique resulted in an accidental masterpiece: the sliced potatoes puffed into balloon-like French fries.

Numerous writers, according to food historians John and Karen Hess, have repeated this story. But the Hesses call it a part of historical fiction and note that the *Larousse Gastronomique* qualifies its judgment of the tale by using the subjunctive tense and also warning the reader of a very hazy attribution ("It is claimed," they write). On the other hand, the encyclopedia also quotes an experiment by "the famous analytical chemist Chevreul," who replicated the whole process and produced a recipe. What seems clear is that Antoine Alciatore, the Frenchman who founded Antoine's Restaurant in 1840, recreated the recipe, no matter how it first began, from a recipe he learned in France and brought to New Orleans. To this day, pommes de terre soufflées are a specialty at Antoine's and at a few other French Quarter destinations for haute Creole cooking. Often patrons order the potatoes as appetizers, with a side of béarnaise sauce for dipping them. And many New Orleans cookbooks contain recipes for the double-fried potatoes.

Because they can be stored for so long, potatoes in all sorts of recipes have remained popular restaurant and home-cooked food for all of New Orleans history. This popularity extended in such a way that Creoles were credited by at least one writer for stretching the use of even potatoes past their prime. In 1885, *The Unrivalled Cook-book and Housekeeper's Guide*, while presenting over a dozen recipes of Creole potatoes in various guises, tells us that one recipe for mashed potatoes (Desirée's Potatoes) is the "Creole method of making poor potatoes palatable."

Another vegetable treatment worth mentioning because it is specific to the cooking of the Gulf South is the "holy trinity" of diced celery, onion, and green bell pepper that cooks use as a base for so many dishes, from red beans and rice to gumbo, from jambalaya to crawfish bisque. These vegetables are not used for their pure flavors. Rather, sautéed or boiled, they form an aromatic background for the larger dish. Garlic, green onions, and parsley, or some combination of the three, often accompany the trinity and are also essential in New Orleans kitchens and cookbooks. The use of this mixture comes to us from the French *mirepoix*, a mixture of diced carrots, celery, onions, and herbs sautéed in butter and used to season various dishes. Soil and weather conditions are very poor for good carrot production in Louisiana. However, sweet pepper production is easy and often year-round. Thus, sweet peppers were substituted for carrots.

Plantains, which New Orleanians sometimes call "cooking bananas," are treated as vegetables as well. Plantains grow more easily than the bananas eaten for dessert, and they are also more robust and darker than bananas. But like bananas, plantains grew first in Malaysia and came to us via Africa, where the Spaniards put some rootstocks on ships to the Caribbean and Latin America in the sixteenth and seventeenth centuries. What New Orleanians (and others) call bananas trees are really not trees at all but herbaceous perennials arising from underground rhizomes. They are kin, thus, to the ginger lilies so ubiquitous in the city's landscape. There are more than 250 cultivars of plantains, but the ones in New Orleans are not that sweet and usually have a dark green, and then a red or black, tint before turning yellow. The Christian Woman's Exchange's *Creole Cookery Book* of 1885 tells us that a ripe plantain is yellow all over, but New Orleanians rarely remember seeing such ripeness. Today they are usually only eaten by the adventuresome, the truly hungry, or those dining in the African restaurant Bennachin. Many Hondurans, who settled here especially in the twentieth century, also pass on plantain recipes for home-cooking.

Fried plantains in Mary Land's *Louisiana Cookery* is a favorite published recipe, although she, like others with plantains, leaves much to the reader's imagination. Some cookbooks writers advise that they are best used as a sweet *entremet*, and almost all recipes, regardless of placement as vegetable, call for frying or sautéing and then sweetening them with syrup or sugar. So, too, however, are many other vegetables in New Orleans; and, indeed, expert cooks here often soak vegetables in sugar and water before cooking. They say it brings out the flavor.

Other vegetable favorites of New Orleans tables are creamed spinach, the same as nationwide though a bit spicier and sometimes here called spinach Creole; southern standbys such as yams, butter beans, and cabbage (cooked in many ways with meat); grits (a starch but here considered a vegetable, at least in many cookbooks); and eggplant, which, as with the mirliton, is a favorite for use with seafood and is found in countless Italian-inspired recipes. A number of visiting cooks believe New Orleans vegetable dishes show the Italian influence more than that of any other ethnic group. Land, on the other hand, places Louisiana vegetable dishes within the Creole tradition since they are usually seared in hot butter before adding water and meat for boiling. To outsiders, the end product may look like a dish from the rest of the South, however.

One unusual taste in New Orleans is for the Jerusalem artichoke. This tuber is a member of the sunflower family and only gained its name because it tasted somewhat like an artichoke to Frenchman and Canadian explorer Marc Lescarbot (1570–1641). The French sometimes call them *artichauts du Canada.* They are also called *topinambours.* By the mid-seventeenth century, they were described as being a suitable food for Lent; and to this day, along the Gulf Coast, they are still considered a delicacy of March and April. They are cooked simply (boiled in water), or puréed, and served with butter and seasonings. The name New Orleanians use, Jerusalem artichoke, is said to be a corruption of the Italian word for sunflower, the *girasole,* thus giving another New Orleans vegetable connection between France and Italy.

Despite the connections of other vegetables to New Orleans cooking, the mirliton remains the most distinctively New Orleanian of vegetables. This is mainly so by default: it is unknown, especially by this name, in most other places in the United States. In the 1997 edition of the *Joy of Cooking,* the authors refer to it as a "chayote"; yet the one recipe they include for preparing it is subtitled Louisiana-Style Chayote, thus confirming that whatever your name for it, the vegetable pear is this region's bijou. So how did the mirliton find its way to New Orleans, and then later to St. Bernard Parish and the river parishes of Louisiana, but not significantly to any other community in the United States outside the Southwest? One can only speculate.

The second edition of *The Picayune's Creole Cook Book* tells us that the mirliton was "commonly grown around Creole homes." By 1901, these vegetables were also sighted in the city as "having been grown for many years" by O. F. Cook, an agent for the U.S. Department of Agriculture, who thought they might be useful elsewhere in the United States with a little encouragement. Another U.S. agricultural agent, L. G. Hoover, similarly noted in 1923 that the chayote had been grown in New Orleans "for more than a generation." Both Cook and Hoover discuss the growth of the mirliton in Jamaica, so one can guess that imports and human migration to New Orleans are likely the key to the mirliton's arrival sometime during the nineteenth century.

Cook guesses this might be so as he traces the chayote's cultivation among the Aztecs in Mexico and gives a description of the first European account of its various uses. In the mid-1500s, Spaniard Francisco Hernandez noted the mirliton vine "for creeping. . . . The fruit is eaten cooked," and "even the bean, or seed, resembles cooked acorns, the rest something marine, such as roasted oysters, sweet potatoes or chestnuts." Cook notes, however, that despite Hernandez's observations, mention of the mirliton does not appear in various other descriptions of plant life in the area at the time of his stay there. Cook speculates that, after discovering the mirliton in Mexico, the Spanish introduced it to Jamaica. By 1756, explorer Patrick Browne had written of the *cho cho* (as they call the mirliton there) vine there. To him, this Jamaican vegetable was "insipid." Another traveler to eighteenth-century Cuba found the mirliton in daily use in soups, stews, and other dishes, thus also showing more about the way it could have spread from Mexico to Louisiana.

Given the reports of these early travelers, the mirliton could easily have arrived with the Acadians and the Saint-Domingue refugees in the late eighteenth and early nineteenth centuries. People from both these groups often sought refuge first in Jamaica or Cuba, before arriving in New Orleans. Similarly, mirlitons could have arrived with no fanfare in a ship transporting other imported foodstuff to New Orleans in the 1850s, or slightly earlier, with returning troops from the Mexican War (1846–1848). After all, peppers, which are so important to Louisiana cooking and history, appeared around this earlier date. Perhaps the mirliton was here but only gained popularity in cooking later, during and after the Civil War, when food was not as plentiful and cooks were forced to be creative. Another possibility is that mirlitons appeared in New Orleans in the 1870s, when sweet bananas arrived here. As mentioned in this volume's chapter on bread pudding, the first banana shipments came from Honduras. Shortly afterwards, they also came from Costa Rica and Jamaica. All three places have a long tradition of chayote production and consumption. In Costa Rica, Minor Keith, whose company later merged with others to form United Fruit, needed freight on a railroad he was building and a product then to sell worldwide: bananas were the answer. Considering the hardships Keith first experienced and his desperation to find food to export, especially to ports in the United States, it is believable that he also sent along a few mirliton plants, which are much hardier than fragile bananas. One final possibility is that mirlitons arrived about the time of the World's Industrial and Cotton Exposition held in 1884 where Audubon Park stands now. For display during this fair, the Mexicans had a garden of their characteristic plants. Urban myth holds that various nations gave plants away during the exhibition; it is conceivable that mirlitons were among these gifts of the fair.

Yet, if Mexico was indeed the originator of New Orleans' mirliton, why were these plants not called by their Spanish name? Furthermore, why does the mirliton have so many other names? There are no answers to these questions, except to think highly of New Orleanians as being loyal to this name that is their own. Moreover, one also can think highly of others in their own allegiance to a local name. This seems especially appropriate in an age where there is so much standardization. The name *chayote* comes from the Nahuatl language, once spoken by the Aztecs in central Mexico. Some thirty-two other names exist for this vegetable-fruit around the world. Most sound like chayote—*camochahyaote, charota, chyotestle, tayote*—and none sounds anything like mirliton, a French word that inexplicably translates to a kazoo-type flute. New Orleanians do tend to know that the mirliton is called *christophene* in France and in the French Caribbean, but no one has ever speculated as to why this name was not adopted despite this city's deep connections to France, the Caribbean, and the French language. In New Orleans, mirliton is pronounced in three ways: milly-tawn, melly-tawn, or merly-tawn, but no geographic placement is found in the various pronunciations. The closest moniker to mirliton in pronunciation is mango pear, used from time to time alongside other names such as the one-seeded cucumber and the vegetable pear.

Not even the mirliton's scientific names have remained consistent from country to country. Its botanical name is *Sechium edule*, though early explorers of South America also called it *Sisyos edulus* or *Chayota eudulis*. It belongs to the gourd family Cucurbitaceae, along with melons, cucumbers, and squash. Most botanists liken it to the cucumber plant above all these others: the mirliton, as noted in the memories of so many here, has the same large and vigorous tendrils, the same climbing and sheltering vines as the cucumber. In the Time-Life volume on Creole and Cajun food (1971), Peter Feibleman called the mirliton "the maverick vegetable of South Louisiana" and likened it to "the illegitimate offspring of an eggplant and a squash with a melon somewhere in its ancestry." Richard Collin described it as "a vegetable somewhat like a combination of green pepper and squash."

Locals, food writers, and scientists alike almost always comment on the vines that make ornamental coverings for fences and arbors. From these vines come also the makings of baskets and hats. The plant's all-round versatility is further demonstrated in the fact that its flowers are said to be rich in honey, and even its roots can be cooked, making it comparable to the true yam. New Orleans growers believe that the mirliton is more tropical than most garden vegetables. After the late nineteenth century, it proved an excellent substitute for summer squash, vegetable marrow, and, especially, artichoke hearts. The agricultural agent O. F. Cook likened the chayote as a fruit to the mangrove because germination takes place before the seed falls from the parent plant. While the mirliton needs a drier soil than does the mangrove, it is still a more tropical plant than most garden vegetables, which may explain its popularity in subtropical New Orleans.

Also somewhat unique, the mirliton plant stays alive after germination and after separation from the parent plant. In this, it is like that other pear among vegetable-like fruits, the alligator pear or avocado. One can sit the large mirliton seed in a small bit of water and watch its vines and leaves emerge. Later, it can be moved to soil. After its harvest, one can preserve the mirliton for the winter by packing it in sand or wrapping it in paper and storing it in a cool and dark place. Likely, this attribute appealed immediately to New Orleanians, along with the fact that the mirliton is relatively disease free. Though it requires growing in loose sandy or loamy substratum soil, it is not a fussy plant at all. There are two varieties of the mirliton, one green and one white, but most New Orleanians today know only the green.

New Orleanians have purchased as well as grown mirlitons now for over a century. Cook tells us that a man described as an agricultural explorer, David Fairchild, found mirlitons in 1898 being sold in the French market for 15 cents a piece, a "price which certainly would not be paid were not the chayote considered a table delicacy superior to the vegetable marrow." About the time of Fairchild's travels, the U.S. Department of Agriculture was trying to introduce the mirliton to Florida, southern Texas, Hawaii, and the Philippines. In California, it had had some success, being introduced from Samoa and grown first in Santa Barbara in the 1880s. But in none of these locales does it remain as popular as it is in New Orleans. Indeed, the 2006 edition of the *Joy of Cooking*, which is said to bring back some of the recipes of the beloved 1975 edition, retains mention of the mirliton and even uses it by its New Orleans name, thus aligning itself with this city rather than the other places where chayote is served. *Joy*'s author Ethan Becker writes, "The mirliton doesn't look like much, but . . . has a firm texture and a hint of sweetness." In her book on southern cooking, Winifred Green Cheney quotes Eudora Welty in attesting to this extra benefit of the mirliton. The famous Mississippi writer calls it Cajun squash, something that yields "a delicate flavor . . . full of life." She could have been discussing *cucuzza*, but since the long green shape of the latter is not mentioned, mirliton is probably what is meant.

As noted above, Jamaicans have enjoyed a long attachment to the mirliton. As in the eighteenth-century work of explorer Patrick Browne, they still call it *chocho* and use it in puddings, tarts, sauces, and other boiled dishes. A favorite among them is chocho fritters, not unlike a mirliton frittata served today in New Orleans. But, the Jamaicans also toast the innermost seeds of the chocho and eat them on toast. The Brazilians eat mirliton as a simple salad, after cooking and then cooling in an oil, vinegar, salt, and pepper base. New Orleanians do this as well, from time to time. And like the nineteenth-century French, who imported the christophene from Algeria, New Orleanians also pickle mirliton as one would green beans, and candy them. In New Orleans restaurants, the mirliton is often fried, sometimes in the manner that Southerners of all stripes batter and fry green tomatoes. It is also paired with shrimp in cream soups: in this sort of preparation, the mirliton's dewy, fruitlike qualities are most prominent.

Chayotes are said to grow along the fences of almost every peasant home in South America today. Costa Rica, the Dominican Republic, and Mexico grow them commercially, and today most New Orleanians buy these imported mirlitons in grocery stores. As in all foods, different cultures have many similar mirliton preparations. But one recipe not likely found in Latin America is a mirliton stuffing for turkey. There are many ways of serving mirliton that New Orleanians have not tried. One calls for mirliton with the addition of lime juice and sugar, or with a mixture of rhubarb or rosella in a dish that is said to be a Caribbean substitute for applesauce. In British India, the mirliton is used in a number of curries. In France, it is boiled in water for an hour, peeled and then mashed with butter and cheese. In Martinique, the flesh is squeezed in a cloth and then mashed with bread soaked in milk to form a sort of paste to spread on toast. Nor have New Orleanians tried to use it in the way that French chefs of the early twentieth century thought would help the poor: as a substitute for artichokes, with the basal part of the fleshy fruit cut into disks. Nor do we treat it like the Mexicans do and think of its roots as a substitute for arrowroot, something to feed sick children or invalids. Nor do New Orleanians talk of it as going well with celery, cauliflower, and kohlrabi, as at least one British chef has noted; nor as superior to potato in the quality and quantity of its various uses as the Hondurans proclaim.

Yet, like the potato, mirlitons do have a hint of sweetness, and perhaps this quality, more than the marine taste first noted by the Spanish explorer, is what makes it a favorite. The mirliton's blandness, too, works in its favor. One upscale New Orleans restaurant experiments from time to time with a shrimp and mirliton napoleon. Today, other new local recipes make it into trendy upscale desserts like mirliton cake, mirliton pie, and mirliton glace.

Of course, as noted, mirlitons make a versatile crop. Historically they are harvested in both fall and spring. And so the mirliton's texture and taste is appreciated just as white shrimp reach their peak in autumn; and brown shrimp, in spring. From the beginning, it appealed to New Orleans' Sicilian community, as it could be used in all the ways of a squash or an eggplant. That is, as one reads the recipe that began this chapter, a mirliton could be stuffed with breadcrumbs, seasonings, and shrimp and/or meat. This is often the way with New Orleans vegetables: they enter the kitchen whole, but are scooped out, paired with other ingredients and then reinserted in their shells. To most people here, the combination demonstrates that "the cook has shown it what it should have tasted like in the first place." Besides its nice fit with shrimp and its suitability to the city's climate and constant growing seasons, New Orleanians like the mirliton for its vine: a single vine will cover a fence six feet high and fifty feet long in just a few months. A seed catalogue from 1900 told of its ability to "cover fences, sheds, or anything else which it is desired to conceal"—certainly an asset in a slowly declining economy.

The annual Mirliton Festival, held in the Bywater section of the city, is a small but gracious and understated tribute to this plant. Return then to the idea that its name is uniquely New Orleanian. As you eat it in the casserole with shrimp, in the dressing with oysters, or even in your ice cream, remember not New Orleans' grand successes or failures, but the humble and industrious backyard farmers of such a city, intent on making a great meal at the end of the day.

CREOLE TOMATO SALAD

Susan Tucker and Karen Trahan Leathem

Most New Orleanians have a certain amount of hubris about all their foods. Yet, for none but the Creole tomato do they claim world standing. Cookbook writer Lee Bailey qualifies his love of this vegetable/fruit stating, "I was born in Louisiana so I guess it's okay for me to say that Creole tomatoes are the best in the world." Writing of his family's restaurant and their recipes, Leon Galatoire makes much the same statement but doesn't worry that his reasoning needs any justification of birthplace: "We have the absolute joy of having what some consider the best tomato grown in the world, the Creole tomato."

But what really is a Creole tomato? It is easiest to begin by defining what it is not: it is not a variety called Creole tomato. Though there is such a type sold in many catalogs, it is not Louisiana's tomato at all. It is not even the one called Creole that was introduced by the Louisiana State University Agricultural Experiment Station in 1989. Instead, a Creole tomato is any tomato planted along the Mississippi River from the St. Bernard and Plaquemines parish lines through Jefferson and Orleans and no farther north than St. Charles or St. John the Baptist parishes. Or, more widely defined, to be a Creole tomato, a tomato must be grown in the river parishes of southeast Louisiana: Plaquemines, St. Bernard, St. Charles, and St. John parishes and along the river in Jefferson and Orleans parishes. Even if grown from the same seeds in other parts of the state, the tomatoes would have a different flavor and would not be Creole tomatoes. Today, Plaquemines Parish reports the largest acreage of Creole tomatoes.

Food writer Gene Bourg, in one of the most loving of all descriptions of the Creole tomato, recalls his visual memory of them as "not *pretty* . . . some were almost as big as grapefruit, and most were gnarled, lumpy, and splotched with reds, yellows and greens." With cracks or with a corona, these tomatoes call forth statements describing them as "imperfectly shaped" to cushion what other people call "downright ugly." On the other hand, according to some, Creole tomatoes are bright red, or tinged with green, and absolutely just what a tomato should be. Regardless of the individuality that all these opinions announce, New Orleanians long for the Creole tomato in almost any size or shape and eat them every chance they are presented. To Bourg, they remain "the juiciest, most luscious tomatoes I can remember eating."

Both Bourg and fellow food writer Marcelle Bienvenu name the Becnel family of Plaquemines Parish among the best known of growers and the purveyors of choice for the Creole tomato. Speaking to these food experts in 2001, Johnny Becnel Sr. specified two deciding influences on the taste: "the alluvial soil and the climate." In addition, according to Becnel, any tomato planted in southern Louisiana is a Creole tomato. Becnel reminisced that his father called anything grown in Plaquemines Parish a *Creole*: Creole cucumbers, okra, corn, and a host of others. "Everything grown in this soil has a totally different taste from anything else in the world whether it's eggplant, squash, or even an Irish potato." This is an interesting observation since, until the 1940s, no cookbook called a tomato specifically a *Creole tomato*. The first two books to show the name Creole tomato in print were Eugénie Lavedan Maylié's *Maylie's Table d'Hôte Recipes* (1941) and Mary Land's *Louisiana Cookery* (1954). It seems, therefore, that *Creole tomato* was a term used in the vernacular first.

The tomato, *Lycopersicon esculentum*, is a tropical perennial and a member of the Solanaceae family, a group that includes potatoes, tobacco, eggplant, and red and green peppers. To make it all the more confusing, this family also includes petunias and a few other flowers. All of these are members of what is called the nightshade family, some of whose species are poisonous. This may have been one reason that well into the nineteenth century some people considered tomatoes poisonous. Botanically, the tomato is a fruit, but in both usage and horticulture, it is treated as a vegetable. A perennial plant, it is grown most often as an annual. Its ability to find sustenance in a variety of soils and climates has helped propel it into one of the most popular vegetables in the world. In North America, it is second only to the potato in terms of vegetables consumed. The tomato owes its worldwide popularity to its versatility. It can be eaten raw and, when cooked, marries well with other ingredients—for example, in Louisiana and throughout the South it is often stewed with okra. However, not until the turn of the twentieth century did most North Americans and Europeans deign to eat it uncooked.

Since it is a New World plant, it is only appropriate that the tomato became such an important part of Creole cuisine. But the route to Louisiana was circuitous, traveling first to Europe before becoming an essential part of the Creole plate. Evidence indicates that approximately two thousand years ago it came from the northwestern coast of South America, then spread to Central America, where it was domesticated, and up to Mexico—a trajectory very similar to that of the chili pepper. Yet even in this journey, Andean cultures did not eat wild tomatoes, and so its cultivation had only a limited role in Central American cuisine when the Spanish arrived. The conquistadors quickly seized upon the tomato after they began to take over Mexico in 1519, disseminating the plant throughout the Caribbean and Europe. The Aztec term *tomatl* meant "plump fruit," and tomatoes were called *xitomatl*. The Spanish settled on *tomate* for the tomato, a word they also used to describe tomatillos.

The Spanish diffusion of tomatoes left a lasting imprint on Mediterranean cuisine, particularly that of southern Italy and Spain, but also that of North Africa and southern France. The tomato most likely entered Europe via the conquistadors returning to Seville in the sixteenth century. Scholars say that for some time after that, the tomato plant was mostly ornamental. Around the same time, the tomato arrived in Sicily and Naples, which were then both under Spanish rule. Spanish cooks probably first concocted tomato sauce, but the first known published tomato recipe appeared in Naples in Antonio Latini's *Lo scalco all moderna*, which includes a recipe for *salsa di pomadoro, alla spagnuala* (which translates as Spanish tomato sauce). By 1800, southern France had embraced tomato sauce and tomatoes as well, laying the foundation for one of the quintessential elements of modern Provençal cuisine.

Meanwhile, in England, the tomato was off to a slow start, with a corresponding trend in the Anglo North American colonies. By the mid-eighteenth century, the tomato, perhaps moving northward from the Caribbean, found its way to South Carolina and North Carolina. The first known American tomato recipe (for a sauce, which bears strong resemblance to a 1795 Provençal manuscript recipe) appeared in a 1770 South Carolina manuscript, and by 1792 tomato recipes were in cookbooks sold in the Unites States. Tomato sauce recipes—used for a variety of meats and fowl as well as for macaroni—were featured in these early cookbooks. The tomato gained popularity throughout the Americas in the nineteenth century, and the late-nineteenth- and early-twentieth-centuries southern Italian immigration gave tomato cookery a new dimension.

How tomatoes came to Louisiana is uncertain, but in all likelihood, the Spanish-French-Caribbean nexus provides a clue. We know that the tomato was grown in eighteenth-century Louisiana. In addition, as in other areas of New Orleans culture, immigrants from Saint-Domingue were doubtless influential. In 1790s Philadelphia, a number of refugees from the Haitian Revolution introduced their neighbors and friends to the cultivation of the tomato and its use in cooking. New Orleans began welcoming Saint-Domingueans fleeing the turmoil on their island beginning in that decade. These new immigrants—enamored of the tomato—were certainly a critical element in helping to establish the tomato's place in Creole cuisine. In the mid-1820s, tomatoes were among the many vegetables sold at the French Market. By 1838, New Orleans bookseller and writer Jacques-Felix Lelièvre referred to the many species of tomatoes in the area, "all of which are used in cooking and equally good."

Like all love denied, tomato lust in New Orleans is all the more dear because the actual time one can find the Creoles is quite short. These tomatoes usually appear at the end of May; they are gone by mid-July. Late May and early June are considered the height of the season, since the optimum daytime temperature range is between seventy and eighty degrees. In hot Louisiana, late growth is not easy. Some years, however, Creole tomatoes can be found as late as September. Urban myth tells us that when the crape myrtles hold their blossoms until September (when there is not as much rain), then tomatoes plants continue producing. That is a city way of interpreting the rural tomato: you find crape myrtles on New Orleans streets; you do not find many people growing tomatoes in their yards. Tomatoes need to be dry on the vine, or they attract insects, and many New Orleans gardens are shaded by mature trees.

When the Creole tomato does appear, there is usually a flurry of newspaper articles on various ways of preparing it. As in the past, the Creole tomato is eaten plain and raw in salads or cooked in soups, casseroles, and sauces. Not surprisingly, there are hundreds of recipes. Yet the only one that can be found in cookbooks from 1885 to the present is for stuffed tomatoes. Newer dishes, such as Upperline Restaurant's Creole Tomatoes with Warm Goat Cheese and Basil Pesto and John Folse's Creole Tomato Basil Pie, show the integration of local tastes with national trends. This is especially so for all those Creole tomato salads paired with Vidalia onions. These latter favorites, of course, do not grow here.

The Creole tomato's centrality in New Orleans' food traditions is also maintained as the only food with its own large festival within the city. (The Mirliton Festival is held in the Bywater District, but it is a strictly neighborhood affair so far.) Whereas nearby towns have strawberry, gumbo, and even a giant omelet festival, New Orleans is strangely quiet about official celebrations of food. True, there is much anticipation of local delicacies at Jazz Fest, but the food there is the sideshow, not the main event. The Creole Tomato Festival began in 1986. Each June, it attracts more than fifty thousand visitors and boasts street performers, jazz bands, celebrity chefs, and plenty of tomatoes to take home. Indeed, in 2006, festival-goers who spent over twenty-five dollars were promised a whole box of Plaquemines Parish tomatoes from famed grower Benny Becnel—while supplies lasted. Before his untimely death in 2004, brother Johnny Becnel annually joined the celebration, too, auctioning off the first of the Creole tomatoes of the year.

The festival's staging at the French Market has emotional as well as tourist appeal. It was here that the Creole tomato was first sold in great quantities, particularly by Italians, who dominated the citrus market by the 1890s and came to be very active in the trade in vegetables and other fruits shortly thereafter. Mildred Cram, a visitor in the early 1900s, found the French Quarter misnamed; there were more Italians than Creoles living there. She found her French language skills of little use: "We went over to the French Market, hoping to capture a little of the local colour that every other traveller has encountered among the vegetable and fruit stalls of the old Halle de Boucheries. But the Creole has abandoned the market to the Italian small grocer. Natives of Reggio, Calabria and the Abruzzi answered my feeble French questions with blank stares or torrents of absolutely unintelligible Calabrese." Venetians and others from what would one day be Italy had come to the city earlier; and, indeed, in 1850 New Orleans had the largest Italian-born population of any U.S. city. But most of the Italians came in the years 1880 to 1910. By 1890, New Orleans was one of the main ports of entry for Italians, especially Sicilians, into the United States.

John Gallo, who today grows Creole tomatoes on a family farm in St. Bernard Parish, remembers his great-grandfather as one of the first generations of Italians associated with the French Market. Vincent Gallo came from Ustica, Sicily, in the early 1880s and began growing tomatoes in 1885 on a plantation in Meraux, a small town ten miles southeast of New Orleans. Like Vincent Gallo, other Sicilians made similar journeys. A drought and an earthquake during the 1870s had resulted in poor crops, soil erosion, and deforestation in all of southern Italy. Intent on escaping the poverty that surrounded them, peasant farmers looked to the United States for new or temporary homes. Businessmen and planters in Louisiana were conscious of these circumstances and sought to attract Italians, especially the Sicilians, to the state. Such publications as the *Manufacturers Record* presented boastful, sometimes near-deceitful accounts of the wealth of sugar cane plantations and cotton fields to attract these farmers.

Known as hard workers, they were considered the answer to any number of problems. The U.S. Department of Labor itself extolled their very "economy" especially in regards to farming: "Nowhere is the Italian's economy more apparent than in the appearance of his garden. Every inch of ground is utilized, and a great deal is crowded into a small space; if there is an orchard, tomatoes, beans, or potatoes are planted between the trees, and small vegetables and berries. . . . He's used to working for long hours with his hands and to labor under a hot sun . . . [and] when he has in the prospect the ownership of a number of acres without heavy taxes, his saving instinct is stimulated to the utmost." This may sound much like the words of the French colonial prefect Laussat, who wrote about the German farmers of the late eighteenth and early nineteenth centuries, quoted in this volume in the chapter on mirlitons. The Italians were sought also, however, for other reasons concerned with ethnicity and race. Neither the French-speaking nor African American farmers already in the state were solicited to migrate to the areas needing farmers. The French-speaking farmers were thought to be too wedded to one particular place. And, as one Daniel Dennett wrote in 1876, "Let the people of Louisiana appreciate the true condition of their state, understand fully her true needs; let them see that she wants tens of thousands of honest, energetic, industrious *white men* to immigrate to her waste places." By 1881, a steamer began going directly between New Orleans and southern Italy to carry the new workers to Louisiana.

Despite being promoted as white workers, the new immigrants suffered from discrimination and often were placed within a racial category that was neither black nor white. In rural parishes, Sicilian agricultural workers were sometimes run out of town, and the infamous 1891 New Orleans lynching of eleven

Italian Americans suspected of killing the police chief offers a tragic example of some of the problems Italians faced. Despite the prejudice they encountered, the Italians found opportunity and land in a climate not unlike southern Italy. In south Louisiana's flat, fertile fields, they grew many of the same crops known to them in their native land and also proved very adaptable both in growing new crops and in adapting old recipes to new ones. They created a considerable agricultural heritage, growing strawberries across Lake Pontchartrain and vegetables, citrus, and, most important to this chapter, Creole tomatoes in the area across the Mississippi River from New Orleans, known as the West Bank.

Many Italians first worked on existing farms, often commuting from the city to outlying areas in an overcrowded train car on Monday morning and returning on Friday night. The most successful immigrants acquired land of their own, with those interested in farming buying outside the city. They began raising vegetables that were then transported by horse and wagon to the French Market. They sold to other Italians who had not yet been able to buy land, who in turn would take tomatoes and other vegetables around the city in carts. These peddlers also carried the many cheeses and olive oil so central to Italian cooking.

Olive oil importation was always important to New Orleans food. Although, like the French, New Orleanians rely heavily on butter, it is not hard to find evidence that the Spanish of the eighteenth century and the first wave of Italians who came in the early nineteenth century did a good job convincing the city of the merits of olive oil. Large pottery olive jars, permanent fixtures in French Quarter patios, are reminders of these early Spanish and Italian connections. And, before the Civil War, novelist William Thackeray had tasted the city's bouillabaisse and found it as good as any in Marseilles. Marseilles has always been both an Italian and French city, and the early bouillabaisse recipes in New Orleans, as elsewhere, begin with olive oil. In the 1880s, Mark Twain met his colorful "drummers," who, "energetic of movement and speech; the dollar their god," spoke of doctored cottonseed oil made in the city and sold as olive oil. "We turn out the whole thing—clean from the word go—in our factory in New Orleans: labels, bottles, oil, everything. Well, no, not labels: been buying them abroad—get them dirt-cheap there." The city was probably divided by ethnic group on the brand of olive oil used. The enterprising Genoese Solari brothers sold Duret Brand Olive Oil, which came from "the South of Europe." But even today New Orleanians discuss how the Mouledoux family sold James Plagniol's

product and how the Lupo/Tusa family at Central Grocery sold primarily Sicilian olive oil.

Two early-twentieth-century peddlers of produce, olive oil, and other goods
from Italy were Antonio Bologna and Frank Taormina. The latter became a well-
known purveyor of canned tomatoes, tomato paste, and pasta. With his brother
he also ran a macaroni factory. The Bologna family also owned a wholesale food
distribution warehouse in the French Quarter. Other peddlers followed their
success. Each produce-seller traveled a set route, so that customers began to
know him. These goods and their vendors influenced the foodways of all the
city. As late as the 1950s, Creole tomatoes were purchased "from the horse (or
mule) drawn produce wagons that rolled through the neighborhoods daily. . . .
The drivers/salesmen would chant the day's wares: "I got tomatahs, watte mel-
lens, okrees," said Maureen Detweiler, an Uptown resident, in an interview.

The peddlers bought their produce directly from the farmers, the most successful of whom arrived at the French or Poydras markets by 3:00 a.m. An early
arrival assured sales to those who ran small grocery stores, to the stands in the
markets, to restaurant owners, or to anyone who could pull themselves out of
bed or, in some cases, send their household servants. By the late nineteenth
century, the Italians had cornered the market in selling produce. The 1898 city
directory listed twenty-nine men involved in wholesale fruit and vegetables and,
of these, at least twenty had Italian names.

However, not all growers were or are Italians. Today Johnny Becnel's brother
Benny is called the "king of Creole tomatoes." The Becnel family goes back five
generations to Vacherie, upriver in St. James Parish. Here, then again, as in the
chapter on mirlitons, the German Coast farmers exert their contributions to
Creole food. To grow their Creole tomatoes, the Becnel family uses the Fantastic variety, a hybrid grown from seeds they obtained "long ago" from California.
Many farmers, along with Becnel, grow also another variety called Celebrity,
also a "determinant, hybrid tomato variety."

Most New Orleanians don't have the same luck growing tomatoes that they
do with mirlitons. As mentioned, this may be because there are too many trees
in the city. Tomatoes need six hours of direct sun a day. It may also be the soil.
Tomatoes need a well-drained loam soil or clay loam, which the city usually
lacks. Still, most city dwellers can tell you that tomatoes are planted as early
as Carnival time (anywhere from early February to early March) and as late as
April. They also know of a tradition among many growers of planting in the

field on or near St. Joseph's Day (March 19). This is considered both safe from freezing and also blessed by the saint, whose feast day is still observed throughout Italy but especially Sicily. St. Joseph's association with food customs runs deep: Sicilians attribute the end of a medieval famine to his intercession.

After planting, the next steps in tomato horticulture concern training the plant to a single stem and removing suckers in the forks between the stem and the leaves. Pruning encourages early fruit development and the growth of larger fruit. To get rid of white flies, the grower Gallo advises wiping the leaves with milk. Growers on the West Bank also advise that one picks the Creole tomatoes later than one does other tomatoes elsewhere; that is, the Creole tomatoes stay on the vine longer. Finally, Creole tomatoes distinguish themselves because most of the people working in the fields and selling them are family members, and the farmers are descendants of several generations of Creole tomato farmers.

The Becnel farm produces as many as one hundred thousand Creole tomatoes a year. They are sold locally and shipped to places as far away as Memphis. However, most growers advise that refrigeration and refrigerated trucks ruin the tomato's flavor. For this reason, New Orleanians, searching for the perfect Creole tomato, take the drive across the river to Belle Chasse. As restaurant reviewer Brett Anderson wrote during the first spring after Hurricane Katrina: "At Ben and Ben Becnel's produce stand you'll find, in the shadow of the Conoco Phillips Alliance Refinery, among jars of fig preserves and locally grown zucchini, okra and cucumbers, the season's truest sign that things are looking up: fresh, ripe Creole tomatoes. Becnel's strike a juicy balance between sweet and tart, and they're sold by the box."

A ripe Creole tomato has "sun-drenched, river-washed flavor," according to journalist John Kemp. Chef Horst Pfeifer of the now-defunct Bella Luna restaurant notes "the flavor and the acidity of it [as] . . . not so sweet and not so mealy." Chef Paul Prudhomme believes they have a "lower acid content than ordinary tomatoes, a better texture—and much more flavor." Many recipes are favored. There are tomato sandwiches, salads, savory tarts, soups, salsa, and casseroles. There are hundreds of ways of making tomato sauce, and tomatoes are used in everything from gumbos to aspics. Crabmeat Courtbouillon with Fire-Roasted Creole Tomatoes, made by Chef Danny Trace of Café Adelaide, and Upperline's Fried Green Tomatoes with Shrimp Remoulade have received recent attention in the national press. Chef John Folse in his *Encyclopedia of Cajun and Creole Cuisine* lists a dozen different recipes, one of which, Chicken and Creole Tomato Pomodori, echoes Antonio Latini's first published tomato recipe (noted earlier in this chapter).

Also, stuffed tomatoes were often featured in early cookbooks and extend chronologically from the two 1885 books, Lafcadio Hearn's *La Cuisine Creole* and the Christian Woman's Exchange's *Creole Cookery Book*, through all the versions of *The Picayune Creole Cook Book* and various other books from each decade of the twentieth century. Recipes for stuffed tomatoes usually call for both chicken and ham, along with parsley, onion, breadcrumbs, thyme, and bay leaf, as well as other seasonings. The addition of both chicken and ham seems to be the dividing line between those recipes called Stuffed Tomatoes à la Créole and plain stuffed tomatoes, or *tomates farcies*, French for "stuffed tomatoes." The earliest versions, such Hearn's, call mainly for ham, "a slice of fat bacon," breadcrumbs, and an egg yolk to hold it all together, so it may well be that the true Creole version is located in simplicity. However, they were not so simple as to lack taste. The *Creole Cookery Book*, written by "American women" (as they and others called them) to tell about the Creole city, does have a Stuffed Tomato, too, but they use only bread crumbs and seasoning. William Kaufman and Sister Mary Ursula Cooper suggested their version of Stuffed Tomatoes à la Créole for a Lenten dish. The Junior League's *Plantation Cookbook* gives two stuffed tomato recipes, one with artichokes. The other is more closely linked to Tomatoes à la Créole and is called Tomato Nests, showing in name as well as affinity to the older recipe the propensity of all Junior League cookbooks to present recipes that are at once appealing to people all over the United States while still incorporating the local. Stuffed tomatoes are also a favorite of community cookbooks in the city.

Tomato salads are not mentioned by either Hearn or the Christian Woman's Exchange. In this respect, they may have been adhering to some concern over raw tomatoes. As mentioned above, eating uncooked tomatoes was not the norm before the early twentieth century. However, Lettice Bryan's *Kentucky Housewife* (1839) recommended raw tomatoes for breakfast and as an accompaniment for roast. Some "raw tomato aficionados recommended seasoning them with sugar, molasses, vinegar, salt, pepper, mustard, or milk." And even at this early time, the "most common way to eat raw tomatoes was sliced and seasoned, like cucumbers, with vinegar, salt, and pepper." The *Picayune* from 1900 onward gives a number of tomato salad recipes. Tomato, Green Pepper and Onion Salad (Salade à la Créole) consists of alternating layers of these different ingredients.

The *Picayune* notes that this is a "great family salad among the Creoles." The *Picayune* also notes that "the Creoles follow the old adage, that the taste of the onion must only lurk within the bowl when using it for salad. More than this renders the salad disagreeable and coarse." For those searching for such a salad, Mary Moore Bremer's Tomatoes Stuffed with Cucumbers, from her 1932 book, and Galatoire's Vine Ripened Tomatoes Stuffed with Boiled Shrimp, in *Galatoire's Cookbook,* are excellent choices. Here, the use of the phrase "vine-ripened" is another way of saying Creole tomato, or rather, of letting others choose their own homegrown tomatoes.

For most New Orleanians, tomato recipes require little speculation. Tomatoes in some form or another are integral to the city's cuisine. Many people tell of a preference for the first Creole tomatoes simply served on French bread or plain white bread, with mayonnaise and salt and pepper, as a tomato poor boy or a tomato sandwich. Still others eat these first ones like apples. A very humble salad represents this simplicity. Jessica Harris, food scholar of Africa and the Americas, notes this need for restraint. She paired the Creole tomato with Vidalia onions, noting, "Combining them demands a simplicity that will let the favors speak for themselves." Or, as Lee Bailey says, they need "nothing more to enhance them than a little salt and a grind of pepper." Almost all New Orleanians remember the ritualistic appearance throughout the season of a platter of sliced Creole tomatoes sprinkled with salt and pepper or with the added drizzle of olive oil and/or red wine vinegar.

This minimalism, buttressed by solid opinions on the virtues of our tomatoes, makes a salad of both modesty and pride. As Chef Chris Montero from Bacco Restaurant stated, "When Louisiana Creoles are in season, there's not much that can surpass that." In this spirit, consider the earlier advice offered by the *Picayune* in 1901: "Serve nicely with a plain French Dressing or any . . . dressings."

CREOLE CREAM CHEESE

Cynthia LeJeune Nobles

Ask any New Orleanian of a "certain maturity" about their fondest breakfast memories and Creole cream cheese will invariably rank high on the list. In its modern heyday, the first half of the twentieth century, this unpretentious farmhouse-style, single-curd, mildly tart artisan cheese was, for many, a morning staple. Bleary-eyed Louisianans usually topped their silky mounds of cheese with cream and sugar. If strawberries were at hand they found their way into the bowl, and the meal was typically rounded out with a side of French bread or "toast bread," the name New Orleanians gave to what others call plain toast. Creole cream cheese was sold by every grocer and was carried on every milk delivery truck. In the 1940s, for example, it was as common to a New Orleans sunrise as *Henry Dupre and the Dawnbusters*. But, unlike radio, this home-grown cheese has a centuries-old history, and its story is one that is as rocky and courageous as the city of New Orleans itself.

No documents exist revealing how Creole cream cheese was invented. Rarely found on nineteenth-century restaurant menus, it was nonetheless an ordinary product sold by street vendors and was also commonly made at home. It was particularly common in households with babies and the infirm, and, although enjoyed any time of day, historical records prove that cream cheese seems to have always been most popular at breakfast. By the twentieth century, the custard-like treat had even become a fixture in restaurant brunches. Writer Peter Feibleman recorded a visit to Brennan's, and proclaimed that Creole cream cheese and fruit "make a wonderful, wakening taste that does for your stomach what the drink just did for your head." Creole cream cheese combats hangovers? In spite of this curative claim, however, it is Creole cream cheese's taste, utility, and familiarity that have kept it enduring through all these years.

According to legend, cheese was accidentally discovered more than five thousand years ago when an Arabian merchant was carrying milk in a pouch made
from a sheep's stomach. The movement of his camel plus the hot desert sun and
the rennet remaining in the pouch (rennet is a natural coagulating agent) forced
the milk to separate into curds and whey. Creole cream cheese's pedigree is not
quite so exotic, but it, too, originated from milk left too long in the heat. Without
refrigeration, pasteurization, or homogenization, milk went bad in the humid
South. Warm buttermilk acid naturally forms *lactobacillus*, a common bacteria
that converts lactose and other sugars to lactic acid, helps with coagulation, and
creates flavor and sourness. After the bacteria attacks, the resulting thickened
and "curdled" milk forms small clumps. Resourceful cooks, anxious to conserve
precious milk, hung these curds in cloth under cool spots like live oak trees or
porches to drain the whey, and the result was a simple, mild, cultured cheese.

Chef John Folse, owner of Bittersweet Plantation Dairy and producer of
artisan cheeses, is convinced that Creole cream cheese was first made in Louisiana by the colonizing French as early as the beginning of the 1700s. In his travels through France, Folse found a long tradition of local production of acid-set
farm-style cheeses that were not meant to last a long while or have tremendous
flavor. He surmises that colonists certainly would have brought the knowledge
of those techniques to New Orleans. The Acadians, who arrived some fifty years
after the first French, were extremely fond of the dish and are often identified
with it. But Folse believes that by the time the Acadians arrived, cream cheese
was already a mainstay of New Orleans cuisine.

Creole cream cheese is usually compared to cottage cheese, firm yogurt,
or soft marscapone. Others besides Folse find more ties to France and relate
it closest to the French soft, white cheeses, especially unripened Neufchatel, a
cheese that originated in Normandy and is commonly molded into shapes like
hearts. The heart shape is often mentioned in early New Orleans cream cheese
writings. Also, it is worth noting that both French Neufchatel and Creole cream
cheese have little in common with the firmer Neufchatel found on U.S. grocery shelves, and Creole cream cheese in particular should not be confused with
"Philadelphia Cream Cheese," a denser product made from milk and milk fat by
a process that was originated by a dairyman in New York in 1872.

The familiar silver foil-wrapped bricks of Philadelphia Cream Cheese were
distributed in 1880 by New Yorker A. L. Reynolds, who gave it its name. At that

time, top-notch food products were often referred to as being "Philadelphia quality." In that vein, it is important to point out the word "Creole" in front of New Orleans' historic cream cheese should not be associated with the burned palates usually (and erroneously) linked with South Louisiana food. Instead, Creole designates that this mild-tasting cheese was originally sold to or made by the Louisiana Creoles or that it is new, a product of the New World, but with parents from the Old. It is also worth mentioning that the word "Creole" was never published in conjunction with the words "cream cheese" until well into the 1900s. Although scarce newspaper articles, pictures, or written recipes from the 1800s exist, those that are available only refer to the dish as "cream cheese."

The word *Creole* (not unlike the attachment of Philadelphia to products) became an icon around the late nineteenth century and was fashionably attached to all sorts of foods, including vegetables, eggs, and coffee. Creole was not only a marketing designation that symbolized the New Orleans aura, but also meant that the product was highly perishable and was meant to be consumed locally. New Orleans creameries also probably embraced the term to help differentiate their product from the increasingly popular Philadelphia Cream Cheese.

Creole cream cheese is made from cow's milk, and to have milk you must first have a cow. Cattle had been brought to the New World by the Spanish soon after 1492, but the first dairy cow didn't arrive in the North American colonies until 1611. In eighteenth-century New Orleans, families with cattle housed them in stables that surrounded in-town gardens, orchards, and chicken yards. Records from 1724 show that Germans living across the Mississippi River thirty miles up from New Orleans also owned cattle and that these immigrants sold excess farm products in the capital. A 1731 record reveals that these same Germans were selling butter and in that same year developed cattle-raising as an industry, the venture specifically aimed at supplying New Orleans with meat and dairy products.

During the early 1800s, the Texas cattle trail along southwest Louisiana's Atascosito/Opelousas Road ended in what is now called Algiers on the west bank of the Mississippi River across from New Orleans. Soon a number of Germans settled in that area, too, and they started dairy farms, but no one became wealthy overnight. For local consumers, milk and cheese were much less trendy than liquor and cigars; newspaper advertisements showed that the two latter products were clearly the hot commodities of the time. Several more substantial reasons for dairy products' lowly status were easy contamination, a short shelf life in summer, and a lack of winter grazing areas. A few writers also infer that French priorities did not include the pampering of milk cows. Cynicism aside, we do know that the German dairies did eventually thrive. We also know that in 1805, a J. Hartwell, a free man of color, owned and operated a dairy in the city limits.

Identification and historical understanding of most products is more closely related to the distributor than the producer, and so it is with New Orleans cream cheese. Back in the colonial era, professional peddlers or *marchands* bought foodstuffs from producers and resold them to consumers in the streets. By the 1780s, the growing volume of trade made traditional price tariffs issued by the Spanish rulers less effective, so in 1784 the government established a marketplace and required food marchands to rent stalls. But some street peddling was still permitted, and it is through remembrances of these roaming vendors that we get a glimpse into the history of early cream cheese.

This July 24, 1846, article in the *Daily Picayune* not only gives an interesting review of cream cheese, but also critiques "Green Sass Men," the early counterparts of the more socially accepted street hawkers:

> The "Green Sass" men. —These individuals are not in the habit of trading on their own hook, and are only "green sass" men by virtue of their calling—nature having put them in continual mourning. Their stock in trade is small, consisting generally of a few vegetables, a small amount of fruit, such as figs, peaches and melons, and, by way of variety, although not strictly a vegetable production, "cream cheeses," so called from their being made of curdled *milk*, and very unwholesome and indigestible, but particularly recommended for children in arms, as calculated to inculcate an early knowledge of book-keeping by enabling them to "cast up their accounts" with facility and at short notice. These commodities are generally transported upon the heads of the vendors in champagne baskets; and their cry, as near as it can possibly be translated, is—"E-a-r-s yerfineniceartaties, artichokes, cantelopes feegs and arnicerkereama-cheeses! Ear! Ear!"

Eliza Ripley (1832–1912) occasionally contributed stories to the New Orleans *Times-Democrat*, and in her published memoirs, *Social Life in Old New Orleans*, she gives a refreshingly joyous view of cream cheese vendors: "in the early morning, when one, *en papillotes*, came down to breakfast, listless and 'out of sorts,' the chant of the cream cheese woman would be heard. A rush to the door with a saucer for cheese, a tiny, heart-shaped cheese, a dash of cream poured from a claret bottle over it—all this for a picayune! How nice and refreshing it was. What a glorious addition to the breakfast that promised to pall on one's appetite." Like most cream cheese ladies, the vendor who crooned at Ripley's door could have also been ringing a bell or tinkling a triangle, and she probably sold products from her family's dairy or a relatively larger commercial dairy. She had also likely earned her status by being reliable and hygienic and had been selling to the family for years. One other reference worth mentioning is found in Kate Chopin's *Awakening*, where the author refers to a late-nineteenth-century vendor, hers a fictional yet accurate description of an old *mulatresse* (a woman of mixed-race heritage) who sold milk and cream cheese.

By the 1850s, the city directory lists several dairies, including one owned by Peter H. Barken on Chippewa and another owned by Jean Louis Aveta on the corner of Prieur and Lapeyrouse. We also know that the penniless widow Margaret Gaffney Haughery (1803–1882) started a dairy business with two cows and a milk cart. Later she bought even more cows and a bakery, and upon her death left a small fortune to the city's orphanages, so someone in nineteenth-century New Orleans was obviously drinking milk.

The small-scale dairy business eventually prospered and the various locations of these enterprises reflect the growth of the city. In 1875, an advertisement ran appealing to gardeners and milkmen to lease land on State Street in the then "far away" region now known as New Orleans' University Section. In 1889, the Jesuits bought a truck and dairy farm on St. Charles Avenue and eventually turned this tract into Loyola University and Holy Name of Jesus Catholic Church. By the early 1900s, approximately 160 mostly family-owned dairies dotted the landscape of the metropolitan area, with about 140 of those located within the city's corporate limits.

Cloverland Dairy, begun in 1889 by pioneer dairyman George Villere, moved from its cramped quarters on Tulane Avenue to 3400 South Carrollton in 1924. Not only did Cloverland sell Creole cream cheese, but from its new location it became the first dairy to offer New Orleanians pasteurized milk. Sealtest bought Cloverland in 1950, but the new owners remained at the Carrollton plant in the landmark terra cotta building with the milk-bottle-shaped water tower. The giant milk bottle was dismantled in 1962, and in 1981 the post office bought the tract and opened an office. A sampling of other early memorable local dairies includes Barbe's (1918), Gold Seal Dairy (1920s–1986), and Godchaux's Belle Pointe Dairy in Reserve, a 1940s era operation.

In the early twentieth century, railroads started crisscrossing the state, prompting the bulk of the dairy industry to congregate thirty to fifty miles north of Lake Pontchartrain in the piney "Florida" parishes (once part of the Republic of West Florida): St. Tammany, Washington, and Tangipahoa. Folse's *Encyclopedia of Cajun and Creole Cooking* says that one of the first large-scale dairies in the South was begun in that region in the early 1900s by Charles Adolph Kent Sr. in Kentwood, the town named for him. Kent shipped milk products to New Orleans and to customers throughout the South but went bankrupt in 1929.

Today, only 308 dairies operate in the whole state, and most of them do not make cream cheese. But dairy industry is still a vital part of the economy and in 2007 provided $198 million in income to the state.

But before the days of labs, research, and iceboxes, a time when milk quickly went bad, Creole cream cheese was as common as magnolias, according to myth and hearsay. Ask any great-grandmother. And although no early recorded local recipes have been found, there are, however, some clues about how it was made. Most of these hints come from several recipes for northern versions of cream cheese. And while most of these writings call for rennet, none of the few historical references to Creole cream cheese mention this coagulating agent. Thus, we can speculate that Creole cream cheese was literally dripped until it was firm and that it coagulated with natural air-born bacteria. Like the name "Creole," rennet seems to have appeared on the New Orleans scene in the early 1900s, when large commercial dairies were looking for consistent product texture. Today the ingredient is called for in virtually all modern Creole cream cheese recipes.

Rennet is the enzyme used to separate the curd (the semisolid portion of coagulated milk) and whey (the watery liquid that separates from the solid curd). According to Chef Joseph Carey in his *Creole Nouvelle*, "the actual active enzyme is something called chymosin or rennin, and was traditionally obtained from the fourth (true) stomach of calves." Today's rennet, both liquid and tablet forms, can indeed come from a young animal's stomach. But cheese-making suppliers do now offer a vegetarian coagulating enzyme that comes from plants such as thistle that have a natural coagulating ability. Most commercially available non-animal rennet, however, is now produced in laboratories from fungal or bacterial sources.

Between 1772 and 1782, Thomas Jefferson's wife, Martha, kept a household book and in it wrote instructions on extracting rennet. Mary Randolph's classic *Virginia House-Wife* (1860 edition, first published in 1824) also graphically details the process by writing that milady should "take the stomach from the calf as soon as it is killed—do not wash it, but hang it in a dry cool place for four or five days; then turn it inside out, slip off all the curd nicely with the hand. . . . You must not wash it—that would weaken the gastric juice, and injure the rennet." Ingredients added to this home-grown version, aside from the calf stomach, include vinegar, salt, cold water, and rose brandy. If made in cold weather, Randolph's coagulator kept for over a year. It is also known that an easier way to make the product was to simply throw a calf stomach into a milk vat, and to let the natural rennet coagulate the milk. Interestingly, Randolph also says that Slip and Curds and Cream, two recipes that combine to create a product similar to Creole cream cheese, are "Arcadian dishes; very delicious, cheap, and easily prepared." Randolph firms up her dish with rennet, and the final product is surrounded with sugar and nutmeg. Later, in 1862, the trendy and nationally circulated Civil War–era ladies magazine *Godey's Lady's Book* published a recipe called Cheese Cream—A Plain Family Way and in it called for draining the resulting curds from warmed milk, cream, and rennet into a mold and serving the finished product with cream and sugar. Could a few adventurous local housewives have taken either *Godey's* advice or Randolph's and used rennet? Unfortunately, we may never know.

Closer to home, Lafcadio Hearn's *La Cuisine Creole* (1885) does not mention rennet or Creole cream cheese in any of his recipes, and his two recipes for cheesecake do not include any kind of cheese at all. But the book does feature the following interesting recipe, the dish a confection similar to frozen Creole cream cheese:

BISCUIT CREAM IN MOULDS

One quart of firm clabber and one quart of sweet cream, make it very sweet with white sugar; flavor with vanilla bean boiled in half a cup of sweet milk. Churn all together ten minutes, then freeze in moulds, or in an ordinary freezer.

Clabber is unrefrigerated, unpasteurized, and unhomogenized soured and curdled whole milk. And like Hearn's Biscuit Cream, the common version of frozen Creole cream cheese is simply Creole cream cheese, cream, sugar, and vanilla mixed together and frozen. This was particularly popular during the era when aluminum ice cube trays were *en vogue*. However, frozen Creole cream cheese should not be confused with today's commercial Creole cream cheese ice creams, products that, though delicious, are based on cooked custard. Although William Kaufman and Sister Mary Cooper's *The Art of Creole Cookery* (1962) does not specifically call for Creole cream cheese, their recipe Frozen Cream Cheese, one of the few printed before the 1990s, does call for cream cheese, along with cream, sugar, and vanilla. It, like Hearn's Biscuit Cream, is uncooked and is close to what locals whipped up at home.

Further tracing this history of cream cheese, one finds that while glass milk bottles were being introduced in Potsdam, New York, in 1884, in New Orleans, Creole cream cheese ladies roamed on foot and mule-driving vendors (men and even women) in chariot-like milk carts carried chest-high cylindrical drums of their products. At homes across the city, the drivers dispensed milk, cream, and Creole cream cheese into customers' pitchers and bowls. Many urban homes had milk rooms, a part of the home locked on the inside to the rest of the house, but open on the outside to the milkman. The second edition of *The Picayune's Creole Cook Book* (1901) gives a lengthy, yet importantly detailed insight into cream cheese street vendors of this era. This record also highlights the importance of "Cream Cheese/*Fromage à la Crème*" to the local Catholics:

> Cream cheese is always made from clabbered milk. The "Cream Cheese Woman" is still as common a sight on our New Orleans streets as the Cala woman was in the days gone by. She carries a covered basket in which are a number of small perforated tins in which the cheeses are. In her other hand she carries a can of fresh cream. She sells her wares to her regular customers, for the old Creoles who do not make their own cream cheese are very particular as to whom they buy from, and when once a good, careful, clean woman gets a "customer" she keeps her during her period of business, coming early every fast day and Friday with her cheese and cream, for this is a great fast-day breakfast and luncheon dish.
>
> Many of the Creoles, however, make their own cream cheese, as follows: The clabber is placed in a long bag of muslin and put to drain, the bag being tied tightly and hung out over night in a cool place. When ready for use, the bag is opened and the cheese is taken out and beaten till light. It is then placed in these perforated molds, and when the time comes for serving, it is taken out, placed in a

dish, and sweet cream is poured over it. It is eaten with sugar or salt, more generally sugar.

Frozen cream cheese is a very delicious summer dish with the Creoles. Some
persons, after skimming the cream from the sour milk, stand the pan on the back
of the stove and scald the clabber with about three quarts of boiling water before
putting in the bag to drain. Again, some use only the perforated tins, instead of
the muslin bag, but the best results are obtained by the former ancient Creole
method. Cream cheese corresponds to the German "Schmier Kase."

The anonymous writers of *The Picayune* here, as in other passages, evoke
the memory of the African American merchants, more commonly known as
the *calas* women, who peddled fried spiced balls made of sugar, flour, eggs, and
boiled rice, and topped with powdered sugar. Traditionally eaten with a cup
of coffee, the sweet breakfast fritter calas is similar to Nigerian Rice Balls, a
dessert made with fewer spices. Célestine Eustis's *Cooking in Old Créole Days*
(1904) gives a detailed French-language recipe for calas. Eustis's cookbook also
gives meticulous instructions for *Fromage A La Crème*. Attributed to one Leo-
nie Penin, the recipe calls for draining milk in linen overnight and beating the
resulting cheese with pinches of salt and sugar, then molding and chilling, and
serving with cream.

In New Orleans in the early 1930s, mules were still delivering milk, but by
then they pulled four-wheeled "dairy wagons," closed-in carts driven mostly by
uniformed men who followed written instructions found on cards left in porch
windows or curled in empty milk bottles. Motorized delivery trucks appeared
later that decade, a time when dairies like Borden's, Brown's Velvet, and Roem-
er's all produced Creole cream cheese. Probably the company most remembered
for this specialty, however, is Gold Seal, a dairy owned by the Centanni family.
The family, long known as the owners of an elaborate Christmas light display
that burned brightly on Canal Street from the 1940s through the 1960s, is representative of the way New Orleanians transform food purveyors into royalty.

Whether Creole cream cheese was purchased or dripped at home, traditional
toppings were cream or half-and-half, sugar, and strawberries. But many who
grew up on Creole cream cheese also had innovative ways of embellishing it.
Some topped it with bananas, grapes, blackberries, oatmeal, dates, and even
cold rice. In German communities, toppings of freshly ground black pepper

and salt were a hit, while more than one adventurous soul ate it with onions. Local writer Errol Laborde records that people "sprinkle cinnamon" and "add blueberries." He also remembers that his mother advised that he should shake the carton before opening it. New Orleans native and food aficionado Maureen Detweiler affirms the religious twist to the dish, and she recalls that she and her mother succumbed to the Creole cream cheese tradition during World War II while her father was off fighting in Europe. Her earliest memories of Creole cream cheese are of her grandmother and great-grandmother having it for breakfast every Friday because Catholics could not eat meat on Fridays. They would have it in a soup bowl, with a little bit of sugar sprinkled on it, along with French bread and café au lait.

In those days before homogenization, uptowner Carolise Rosen remembers cream cheese draining in her mother's big bowl on the countertop. Martin Spindel, retired veterinarian and guide and cook at Destrehan Plantation, says that home cooks didn't use fancy molds. His family mostly used white, bleached feed sacks and hung them from trees. He recalls that ice used to be delivered only three days a week, and that his kin became prolific cream cheese makers in the heat of the summer. He also affirms that home cooks did not use rennet and explains that the higher fat content that came from the era's Jersey and Guernsey cows (compared to today's Holsteins) was more conducive to creating creamy cheeses.

Creole cream cheese was also common in rural areas. Laura Locoul Gore, Laura Plantation's namesake, grew up in the 1870s, and as a child she was put off by fig preserves and cream cheese. In her memoirs, she notes that her cheese was molded into heart shapes and was topped with thick, yellow cream. But even though she found it repulsive, in the years before her death she writes that she longed for her comforting cream cheese. In Gore's case, as was typical on most plantations, an on-site dairy provided milk. Gore chronicles the processes of making butter and remembers that her family would give the African American workers the extra milk and clabber every morning.

During the twentieth century, the delicacy was still made prolifically in Louisiana's Acadian parishes, where family milk cows still provided milk, butter, and cream and where some Acadians called cream cheese *caillé gouté* or "creamed clabber." Acadia Parish native Clarice Zaunbrecher LeJeune remembers taking clabber that originated from her family's herd (clabber being a favorite drink of her first-generation German father), tying it in a feed sack or cheesecloth and onto the kitchen faucet, and letting it drip overnight. She did not add salt or rennet, and her family ate the finished product with cane syrup. Food columnist and author Marcelle Bienvenu also grew up in the Acadian part of the state and was a local consultant on Feibleman's *American Cooking: Creole and Acadian*, a volume that features a terrific photograph of an elderly woman named Grace Broussard draining Creole cream cheese, her product firmed up with rennet. Bienvenu later writes in *Stir the Pot* that her Aunt Grace, presumably the same Grace from *American Cooking*, didn't buy cream cheese at the store; she made it herself. Octavia Sansovich grew up north of New Orleans in Bogalusa, and her mother put the family cow's excess milk in crockery bowls to sour and hung the resulting clabber on a line on the back porch. Chef Folse vividly remembers that cream cheese was his grandmother's every night food. In the days before trucks delivered the staple to her St. James Parish home, she would take leftover buttermilk, skim the cream off, and mix the acidified buttermilk with milk in her cream bowl on the table and, *voila*, the next morning she had cream cheese.

In the early 1970s, Creole cream cheese was still a familiar item in grocery dairy cases. Rima and Richard Collin wrote in *The New Orleans Cookbook* (1975) that Creole cream cheese with fresh fruit was the traditional first breakfast course. According to the couple, Creole cream cheese was still prepared by all the local dairies and was typically packed in eleven-ounce containers similar to those used for cottage cheese. Like that sold today, it was a single large curd made from milk and was surrounded by cream. But soon the frenetic hand of popular culture made even southern life faster. As a result, habits quickly changed, and by 1981 most local dairies had eliminated home milk delivery. Only Gold Seal was delivering in some neighborhoods, but that ended in early 1986 when competition shut Gold Seal's doors. And although memories affirm that Creole cream cheese was still wildly popular, by the 1980s the delicacy, like Gold Seal Dairy, was facing extinction.

This tragedy occurred for several reasons. First, a government prohibition on selling raw milk had long since stopped city-dwelling home cooks from making their own product. Health consciousness rose, and everyone seemed to be on a diet. Creole cream cheese was also suffering from competition from the growing use of mass-produced processed foods. Creole cream cheese was shunned by early-twentieth-century cookbook writers, whose recipes reflected the times, favoring cheeses like American and Philadelphia brand cream cheese. Even local writers were guilty of neglect. The *New Orleans States-Item* in 1958, for example, ran an eleven-page special on Dairy Month that did not once mention Creole cream cheese. As a final blow, in the 1970s regulations were adopted banning dairies from producing bottled fluid milk and cheese at the same facility. By the 1980s no commercial dairies were manufacturing cream cheese. Writing in 1997, *Times-Picayune* columnist Lolis Eric Elie documented that Brown's Velvet Dairy stopped making the delicacy around 1980. Temple Brown, the company's president, gave a no-nonsense version of Creole cream cheese's sudden end when he told Elie that sour cream and cottage cheese were easier to make and sell; and besides, there was a generation that had never even tasted it; the market was limited. Elie's article also mentioned that Chicory Farm in Mount Hermon tried to revitalize the product, but abandoned their plans when they learned that Creole cream cheese was highly perishable. This shelf-life problem is echoed by various producers and state health agencies.

In 1986, Frank Schneider of the *Times-Picayune* was lamenting the lack of cream cheese when he wrote that it was impossible to make good old-fashioned clabber. Schneider pointed out that the homogenized milk of the time had so many preservatives it would not sour right and instead turned slimy. At the end of that same article, however, Schneider tacked on a late flash. He had just learned that Dorignac's Grocery Store of Metairie had been testing batches and had solved Schneider's Creole cream cheese crisis by releasing an initial order of 140 pints that were swooped up from the dairy case. Dorignac's, using its version of the old Gold Seal Dairy recipe, still makes Creole cream cheese in-house and still sells it in sixteen-ounce round, white plastic containers. Lorin Gaudin, a writer for Emeril Lagasse's Web site, wrote in 2000 that Dorignac's uses slightly warmed milk and rennet tablets and wet packs their Creole cream cheese with half-and-half. She also mentions that the grocer makes it fresh daily and sells around three thousand containers a week. A recent visit to the Veterans Highway store revealed a freshly replenished mountain of white plastic cartons sans labels (the guys in the back had run out). No matter. Happy customers were piling cartons in their shopping carts, no one questioning their precious cargo's contents.

Gaudin's article also credits chef and food preservationist Poppy Tooker with resurrecting Creole cream cheese as a food item very easily made at home and something worth preserving as part of New Orleans' food heritage. In the 1990s, Tooker reintroduced the city to Creole cream cheese through farmer's markets and cooking classes. Devoted to tradition, she does not warm her milk and recommends molding the homemade product in plastic butter tubs punctured with holes. She is another fan of the Gold Seal Dairy recipe, though her version uses a different rennet from Dorignac's. Tooker is also an engaged member of Slow Food USA, an organization based in Italy that ferrets out important foods and regional cuisines and works to preserve them by placing them in a figurative "Ark of Taste." Along with foods like the Louisiana Satsuma and the Louisiana Heritage Strawberry, Creole cream cheese has been placed on this group's list of culinary endangered species.

Dorignac's success seems to have inspired a few commercial dairies to also give Creole cream cheese a reprieve. In 2001, Mauthe's Dairy of McComb, Mississippi, consulted with Slow Foods USA and bought forty thousand dollars' worth of secondhand equipment. The tiny dairy started making Creole cream cheese at their Folsom, Louisiana, plant and began selling most of their product to a rabidly receptive clientele at farmers' markets in New Orleans. At the time, Mauthe's had also been selling skim milk to Commander's Palace, the world-renowned restaurant that had been using the product to make its own cream cheese. Like most manufacturers, the Mauthe family had its own ideas about why cream cheese lost favor in the first place. Kenny Mauthe believes that the product may have been phased out because of a trend toward low-fat foods. In 2003, he told Dale Curry of the *Times-Picayune* that older south Louisianans still had a love affair with Creole cream cheese, but that the younger generation, although familiar with it, did not want to ingest the calories. This same article goes on to reveal that a half-cup serving yields 207 calories and thirteen grams of fat and has become a favorite of those on the low-carbohydrate Atkins diet.

Since 2001, Smith's Creamery in rural Washington Parish has been selling Creole cream cheese commercially, mostly to specialty food stores and at farmers' markets. Warren Smith, the creamery's owner, takes pride in the fact that his thirty-eight-year-old dairy produces milk without hormones, additives, or homogenization, and that the cream on the top of a bottle of Smith's milk brings back old times. He is also proud of his company's extra-smooth, rich cream cheese topped with full cream, but he does admit that producing consistent batches is sometimes difficult. It took Smith nine months to develop a workable recipe. And even though he mixes the exact same proportions of ingredients and religiously follows the same processing method, he still finds himself occasionally having to throw batches away.

Could the air be part of Smith's problem? Much has been made about the unique atmosphere surrounding New Orleans and its positive effects on cultured foods. Collin and Collin (*The New Orleans Cookbook*) note that the culture that produces Creole cream cheese cannot be duplicated successfully outside southeastern Louisiana. It has long been speculated that Creole cream cheese is difficult to duplicate in other parts of the country because of the lack of an unknown but necessary bacteria that lives in either the milk or the air. Warren Smith laughingly says that it is possible that whatever makes Creole cream cheese taste so great may be the same villain that from time to time sabotages his product's consistency.

Probably the most ambitious Creole cream cheese undertaking comes from Chef John Folse's Bittersweet Dairy. Regarding the near death of Creole cream cheese, Folse cites a perfect storm of unlucky events, yet mostly puts the blame on the USDA's "separate plants for different products" regulations. He points out that every dairy was making cream cheese before the new laws forbidding cheese and milk production in the same plant. Folse produces specialty products like cow's milk triple cream cheeses and goat's milk cheeses, and he has plans for building a plant in Donaldsonville that will exclusively process Louisiana milk. When he first decided to get into the dairy business, however, a tangy Creole cream cheese topped with half-and half was the first cheese out of his plant. While researching recipes for his new product at Dorignac's, an employee put Folse in touch with a former owner of the Gold Seal Dairy who, in turn, gave Folse that ever-popular formula. Folse's *Encyclopedia of Cajun and Creole Cuisine* offers these directions to the home cook:

CREOLE CREAM CHEESE

Prep Time: 4 Hours
Yields: 10–12 Cups

2 gallons skim milk
½ quart buttermilk
½ rennet tablet (available at cheese specialty stores)
Half-and-half (optional)

In a stainless steel pot, combine skim milk, buttermilk and rennet, stirring constantly. Carefully monitor temperature with a thermometer until milk reaches 80° F. Continuing to stir, hold milk at 80° F for 5 minutes. Remove from heat, cover tightly and let sit 3 hours. Drain off whey

(liquid remaining after curds are formed) and discard. Pack solids (curds) in 8-ounce portions.
Top each portion with equal parts half-and-half, if desired. Chill and serve with sugar or fruit.
Creole cream cheese is excellent in ice creams and pastries.

The first cream cheese molds were woven wicker baskets, and through the years have included fine netting or cloth, wood, porcelain, and tin. At his processing plant, Folse created three hundred wash-pan-size filtered molds that hold ten-pound cheeses that are portioned into 11.5-ounce containers. But the historian in Folse led him to track down Gold Seal's original cream cheese molds, containers that had ended up stored at Louisiana State University in Baton Rouge. After a little cajoling, LSU turned the molds over to Folse. Although he does not use them commercially, he is now the proud owner of this important part of Louisiana history.

Folse's initial Creole cream cheese success was spurred by a partnership with mega-dairy Borden, which, for three to four years, contracted with Bittersweet Dairy to make cream cheese for their label. Folse now sells only his own product through grocery stores and online, while the Brown's Dairy network distributes three hundred cases of Bittersweet's Creole cream cheese a week. Thanks to the efforts of local food visionaries and brave cheese artisans, the future looks bright for Creole cream cheese. Folse says that his sales are steadily improving. However, he does not sense the revival of cream cheese as a breakfast dish, but instead sees a growing interest in using Creole cream cheese as a cooking ingredient. Indeed, recipes specifically calling for Creole cream cheese are popping up in everything from hors d'eouvres to cheesecake, and Louisiana's numerous TV chefs are touting the specialty on the nation's airwaves. Many local grocery shelves offer more than one brand; and, although it is hard to find outside Louisiana, a few dairies, like Bittersweet, do ship out of state. If all else fails, Creole cream cheese is super easy to make at home. And without cream and toppings, a typical half-cup serving is actually kind to the waist.

No one knows for sure if it cures a hangover, but we do know that more and more folks are reaching back in time for "real" foods, and few American dishes are as simple and authentic as Creole cream cheese. Slow re-acceptance seems to be due to a lack of education, so, who knows—with a little more advertising, Creole cream cheese might soon find itself an idol of the ever-changing national pop culture.

BREAD PUDDING

Susan Tucker

Dessert in New Orleans is not as often discussed as the other courses set upon the table. Yet bread pudding is one of those dishes lately associated with the city. Evocative in its simplicity and embellished with a sauce of butter, liquor, and sweetness, this particular sweet holds center stage on the dessert table, and any investigation of it tells a story that is revealing of the multiple meanings that New Orleanians attach to their favorite foods. Here is one recipe:

BREAD PUDDING WITH AMARETTO SAUCE

1 loaf of French bread, stale

1 quart of milk

½ cup of sugar

6 eggs

1 cup raisins

1 Tbsp. vanilla

Splash of amaretto

In large bowl, soak bread in milk. Mix lightly and place in well-buttered baking dish. Bake at 375° for 30–45 minutes.

AMARETTO SAUCE:

1 stick butter

1 cup powdered sugar

¼ cup amaretto or other liqueur

1 egg yolk

Over low heat, melt butter and sugar, stirring constantly. Add amaretto and egg yolk. Heat
slowly for one or two minutes to set egg. Pour sauce over pudding.

Cooking school instructor Lee Barnes scratched out this version on a piece of
paper in the late 1970s and photocopied it for her classes. A petite redhead who
had been trained as a painter, the late Barnes is credited with saving many traditional New Orleans dishes, and her cooking school (1975–1985) was the first in
New Orleans to reach a wide audience. Earlier cooking schools were segregated
by race, class, and sex.

Cooking schools in the city had never advertised before, but Barnes placed
ads for lessons at her store on the sides of streetcars that circulated through Uptown and the central business district. From Barnes's Maple Street and later Oak
Street locations, such internationally known culinary luminaries as Madeleine
Kamman taught how to make a perfect buttercream icing to what was probably
one of very few racially integrated New Orleans groups of its time. Evening and
Saturday classes taught by such locals as Paul Prudhomme and Leah Chase
accommodated gourmets from all sorts of backgrounds. Newcomers to cuisine,
including many newly divorced men, enjoyed her Cooking 101 class, sometimes
called "How to Boil an Egg." Barnes showed new ways to use one of the city's
favorite starches, rice, including lessons in the exotic foods of Asia. She also
taught classic French cuisine, showed neophytes how to make pasta, and made
sure those new to the city learned Creole cooking.

The story of Lee Barnes's Cooking School and her bread pudding recipe
bring insight into the 1970s, national food trends, and the renewed interest in
New Orleans food favorites. The amaretto sauce suggests the spread of coffee houses and ethnic cuisine, both of which provided a stimulus for tasting
various liqueurs. A number of other forces also influenced the type of school
she ran and the types of recipes she taught—the integration of public spaces,
the rising divorce rate, and the increasing number of women in the workforce.
Thus, the recipe itself embodies a tale of social change. But Barnes and her
bread pudding recipe also point to New Orleanians' love of bread and butter,
old-fashioned Creole frugality, and the penchant for crafting new meals from
leftovers.

Bread pudding recipes appear in the very first New Orleans cookbooks, but the dessert was not closely identified with Creole cuisine for a very long time. The dish is not unique to the region and is found in some form across many cultures. Between 1880 and 1970, it appeared mainly on the menus of New Orleans neighborhood restaurants. Even today, many locals don't give much thought to the place of bread pudding in our cuisine. Some New Orleanians express surprise that both the 1997 and the 2006 editions of *Joy of Cooking* include a named recipe, New Orleans Bread Pudding. These natives don't know that the city's pudding is different or that bread pudding somehow belongs to New Orleans.

Both *The Creole Cookery Book* by the Christian Woman's Exchange (1885) and *La Cuisine Creole* by Lafcadio Hearn (1885) give bread pudding a singularly slight place in their listings. Hearn makes it sound like a comfort food for a very slow night: "Butter some slices of bread," he begins, "and lay them in a dish, with currants and citrus between." Then pour a quart of milk "with 4 well-beaten eggs, and sugar sufficient to taste and bake."

By 1900, North American bread pudding in general had acquired a more complicated identity, and variations abounded. Recipes urged cooks to try chocolate bread pudding, bread pudding with meringue, or other dressed-up versions. Nationally, Fannie Farmer spread the fame of bread pudding, and though hers was a plain one, she added a vanilla sauce; and those writers immediately following her often added a lemon one. The first and second editions of *The Picayune's Creole Cook Book* (1900 and 1901) followed this trend, suggesting that bread pudding be accompanied by hard, cream, brandy, or lemon sauce. At the same time, the *Picayune* also takes pains to inform readers that there is no French word for pudding, a point often repeated by the French themselves. In this manner, the *Picayune* continued in allowing readers to see New Orleans as a place related to France, even as they presented bread pudding as an acquired or assimilated taste. The *Picayune's* writers made sure that readers knew that the dish was a bit unusual for the city. This distancing is part of the compilers' efforts to provide a larger overview of French and Creole traditions than earlier New Orleans cookbooks had. Their bread pudding recipe imitates, in fact, a dish Escoffier called (in various books written since 1886) Pouding au Pain à la Française. His recipe called for four whole eggs, six egg yolks, four egg whites, milk, vanilla, sugar, and bread crumbs. But he also included Pouding au Pain à l'Anglaise, a recipe not unlike Hearn's version of buttered slices of bread spread with currants and sultana raisins.

The double identity of bread pudding as part of both a national trend and Francophile New Orleans continues until the present day, with recipes always displaying a sort of linguistic blandness and only an occasional word of excitement. Even bread pudding soufflé retains the homely words of bread and pudding. One notable exception is "heavy devil," the name riverboat cooks are said to have called bread pudding. In her 1904 cookbook, Célestine Eustis gives no recipe for a simple bread pudding, probably supposing it was known to all and certainly not worthy of an expensive sauce. She does, however, give a recipe for a meringue pudding made from stale breadcrumbs and a fancy dessert version of French toast or *pain perdu*, called Custard Bread. She, too, then, shows a tendency to link Creole food to the larger American scene, despite the fact that her book contains both English and French texts.

In New Orleans cookbooks from the 1910s through the 1960s, bread pudding continues to appear, especially in its more dressed-up versions. For example, Mary Moore Bremer in 1932 gives Butter Scotch Bread Pudding, and a year later, *The Gourmet's Guide to New Orleans* includes a chocolate bread pudding but not plain bread pudding. The Depression and World War II seem to have had little effect on the frequency of bread pudding recipes. During the 1950s and 1960s, bread pudding recipes lived on as a plain family dessert but also added the use of new convenience foods, such as canned pineapple or fruit cocktail. According to a query of cooks who attended a 1993 seminar at the Newcomb Center for Research on Women, where African Americans Jessica Harris and Leah Chase spoke, the use of fruit cocktail is still important to bread pudding, especially that made in African American homes and restaurants. Bread pudding made with fruit cocktail or canned pineapple was also a regular on the menus of neighborhood restaurants in the 1960s and the 1970s.

But what happened between its 1960s kitchen-table place and its 1970s epiphany on all types of restaurant menus? Its presence on menus may be attributed to the fact that, at least according to bakers in the city, bread consumption in New Orleans was central to the history of the city itself. As noted in the chapter on French bread, flour itself was hard to come by in the nineteenth-century South; and to most Southerners, bread was cornbread and, on special occasions, biscuits. Visiting New Orleans, country cousins were struck by early Alsatian, German, French, and Italian bakers who made good use of imported flour and produced loaves of the round or cap type. Leftover bread was rare, but when it did appear, housewives here knew how to make good use of it, even its crumbs, in bread pudding.

The main bread consumed in the twentieth and early twenty-first centuries, known as French bread, is shaped like a baguette but is characterized by an airiness and thin crisp crust. These qualities make it ideal for both breadcrumbs and a custard base. New Orleans French bread combined with the ten eggs of Escoffier's recipe makes for a very different pudding from those using other types of bread and the typical four eggs called for in U.S. cookbooks. Significantly, now that most New Orleans bakeries are out of business, new recipes assume that cooks are starting with fresh bread rather than leftover, stale bread. Emeril Lagasse's *From Emeril's Kitchen* (2003), for example, says that fresh bread simply means that the bread should not be soaked as long in milk as stale bread would be.

The adaptability of bread pudding to various sauces, trends, and occasions was not lost on cooks here. Whiskey sauce, an early and continuing favorite since alcohol was so associated with the city, would have made the dish one prized by visitors and by local hosts. Other trends were such sweeteners as bananas, butterscotch, chocolate, white chocolate, and, as mentioned above, canned pineapple and fruit salad. Today, restaurants experiment with both old standbys to add to the puddings, such as seasonal fruit, and more trendy ones, such as Chunky Monkey ice cream. In summer, Clancy's restaurant makes a superb peach bread pudding. At home, a meringue topping still makes the dish all the more special.

With or without extra touches, bread pudding retains its centrality because it can be either *en famille*-plain or dressed up for company. New Orleanians know well what Eliza Acton meant when she spoke of bread pudding as allowing "a transition from a common version to a rich version of a dessert, effected without compromising the essential simplicity of the dish." New Orleanians also follow both French and English culinary practices in understanding that hot bread pudding is a custard, and cold bread pudding is a fine cake or breakfast dish. They also understand that bread pudding has to have a balance of smoothness and firmness in general.

In its very plainness, bread pudding has importance to New Orleanians and their love of home cooking. The latter, as noted throughout the chapters in this book, was governed by thrift and simplicity. As Hearn noted, "The Creole housewife often makes delicious *morceaux* from things usually thrown away by the extravagant servant." Red beans, as the Monday dish to follow the use of the ham on Sunday, remains a more often touted example of this tradition of frugality, but bread pudding is a close second.

As a part of this frugality and simplicity, New Orleans dessert cooking also long retained, and to some extent still retains, a reliance on molasses and other local ingredients. Molasses and sugar, of course, were central to the New Orleans economy, and Louisiana proclaims itself the oldest and most historic sugar-producing area in the United States. Jesuit priests planted the first sugarcane in the city in the 1750s. In the late 1790s, Etienne de Boré (at a plantation where Audubon Park now sits and at the more distant Destrehan Plantation) perfected his method for crystallizing brown sugar from cane. Soon, for residents in many parts of the United States, molasses from sugarcane began to replace sorghum molasses and maple syrup from the Upper South. Cookbook writers of the late nineteenth century praised New Orleans molasses as second only to that from Puerto Rico. Improved methods of production and the centralization of mills meant that by the 1950s Louisiana produced about 80 percent of the sugarcane grown in the continental United States. New Orleanians always were involved in marketing and processing sugar, a fact that still has an impact today. For example, elderly residents in the area near the Uptown Square shopping center still recall the smell of burnt sugar from the whiskey and molasses factory located there in the early twentieth century. Both Domino and Imperial operate sugar-processing plants in Louisiana, and many New Orleans families have ties to the rural areas where sugarcane is grown. Overall, Louisiana today produces about 25 percent of the sugarcane grown in the United States.

In early New Orleans cookbooks, molasses was usually, though not always, called "Louisiana molasses." Molasses pie, for example, is a favorite. Food writer John Egerton notes that this was a precursor to pecan pie, which does not appear in New Orleans cookbooks until the 1920s and never makes its way into the *The Picayune's Creole Cook Book*. The Christian Woman's Exchange cookbook gives nineteen ginger- and molasses-based sweet recipes. *The Picayune Creole Cook Book* of 1900 has five recipes for molasses cakes, and Eustis (1904) has three such recipes.

Of all the molasses recipes, the one most important was that for stage planks, sometimes called gingerbread tiles. As the name suggests, these treats are rather hard gingerbread and molasses rectangles uniformly proclaimed as a sweet for the masses. The name of these cookies was also Estomac Mulâtre, French for "mulatto's stomach." Different writers assign different meanings to these names, some giving a racist twist and saying the gingerbread was fit only for the stomach of a mulatto to digest, while others talk about the color of the gingerbread and its resemblance to the skin color of people of mixed racial descent.

Mary Land, writing in the 1960s, recalled that stage planks were once the most popular of all snack food sold by French Quarter street vendors and in small stores throughout the city. Sometimes called ginger cakes, stage planks are still available, though not as ubiquitous. Indeed, one sees them in outlying areas such as Houma more so than in New Orleans. Other molasses sweets are very rarely seen today, such as *la colle* (a cake made from molasses and roasted peanuts or pecans), *tac-tac* (popcorn and molasses), and *maïs tac-tac* (parched Indian corn and molasses). Eliza Ripley, writing her memoirs of the 1840s, recalled the "the colored *marchandes* who walked the street with trays, deftly balanced on their heads, arms akimbo, calling out their dainties, which were in picayune piles on the trays—six small celesto figs, or five large blue ones, nestling on fig leaves; lovely popcorn tic tac balls made with that luscious 'open kettle' sugar, that dear, fragrant brown sugar no one sees now."

It was not until after the Civil War that Louisiana began producing white sugar, though imported white sugar was used earlier on special occasions. White sugar was, of course, treasured and demanded in early favorites such as *babas*, snap dragons, and pralines. Babas, though Polish in origin, built upon the French love of buttery brioches, which they somewhat resemble. Land makes a further argument for their origin in France, the French name for them being *savarins*. Snap dragons, which Land also described as a party favorite of the past, were made of "raisins, which had been plumped by hot water . . . in a chafing dish . . . with brandy . . . to cover and whole walnuts or pecans sprinkled with sugar. The partygoers then watched as the brandy was set aflame and delighted when they pulled their confection from the blaze." Babas, except as a restaurant dish, rarely are described in cookbooks of later periods, and though snap dragons were still popular in the 1930s, they are not mentioned in later cookbooks.

Other early sweets that draw upon Louisiana ingredients are rice puddings, ambrosias, and lace cookies. Although at least one writer and custom have long dictated that people who eat rice with meats tend to avoid sweet rice dishes, New Orleans cookbooks have had no shortage of rice puddings. The Christian

Woman's Exchange cookbook has a rice *blanc mange* (a jellied dessert made with milk) and a plain rice pudding. Hearn has a recipe for rice pudding and rice custard as well as baked rice cakes and rice milk for children. His rice pudding calls for a meringue topping, thus making one believe that the dish might have been served to company. All editions of *The Picayune Creole Cook Book* include many custards, fritters, puddings, dumplings, ice creams, and meringues made with rice, and the authors specifically attribute the rice dumplings to the "old Creole cook." Eustis gives a recipe for plain rice pudding, so named, one assumes, to show that it was for everyday use and even a way to use leftover rice. Recall then that all these sweet dishes come from a state that is a leading U.S. rice producer and whose inhabitants are famously known for their consumption of savory rice dishes. And there are also others: one sometimes named "snowballs" (not the ones that are shaved ice and syrup) with coconut and also a sweetened popped rice, eaten like popcorn. In one of the few books to discuss food brought by refugees from Saint-Domingue in the late eighteenth and early nineteenth centuries, Land's *New Orleans Cuisine* mentions these treats. In *La Bouche Creole* (1981), Leon Soniat Jr. includes not only a rice pudding recipe, but also *riz au lait*, a traditional breakfast dish cooked with leftover rice, milk, and sugar.

A number of other early desserts use Louisiana oranges, a fruit specified repeatedly in the 1900 *Picayune's Creole Cook Book*. The special favorite among orange desserts remains ambrosia: oranges, coconut, and sugar chilled and served in a cut-glass bowl. Hearn pronounced it a "pretty dessert" or "supper dish," and New Orleanians have not changed in their belief that its simple beauty should follow a heavy Christmas meal. Although this preference holds true all over the South, many New Orleanians continue to demonstrate a special affinity for ambrosia, and each fall they search out Plaquemines Parish oranges or use their own garden-grown satsumas and tangerines as key ingredients for this holiday dish.

An early recipe for lace cookies appears in Natalie Scott's 1931 *200 Years of New Orleans Cooking*. The name of the recipe, Lace Cookies Hélène, links Scott's theme of the African American cook, known only by her first name, with a dish made of molasses, butter, and rum. A similar recipe, calling mainly for butter and flour, with no pecans, appears in the Junior League of New Orleans' *Plantation Cookbook* (1972) and in Suzanne Ormond, Mary Irvine, and Denyse Cantin's *Favorite New Orleans Recipes* (1979). Lace cookies originated in South

Carolina and there and elsewhere seem to have been centered around the use of pecans. In New Orleans, oddly, pecans are optional, but the cookies are popular for entertaining because of their ease of preparation, at least according to Emeril Lagasse. With their crisp, gold color, they are not unlike beignets or calas, long associated with the romance of the Vieux Carré.

Other contemporary sweets derived from past traditions of the city are flamboyant and fire related—importantly so since one of the definitions of Creole food always includes a nod to *joie de vivre* and festivity, often proclaimed a part of life in New Orleans cookbooks. "Joy is one of the duties of life," write Natalie Scott and Caroline Jones in *The Gourmet's Guide to New Orleans*. "The characteristic nature of the city . . . is a feeling of enchantment," says Land. Descendants of the flaming snap dragons are part of this tradition, as is crème brûlée, which Emeril Lagasse, among others, has transformed to a staple of the dessert table in many restaurants and homes. This dish, with its ingenious use of burnt sugar over the homely cup custard—itself a favorite of early twentieth-century sick rooms—is often claimed as having originated in New Orleans. But, actually, it appeared in French cookbooks as early as 1691. Early editions of *The Picayune's Creole Cook Book* call the dish "burnt cream," its traditional British name.

Crème brûlée, then, is not as distinctively New Orleans as bananas Foster, cherries jubilee, and crêpes Suzette. These are fancy restaurant desserts, promoted to starring roles in the 1960s. At this time, the interplay of national focus on New Orleans and New Orleanians' own self-perception also led to the reappearance of older dessert favorites such as *pain perdu* (arguably the dessert that most frequently appeared over the years on restaurant menus, though today thought of primarily as a breakfast dish) and *gateau de sirop*. But, in a poll done by members of the Culinary History Group, bananas Foster places second only to bread pudding as the most representative of the city's sweets. That dessert was first created in the 1950s by Chef Paul Blangé for Brennan's at the request of Owen Edward Brennan, who wanted to make use of the bananas coming into the port. Named for Richard Foster, the owner of Foster Awning Company, the recipe suggests a story of commerce, friendship, and creativity. It also suggests the ties between New Orleans' grand restaurants, the local business community, and the national press. Peter Feibleman described bananas Fosters in his 1971 Time-Life cookbook as "taking advantage of the smoothness of bananas and the not too sweet taste" that seems to occur with cooking. Flamed with rum, most often right at the table, and served over ice cream, Bananas Foster is said to be both hot and cold.

Bananas also appear in countless other New Orleans recipes, including a contemporary bananas Foster bread pudding from Dickie Brennan's Steakhouse and Chocolate Bread Pudding with Drunken Monkey ice cream (white chocolate, bananas, rum, cashews, and dark chocolate) from Emeril Lagasse's restaurant called NOLA. Earlier favorites were standards across the United States, such as banana pudding and banana meringue cake, though fried bananas do appear in New Orleans cookbooks more often than in those from other places.

An 1866 reporter for *Harper's Weekly* noted that bananas (albeit, in his opinion, "inferior" ones) could be found at the French Market. Santo Oteri and Salvador D'Antoni brought the first large shipments of bananas from Honduras to New Orleans in the 1880s, and by 1900 D'Antoni and the Vaccaro family were bringing in regular shipments via their Standard Fruit and Steamship Company. Thus, New Orleanians were probably among the first North Americans to taste bananas. In the early twentieth century, bananas were purchased from street vendors, but also directly from banana boats. Families along Esplanade and in the French Quarter walked to the boats to get what they called *bananes figues*, short and small brown-spotted bananas.

Flaming desserts with a more tenuous link to the city are cherries jubilee and crêpes Suzette, both of which originated in Europe, yet appear consistently on the tables and in the cookbooks of the famous New Orleans restaurants of the late twentieth century: Antoine's, Galatoire's, Arnaud's, and others. For special occasions, New Orleanians are also fond of Antoine's Restaurant's Baked Alaska (Omelette Alaska Antoine), featuring honorees' names written across the meringue.

New Orleanians' reactions to such displays are taken in stride, but these desserts are not as prized as either a good gumbo or a home dessert. For the most part, locals retain their love of simple desserts. Street sweets are another example of this propensity. Cooled fruit, for example, is a summer dessert often recalled by New Orleanians, but rarely given attention in cookbooks or travel accounts. This specialty seems to have originated with Italian immigrants who arrived in the late nineteenth century and remembered cut fruit slices sold on summer nights on Sicilian streets. When asked about this tradition, New Orleanians tell that it lasted in the French Quarter, Bywater, the Ninth Ward, and Uptown until the 1960s.

Another of these obscured street traditions with a more lasting presence is the snowball—shaved ice with syrup, served today at neighborhood snowball stands that operate only in the warmer months. From 1920 to the end of World War II, neighborhoods had snowball stands on nearly every block, and today a few families as well as established stands still follow this summer ritual to earn extra dollars. Like other street foods, snowball recipes are not featured in any cookbook and are described sparingly as part of the culinary tradition in various New Orleans travel guides. Italian ice cream also remains a favorite, still sought after at Brocato's and well described in a now historic account by Richard Collin in his *Revised New Orleans Underground Gourmet* (1973).

Not exactly a street sweet, but a public one in the sense that it was available in bottles and in drugstores, is the nectar soda, especially remembered by those who sat at the counters in Katz and Bestoff. First invented in the late nineteenth century by a local pharmacist, I. L. Lyons, nectar soda is a very sweet, reddish-pink-colored concoction with almond and a hint of vanilla. Mixed with ice cream and cherry syrup to make it even sweeter, it was a favorite until the 1970s. Collin called it "a magic potion" and instructed readers that it could "cure almost anything." A bottled version is sold today by the Nectar Soda Company of Mandeville, Louisiana, and in such stores as Dorignac's of Metairie (always worth a stop for anyone wanting local foods).

Of course, the most familiar of all street sweets remains pralines (pronounced here with an *au* sound or, as some say, to sound like praw-leens, never ever with a long *a*). The name is attributed to a chef employed by the Maréchal du Plessis-Praslin (César, later Duc de Choiseul) in the 1600s; the *amandée risollée dans du sucre* took on the name of du Plessis-Praslin. New Orleans pralines, unlike bread pudding, have enjoyed a consistent though rarely passionate love affair with locals and visitors. Pralines also have been less sullied with ingredient substitutions. The basic recipe of the first pralines made here in the eighteenth century remains caramelized sugar with a slight bitterness coming from pecans. This version is very different from French confectionery by the same name, which is a cooked mixture of sugar, almonds or hazelnuts, and vanilla. Often ground to a paste, this mixture is most likely to be found as a pastry or candy filling.

Oral tradition holds that both the Ursuline nuns and later émigrés fleeing the French Revolution contributed to the appearance of the praline in settlements all along the Gulf Coast. The Louisiana settlers used the native pecans and at first only brown sugar in their rendition of this French candy. Pralines were said to have been sold on the streets of New Orleans by free women of color and slaves. The basic recipe remains sugar, nuts, butter, cream or milk, and vanilla. Variations include the type of sugar added and the occasional substitution of peanuts or coconut for pecans. In addition, various editions of *The Picayune Creole Cook Book* and other cookbooks added such faddish recipes as white and pink pralines, the latter using cochineal, made from lady bugs and other insects, which generally imparted a red color but could result in pink, thus bolstering the national propensity of serving all white, all pink, or all green foods at parties during the early twentieth century. Praline parfaits, praline cookies, and other desserts made from pralines seem to be a phenomenon of recent times, though praline ice cream was given a place in a number of early cookbooks.

There is also doberge cake, something not found as commonly elsewhere as here. This is a beloved multilayered sponge or butter cake with a custard filling of chocolate, lemon, or caramel, a finish of a slight layer of butter cream, and then poured fondant. First modified in the 1930s from an Austro-Hungarian recipe, this cake is a favorite for all sorts of holidays. Doberge stands among the few sweets that evoke passion from natives. Parents ship this cake by overnight delivery to their children who have left the city, and it was one of the first cakes that Gambino's Bakery made again after Hurricane Katrina.

Despite this pleasure with doberge cake, the rich butter and cream of pralines, and the occasional festivity of flaming desserts, New Orleanians seem to have stayed true to a plain French-style bread pudding. And even though the city is filled with fancy versions, such as Jamie Shannon's White Chocolate Bread Pudding and Commander's Palace Bread Pudding Soufflé, plain bread pudding remains identified with New Orleans more so than with other places. This association was made permanent long before televised cooking shows took New Orleans cuisine around the world in the 1990s and early 2000s. In a talk at the Jewish Community Center in 1985, for example, Nora Ephron apologized profusely to the city's audience, who had turned out to hear her read from her novel, *Heartburn*. It seems that the first edition had printed the wrong recipe for bread pudding. "In this, of all cities," she stated, "I sincerely apologize."

This association of bread pudding with New Orleans may be best understood by looking to the retention of French culinary traditions—thrifty in the home and grand in the public spaces. To borrow from the vocabulary of such theorists as Pierre Bourdieu, bread pudding is of economic and linguistic importance to an understanding of New Orleans. To Bourdieu, food is the "archetype of all taste." The popularity of certain foods, their consumption, and their recipes reveal internalized ideas about where a person or a group of people fit in a social structure. Bourdieu also differentiates between tastes of luxury (something he also called, as did Sidney Mintz in writing about sugar, "tastes of freedom") and tastes of necessity. Bread pudding falls between these two; that is, bread pudding can be both a taste of luxury and a taste of necessity or homeliness.

Bread pudding is sold today in New Orleans grocery stores, even in national chains like Winn-Dixie. A simple bread pudding, even store-bought, dresses up the end of a meal quite gracefully, a trick that has been consistent in New Orleans food since the city's early days. This may be yet another marker of a love of both a high and low cuisine, discussed in various chapters of this book. Bread pudding is all at once a fancy restaurant dish, a convenient grocery store item, and a make-it-yourself favorite because New Orleanians find in it something that speaks to their identity as thrifty cooks and as descendants of people who happened to eat very good bread when other Americans did not. This is one of the key roles of New Orleans food—to maintain ties with older, esteemed traditions.

Return now to the recipe of Lee Barnes at the beginning of this chapter. Its inclusion of more eggs than most recipes and its choice of amaretto are reminders of yet again the subtle richness of culinary history. This recipe differs from Barnes's bread pudding recipes that appear in her two cookbooks and is, therefore, inaccessible to most people. Barnes gave this recipe to people who attended her cooking school, thus letting them become part of an inner, privileged circle of those who knew New Orleans cuisine. Overall, the gift of the recipe was a reminder of the way New Orleanian cooks have chosen to live—between a grand culinary tradition and a relatively depressed economy, in a ceremonial yet essentially private culinary tradition.

CAFÉ BRÛLOT

Sharon Stallworth Nossiter

CAFÉ BRÛLOT DIABOLIQUE

8 cloves

1 tablespoon sugar

2 cinnamon sticks

The thin outer rind of a lemon

3 oz. brandy

3 cups hot black coffee

Combine the first five ingredients in a bowl that can withstand direct flame, and heat almost to boiling. When all is hot, remove the bowl from the stove, bring it to the table and set it aflame with a match. Use a silver ladle to stir the contents for a minute or two. Pour the coffee into the flaming bowl, stir, then ladle into small coffee cups.

"A good cup of Creole Coffee! Is there anything in the whole range of food substances to be compared with it?" So begins the first chapter of second edition of *The Picayune's Creole Cookbook*, which devotes two and a half closely written pages to the proper making and healthful benefits of the same. By the time those words were published in 1901, coffee had been shipped to and through New Orleans for almost 150 years, and residents had acquired a taste for a chicory additive and a uniquely dark roast. Black coffee is a "powerful aid" to long life and relieves "the sense of oppression" brought on by a heavy meal, wrote the anonymous editors of the cookbook. Local custom dictated black coffee in the early morning and afternoon, but café au lait was the city's favorite breakfast drink. The ancient Creoles of New Orleans expected other marvelous things of their coffee. It was also thought to counteract various poisons and to prevent infections. They burned grains of coffee in a chafing dish to deodorize the sickroom.

French doctors recommended it to inhabitants of moist countries, so perhaps this helps account for its early popularity here.

"Café au lait (strong chicory coffee and hot milk, about half and half) is the apotheosis of coffee," wrote Richard Collin, a romantic on the subject of New Orleans food traditions. "The visitor to the city should not miss the experience of drinking steaming café au lait with the freshly baked beignets within a stone's throw of the Mississippi River in the heart of a great city. It is one of the truly memorable experiences New Orleans has to offer." The combination of coffee and chicory is much enjoyed in New Orleans and Acadiana as well as in the Cuban neighborhoods of south Florida, but other parts of Louisiana remain immune. Mid-century food writer Mary Land, who lived all around Louisiana, identified coffee brewed with chicory as specifically a New Orleans custom: "Southern Louisiana prefers pure coffee as does northern Louisiana." One New Orleanian, fleeing Hurricane Katrina, realized how far she was from home (185 miles, in Lake Charles, Louisiana) when she went to the local super-store to buy the coffee and chicory blend she drank, only to discover it wasn't stocked. She burst into tears.

Chicory is not the only additive or coffee substitute ever attempted here, although it is the only one that has persisted. An 1805 edition of the *Louisiana Gazette*, published in New Orleans, recommended drying, roasting, and grinding potatoes, presumably sweet potatoes, which were often recommended, to make coffee. "Few persons can distinguish one from the other," wrote the editor, adding that it was a cheap, plentiful, and nourishing vegetable, and partakers would not be dependent on foreign commerce to enjoy it. Anecdotally, most New Orleanians date the popularity of chicory to the shortage of coffee during the Civil War, when Union blockades of southern ports and the occupation of New Orleans from 1862 onwards severely limited its availability and caused prices to soar. Chicory, many say, was a cheap filler for coffee. However, until 1897, all the chicory used in the United States was imported from Europe and presumably would have been equally unavailable. Europeans had been adding chicory to coffee since the latter half of the eighteenth century, not long after coffee became a fashionable and expensive drink on the Continent.

Chicory "prevents caffeine poisoning which would frequently occur if a person drank an excess of coffee, correctly made. But coffee addicts do not admit of the slightest addition of chicory in coffee, and they are justified," sniffed the *Larousse Gastronomique*. Other Frenchmen begged to differ. The French surgeon

Saint-Arroman concluded that coffee of "succory . . . agrees with the bilious; taken fasting it promotes appetite, and taken after meals it facilitates digestion without causing any excitement." However, he disapproved greatly of café au lait, which he said was "bad nourishment."

All this might lead one to suppose that chicory was a French-inspired habit. But perhaps not. "The addition of chicory was always a bone of contention in our house, and neither *Mémére* nor my mother used it and neither do I," wrote Henri Gandolfo, descendant of an old Creole family. "Some Creoles looked upon it as an invention of *les Américains*." However, this is refuted by Alexandre Dumas, *pere*. He puts the blame on Napoleon, who in 1808 decreed a blockade that deprived France of both coffee and sugar. "Beet sugar was substituted for cane sugar, and coffee was eked out by mixing it half and half with chicory. This was completely to the advantage of the grocers and cooks who took to chicory with passion and maintained that chicory with coffee tasted better and was healthier."

Food writer John Thorne posits the theory that it was the Depression that popularized chicory in New Orleans coffee. "The most important aspect of dark-roasted, chicory-flavored coffee may be that it allows the impression of a conscious choice," he wrote. "It is the preferred choice of the poor but proud, who can justly claim to like what poverty forces them to choose. Louisiana had its first taste of this method during the Civil War, when the Northern blockade cut off regular coffee shipments." "Even so if one can trust the evidence of later cookbooks and visitors, there was no lingering affection for it," Thorne continues, noting that the late-nineteenth-century and early-twentieth-century Creole cookbooks do not mention chicory. On the other hand, as early as 1906 companies like Charles Feahney Importers and Roasters were marketing their Poydras Market brand of "Roasted Coffee and Chicory."

Thorne's theory would accord with the Creole tradition of making a virtue of necessity, although occasionally some made a vice of the virtue. In 1907, one New Orleans coffee company sued another over suspiciously similar labeling—French Market Coffee versus French Opera Coffee. Part of the defense was that the plaintiff wasn't entitled to protection of the law because he sold as "Java blend" a coffee that contained no Java beans at all, only "a cheap grade of Rio coffee mixed with chicory." However, as it turned out, the defendant company was doing exactly the same thing. "Strange to say, its president admits that the purpose of defendant in using these words was to deceive the public," wrote

Louisiana Supreme Court Justice Joseph A. Breaux, author of a June 7, 1909, decision on the case.

The chicory used in New Orleans coffee is the root of the *Chicorium intybus*, subspecies sativum. It is chopped, roasted to a dark brown, ground, then packaged and exported here for blending. The best chicory comes from France, although today it is also grown in Belgium, Poland, Russia, and India said longtime coffee industry executive Tommy Westfeldt in an interview in May of 2007. New Orleans shoppers can find ground chicory on some grocery store shelves, in packages ranging from four to six and a half ounces, each recommended to be mixed with a pound of coffee. Westfeldt recommends adding no more than 10 percent chicory to a coffee mix unless it is to be used for café au lait, in which case the chicory can make up to 20 percent of the mixture. For those who want their chicory already blended, Community Coffee, Luzianne, French Market, and Mello Joy fill that niche. Chicory is marketed as a coffee extender that "mellows, enriches and helps make coffee go twice as far," with the added benefit of no caffeine. Given the amount of coffee New Orleanians have been reputed to drink, limiting the caffeine consumption could be beneficial.

"The Louisianian drinks coffee all day," wrote a local graduate student in 1931. "It is claimed that the creoles who are at the French Market in New Orleans drink from ten to fifteen cups a day." Mary Barton Reed went on to cite the early morning cup, the breakfast cup, the mid-morning cup, the after-dinner (mid-day) cup, the afternoon cup, and the coffee served with or after the evening meal as a normal amount of coffee consumption. Louisiana coffee is "a thick liquid strong enough to stain a china cup," she said, noting that it was roasted a very dark brown, ground fine, used liberally, and dripped slowly, using only a tablespoon or two of water at a time, through mesh or muslin. Mrs. Henry A. Steckler refined consumption to four cups a day, with an interesting note on restaurant etiquette for the after-dinner cup. "These are called 'small blacks.' The signal for a small black that is understood by any waiter in any restaurant is to lift the right hand, hold thumb and first finger about an inch apart, keeping the other fingers closed into the palm of the hand. The after dinner cup may take the form of a Café Brûlot." Perhaps the endless drinking of strong coffee has contributed to the feeling of those who visit New Orleans that they are somewhere outside the usual American experience. "Taken in large quantities, at once, it not only produces morbid vigilance, but affects the brain so as to occasion vertigo, and a sort of altered consciousness, or confusion of ideas, not amounting to delirium; which I can compare to nothing so well as the feeling when one is lost amid familiar objects. . . . I have experienced these feelings myself after a cup of café à la française, early in the morning, in New Orleans," wrote Dr. Daniel Drake in his 1850's *Principal Diseases of the Interior Valley of North America.*

Peter Feibleman, in the wire-bound recipe book accompanying his 1971 *American Cooking: Creole and Acadian,* recommends using six tablespoons of ground coffee to three eight-ounce measuring cups of water. The water is brought to a boil while the coffee goes into the top of the drip pot that all good Creoles used. Then, as Reed also observed, the boiling water is dripped through a tablespoonful at a time—all three cups of it. "Since the procedure may take as long as 20 minutes, you may keep the coffee hot by setting the pot in a saucepan partly filled with boiling water," Feibleman suggests. ""Never set the drip pot directly on the stove to heat the coffee."

Coffeehouses have assumed public importance since the first one opened some five hundred years ago in Persia—"a respectable retreat for idle persons, and a place of relaxation for persons engaged in business. The politicians talked of the news there, the poets there recited their verses and the mollahs their sermons." Although the Turks, and later also the English, found that coffeehouses were "seminaries of sedition," the popularity of coffee was such that attempts to outlaw coffeehouses were ultimately unsuccessful.

Downtown New Orleans office workers of the early to mid-twentieth century had an institutionally recognized morning coffee break—some claim it as the country's first—when business would stop and everyone would gather nearby to drink coffee. That would be a direct inversion of the nineteenth-century habit of Creole bankers, brokers, importers, and exporters, who would gather each day for a coffee break in order to *conduct* business on Exchange Alley. Originally, an exchange was a building where the town's merchants met to do business. In the early years of New Orleans, as a flurry of fortune-seekers bought and sold goods of all descriptions, some of the coffeehouses took the name "exchange," as in the Exchange Coffee House, which first sought subscribers in 1806. Exchanges and coffeehouses fulfilled a variety of functions, selling alcohol as well as coffee and providing public meeting places. Some rented out rooms and provisioned meals. Slaves were among the goods that were traded at some exchanges.

Before the Americans established their exchanges, the Spanish had regulated the sale of coffee and other drinks through the *limonadier*. In 1769, the Cabildo of the newly arrived Spanish governor, Alejandro O'Reilly, established a "master lemonadier [*sic*]," who sold "lemonade, liquors, fruit brandies, orgeats, syrups, liqueurs, sugared almonds, coffee beans, powder and in beverages, as well as chocolate; the entire lot of good quality & well-made."

The French traveler C. C. Robin, who settled for a short time in Louisiana, recorded his observations on commerce in the New Orleans of 1802–1806, including the trade of wine, olive oil, and other luxuries. But he omits any mention of coffee until a discussion of boatmen peddlers, who supplied the settlements outside New Orleans with "sugar, coffee, tafia, china and some cloth goods. . . . They take in payment, chickens, eggs, tallow, lard, hides, honey, bear-oil, corn, rice, beans, in fact anything that they can sell in town, and they are the principal victuallers of the city." He also noted, "The Louisianians, whose palates are continually coated with the grease of the meat which so abundantly fills their stomachs and who never, as we do, finish their meals with desserts of tart fruits to clean the mouth and restore to the nerve endings of taste their tone and sensitivity, require more than we do, restoratives of a hot, spirituous, or stimulating nature." These presumably included coffee.

At roughly the same time Robin was keeping his account, a free woman of color was making her mark on the city, one not often recalled. Rose Nicaud, acute enough to have earned her freedom from slavery, recognized a common need for an early morning stimulant that was not an intoxicant and set up a small coffee stand near the central French Quarter market and St. Louis Cathedral. She thus energized other free women of color, who were soon brewing their own personal blends and selling them from similar stands. A monument to Rose Nicaud exists today only in the form of a coffeehouse in the Faubourg Marigny that bears her name; but surely, in a city as fond of coffee as New Orleans, a statue could stand in a prominent place!

The early to mid-1800s were a boom time for New Orleans, where fortunes were made, and coffee helped fuel the men and women whose industry made the city the second largest port in the country and the fourth largest in the world by the 1840s. "New Orleans is destined, unquestionably, to become the great coffee mart of the United States," opined J. S. Duke in *DeBow's Commercial Review* of November 1846. "Twelve years ago, and scarcely more than one cargo of Rio coffee was imported direct into our city. Everything now indicates that very nearly, if not the whole of this trade, must very soon be ours."

A few years before the Civil War began, the city directory listed more than five hundred coffeehouses in New Orleans, but, as previously noted, those met a variety of needs and coffee may not have been the primary beverage they poured. The city's neighborhood markets had their coffee stalls as well, some with marble-topped counters and stools for the convenience of their patrons. Lafcadio Hearn, in his *Historical Sketch Book* (1885), describes a coffee stall at the entrance of the French Market:

> The keepers of these stands are semi-neat looking, too. Their shirts are as white as
> the marble tops of the tables, their buttons as bright as the little cups and saucers,
> and their countenances fresh and healthy-looking as the steaming dishes of bacon
> and greens. . . . They are acknowledged as the elite of market society by the com-
> mon consent of their humbler neighbors, of the vegetable and poultry trades. . . .
> They seem to feel a pity for those poor vegetable sellers; for some of them were
> once vegetable men themselves and they can appreciate the position. They are
> proportionately urbane as their customers are respectable. They pour out their
> coffee in dignified silence for the poor market men and women who come up
> and lean their elbows on the marble tops of the tables. When monsieur from
> the steamboats, or his desk, or his loafing place at the corner, comes up to get his
> breakfast, the coffee-vendor is all politeness.

As Hearn indicates, some coffee stands sold more than coffee. They also pro-vided cheap meals for the working class. In an earlier letter from 1878, he esti-mates that half of New Orleans ate at the markets, where coffee stands provided a cup of coffee, a plate of doughnuts, and a long loaf of French bread for a good ten-cent breakfast. Fifteen cents bought plenty of meat, vegetables, coffee, and bread for dinner.

In the early twentieth century, every one of the more than thirty pub-lic markets had a coffee stand. Some of these stands were merely "marbled-topped tables suspended between the ponderous columns of the hall." Others were "replete with chairs and tables, ceiling fans, barrels of frying oil, frying pans and bread knives, in addition to nickel-plated coffee urns. . . . The culture of these stands typified the strong association between markets and drink-ing coffee, that was a staple of life in France and all around Europe." Some of the coffee stands with more exceptional cooking expanded their menus and premises and became known for more than coffee. The Café du Monde has anchored the French Market since 1862 and continues to thrive today, serving black coffee with chicory, café au lait, milk, orange juice, and beignets to tourists and locals alike twenty-four hours a day. Morning Call, which opened in 1870, is still run by descendants of its Croatian founder but in 1974 decamped to the suburbs.

In the mid-1920s, the French Market coffee stands became chic. "All night long Decatur street is thronged with automobiles," wrote a reporter for the *Morning Tribune* in 1928. "From 11 to 3 is the most popular time for society, who drop in for coffee after the theatre and following parties. Along toward the fag end of this period is when the artists generally break loose from their studio parties and stroll out for a bit of refreshment. Cabaret performers and night club patrons favor even later hours. They occur from about 3 to 5 o'clock. From 5 o'clock on most of the coffee drinking is done by truck gardeners and office people on their way to work."

Not everyone, however, has enjoyed the New Orleans coffee experience. Duncan Hines, whose name for many signifies the sort of tasteless, insipid coffee one finds in many restaurants, pronounced his cup of coffee and chicory to be "syrupy mud" until his travels took him to Italy, where he had some sort of epiphany after drinking espresso for the first time. His European coffee-drinking and subsequent return on a French ocean liner serving what Hines called "New Orleans–type coffee" resulted in a change of habit so profound that "good old American coffee" no longer satisfied. Today people recall how Hines apologized to the city for criticizing its coffee, but he is doubtless not the only traveler here to find it too strong for his taste.

The coffee trade in New Orleans dates to the earliest years of the city. Its position at the base of the Mississippi Valley earned it a nickname, the "Logical Port," for coffee imports from Latin America and the Caribbean islands. In 1802, 1,438 bags of coffee were imported; by 1857, more than 530,000 bags entered the port of New Orleans. The Civil War dealt a heavy blow to the coffee business, as it did to the city's economy in general. The city was under Federal military rule from April 1862 on, and businessmen were required to take loyalty oaths. Many responded by closing their businesses and leaving New Orleans. In 1859 and 1860, more than 285,000 bags of coffee were imported from Rio and Cuba; in 1862 and 1863, it was fewer than 11,000.

Lyle Saxon wrote that the history of old New Orleans ended with the Civil War. After that, it was no longer a Creole city, but an American city, he said. But there were pockets of tradition that still existed. "Visitors never fail to comment upon the coffee-houses tucked away in corners. For French drip-coffee is the favorite legal beverage of the men of New Orleans. And it is no unusual thing for a business-man to say casually: 'Well, let's go and get a cup of coffee,' as a visitor in his office is making ready to depart. It is a little thing perhaps, this drinking of coffee at odd times, but it is very characteristic of the city itself. Men in New Orleans give more thought to the business of living than men in other American cities, I believe."

The port and the coffee business recovered slowly, but by the early twentieth century riverfront warehouses were again full of coffee beans. In 1925, huge crowds turned out to witness a wind-blown fire that burned from the Girod Street docks down to Canal Street, taking with it $1 million worth of green coffee beans. Six large-scale roasters as well as several specialty roasters call New Orleans home today, but the dozens of independent roasters who used to perfume neighborhoods of Magazine, Gravier, and Tchoupitoulas streets are much reduced in number, absorbed by larger concerns. Gone, too, are the dozens of names of coffee brands they produced, many evocative of New Orleans themes and institutions: St. Charles, Honeymoon, French Opera, Tulane, Dixieland, Loyola, and Monteleone all once appeared on coffee labels. The Port of New Orleans, at times the top coffee port in the country, has lost business in recent years to the Port of New York and faces new competition from Houston, which was recently certified for coffee. But with the world's largest bulk coffee processor, Silocaf, located on the Uptown riverfront, it is likely that when the wind is right, New Orleanians will continue to smell the green coffee beans moving through the roasters in the Faubourg Marigny.

While the number of roasters and importers has declined, the number of coffeehouses has increased dramatically. For much of the twentieth century, after the last neighborhood markets closed, taking their coffee stands with them, New Orleans coffeehouses were concentrated downtown. There were a few outposts of beatnik individualism, such as the Penny Post Coffeehouse, now the Neutral Ground, Barsodi's, and the Quorum Coffee Shop, which was busted in the summer of 1964 "for offenses apparently no greater than playing bongo drums, reciting bad poetry and mixing with people of other races." Others fondly remembered are Croissant d'Or, still doing business on Ursulines, and its predecessor, La Marquis, and Kaldi's Coffeehouse and Museum. Today there are coffeehouses scattered throughout the city. The ubiquitous Starbucks competes for coffee dollars with homegrown concerns such as Café Luna, Rue de la Course, C. C.'s (a division of Community Coffee), PJ's, City Perk, Fair Grinds, and True Brew. Post-Katrina, the July 2007 *Polk City Directory* for New Orleans lists three coffee mills, thirty-eight entries under coffee shops, and fourteen more under coffee and tea, although some of those are blenders, roasters, and distributors. It rather surprises a New Orleans resident to go to other large southern cities—Memphis, for example—and note the absence of coffeehouses, particularly shops that are locally owned.

Besides offering a welcome break in the business day, coffee is also a social element in New Orleans homes. Marcelle Bienvenu, chronicler of current-day Creole traditions, wrote of her Aunt Cina's coffee party recipes, sweets produced to accompany the presentation of coffee in a silver pot and cream and sugar in heirloom porcelain sets. Fig cake, praline cookies, *ti gateau sec,* and *soupirs* (meringues) are among the treats that would appear on such an occasion. Café brûlot is a more ornate presentation. An admiring *Times-Picayune* columnist wrote in 1958 of a café brûlot ceremony he witnessed at an Esplanade Avenue guest house, "a carryover from the genteel existence of another era." The hostess, Mrs. Edward Preston Munson, "poured alcohol on the platter under the big bowl. The lights were extinguished and a match applied to the fuel. Great orange and blue flames leaped up and enveloped the bowl, and within a minute or so the contents ignited and the bowl and platter became a towering mass of fire. The flickering light cast weird shadows upon the massive crystal chandeliers and the ornate gilt mirrors in the darkened room." A spectacle more calculated to appeal to the dramatic and risk-taking spirit of New Orleanians can hardly be imagined. Most recipes, however, do not recommend setting fire to the platter, but only to the bowl, or even to a ladle of liqueurs which can then be poured into the bowl.

Hearn, in his *La Cuisine Creole,* gives a recipe for a *grand brulé a la boulanger,* although what the baker has to do with it is not immediately clear. Perhaps it was a reference to Monsieur Boulanger, the eighteenth-century Parisian café owner who was the first to branch out from serving drinks to offering restaurant meals. The recipe contains no coffee, but is composed of brandy, kirsch, maraschino, cinnamon, allspice, and sugar, which is saturated in the liqueurs and flamed with brandy. "As it burns it sheds its weird light upon the faces of the company, making them appear like ghouls in striking contrast to the gay surroundings," Hearn wrote. "The stillness that follows gives an opportunity for thoughts that break out in ripples of laughter which pave the way for the exhilaration that ensues." Amidst the exhilaration, however, one should keep in mind the story, possibly apocryphal, of the French Quarter restaurant that burned when a flame escaping from the café brûlot leapt undetected into the draperies, where it reasserted itself after the restaurant closed. Some recipes note that a chafing dish can be substituted for a brûlot bowl, and New Orleans cook and writer Christopher Blake comments that the whole business can be accomplished in the kitchen and heated in a coffeepot without flaming it.

There is a legend that the pirate Jean Lafitte was the originator of café brûlot, but there are more recent claimants to this title as well. Antoine's restaurant, for example, is often credited with creation of this drink. Roy F. Guste Jr. wrote in 1988, "Café Brûlot was created by my great grandfather, Jules Alciatore for his patrons at Antoine's." But café brûlot does not appear on a menu used at Antoine's from 1910 to 1940 and is also absent from Guste's book *Antoine's Restaurant since 1840 Cookbook*. Still, Guste does mention that Antoine's uses a special copper brûlot bowl and cups that were designed by his great-grandfather Jules Alciatore, who ran the restaurant from 1887 to 1933. Adler's, the venerable Canal Street jewelry and china shop where gifts for many occasions of ritual can be found, sells a silver brûlot bowl and cups decorated with the traditional red *diable* for serving it.

Café brûlot recipes vary in the amount of spices and sweetening. Some use different liqueurs or oranges instead of lemons. An unusual recipe for Orange Brûlot appears in the *Gourmet's Guide to New Orleans*, one very similar to Hearn's Petit Brulé in *La Cuisine Creole*. The pulp and skin of an orange are separated with a thin, sharp knife and spoon. The skin is carefully rolled back from the pulp, "turning it inside out, half making a cup, and the lower half making a stand. Fill cup with cognac, take a small lump of sugar, put it in a teaspoon filled with cognac, light it, then put it with the cognac in the cup, setting fire to the whole thing, and perhaps your tablecloth. The heat extracts the oil from the orange peel, making a delicious liqueur, said Mrs. Joel Harris Lawrence."

A sort of bookend to café brûlot is coffee punch, often served in summer at parties. Here is one that appeared in the *Times-Picayune* on January 8, 2004, devised by Uptown resident Rita Bielenberg Lapara, who serves it at teas but also as a dessert:

COFFEE PUNCH FOR 25

10 cups freshly-brewed strong coffee (not decaf), made with ½ c. regular-grind CDM Coffee and Chicory to 10 cups water

1 cup sugar (or the equivalent of sugar substitute)

3 tablespoons pure vanilla extract

½ gallon vanilla ice cream (Lapara uses Sugar Busters!)

1 quart chocolate ice cream

2 quarts half-and-half (don't skimp)

½ gallon milk

1 12-ounce container Cool Whip

To the freshly-brewed coffee, add sugar and vanilla, stirring until sugar dissolves. Cover and refrigerate until very cold. (This can be done a day ahead.)

About 30 minutes before serving time, remove both ice creams from freezer to soften slightly. Fifteen minutes before serving, place chilled coffee in a large punch bowl. Add half-and-half and milk to bowl, stirring lightly. Add small scoops of ice cream, using all of both. Add dollops of Cool Whip, mixing them in slightly. Serve immediately. The punch will hold a good hour in the punch bowl at cool room temperature; don't add ice or it will get watered down.

SOURCES

The following abbreviations are used in the notes to denote libraries and archives:

HNOC   Historic New Orleans Collection, New Orleans, LA
NOPL   New Orleans Public Library, New Orleans, LA
NCCRW   Newcomb Center for Research on Women, Tulane University, New Orleans, LA
Other abbreviations used in the notes concern cookbooks:
CWE   Christian Woman's Exchange (a New Orleans women's philanthropic and service organiza-
        tion whose members compiled *The Creole Cookery Book* in 1885)
PCCB   *The Picayune Creole Cook Book* (a cookbook published in fifteen different editions between
        1900 and 1987 by the newspaper, the *New Orleans Times-Picayune*) Many facsimile editions
        have also been published. Unless otherwise specified, the chapters refer to the second edi-
        tion, published in 1901, which was called *The Picayune's Creole Cook Book*. Beginning with
        the fifth edition in 1916, the title was changed to *The Picayune Creole Cook Book*.

The major sources used in this book were cookbooks; histories of the city; and archival and manuscript
collections concerned with dining, selling food, and living in the city of New Orleans. The cookbook
collections of the Vorhoff Library at the NCCRW, the HNOC, and the NOPL were used extensively.
Menus at HNOC and NOPL and city guides and directories at NOPL were also consulted. All references to the *PCCB* are from the 1901 edition, unless noted in the text otherwise.

SETTING THE TABLE IN NEW ORLEANS

Food history on New Orleans is found in a wide array of sources. Cookbooks offer extensive back-
ground materials. Especially helpful are Collin and Collin, *The New Orleans Cookbook*; Feibleman,
American Cooking: Creole and Acadian; Land, *New Orleans Cuisine*; and the many editions of *The
Picayune's Creole Cook Book*. Menus found at the HNOC and the NOPL offer insight into the past. At
HNOC, see also their taped programs from "Food for Thought: Culinary Traditions of New Orleans,"
held January 19, 2007, and their events on this theme during 2007, notably Walker, "Reporting on
New Orleans Food," October 8, 2007. At HNOC, see also Laudeman, "A Preliminary Report on the
Historic New Orleans Collection (HNOC) Project, *A Dollop of History in Every Bite, 2005–2007*"; and
Lawrence, Arcenaux, Laudeman, Magill, and Patout, *What's Cooking in New Orleans? Culinary Tradi-
tions of the Crescent City*. At the Newcomb Archives, NCCRW, see the papers of Ann Bruce, Mary

Land, and Mary Nelson, and the "Three Women and Their Restaurant" files. See also notes collected from the panel discussion on the History of Ice and Refrigeration, summer 1999; Culinary History Study Notebooks; oral histories and taped lectures for Chase, Covert, Gothard, and Reeves; Leathem's *Two Women and Their Cookbooks*; and Nossiter's "Food Supply and Markets in Colonial New Orleans."

For definitions of "Creole," see Kein, *Creole*; Dominguez, "Social Classification in Creole Louisiana"; Tinker, *Creole City*; Tregle, "Creoles and Americans"; Tregle, "Early New Orleans Society"; and various online publications of the Creole Heritage Center at Northwestern State University, http:// www.nsula.edu/creole/default.asp. Definitions of cuisine in general and theories on food and foodways are found in Appadurai, "How to Make a National Cuisine"; Belasco, "Ethnic Fast Foods"; Farb and Armelagos, *Consuming Passions*; Lovegren, *Fashionable Food*; Mintz, "Cuisine and Haute Cuisine"; Mintz, *Tasting Food, Tasting Freedom*; Rozin, "The Structure of Cuisine"; and Trubek, *Haute Cuisine*.

For food writing in general, with a few excerpts on New Orleans, see O'Neill, *American Food Writing*; Paddleford, *How America Eats*; Paddleford, *Recipes from Antoine's Kitchen*; and the Clementine Paddleford Papers, University Archives and Manuscripts, Kansas State University, http://www.lib.k-state.edu /depts/spec/findaids/pc1988-19.html.

Articles and books on the history of New Orleans are a good source for the study of food. Accounts from travelers, explorers, and early residents include Busstry, *Men and Manners in America*; Galsworthy, *The Inn of Tranquility*; Hammond, *Winter Journeys in the South*; Laussat, *Memoirs of My Life*; McWilliams, *Iberville's Gulf Journal*; Toklas, "Food in the United States in 1934 and 1935"; Shippee, *Bishop Whipple's Southern Diary*. For an overview of travelers' accounts, as well as a thorough history of early foodways and agricultural concerns, see Block, "The Evolution of the Cuisine in New Orleans"; and Stephenson, "Antebellum New Orleans as an Agricultural Focus."

For information on the city's residents, see Bourg, "Germans Left Mark on N.O. Food"; Cable, *Lost New Orleans*; Clark, "New Orleans as an Entrepot"; Cowan, *New Orleans*; Deiler, *The Settlement of the German Coast of Louisiana and the Creoles of German Descent*; G. M. Hall, *Africans in Colonial Louisiana*; Huber, *Creole Collage*; Lewis, *New Orleans*; Saxon, *Fabulous New Orleans*; Turley, "The Ecological and Social Determinants of the Production of Dixieland Jazz in New Orleans"; Widmer, *New Orleans in the Forties*.

Information on food and African Americans is found in Block, "The Evolution of the Cuisine in New Orleans"; Curtin, *Economic Change in Precolonial Africa*; G. M. Hall, *Africans in Colonial Louisiana*; Genovese, *Roll Jordan, Roll*; Hanger, *Bounded Lives, Bounded Places*; Harris, *Beyond Gumbo*; Harris, *The Welcome Table*; Mintz, *Tasting Food, Tasting Freedom*; Northup, *Twelve Years a Slave*.

Biographies, essays and articles, guide books, local histories, and scholarly accounts consulted for accounts of food include Allen, *Leah Chase*; Blount, *Feet on the Street*: Campanella, *Geographies of New Orleans*; Collin, *The Revised New Orleans Underground Gourmet*; Folse, *The Encyclopedia of Cajun and Creole Cuisine*; Gehman, *Women and New Orleans*; Hearn, *Gombo Zherbes*; Johnson, *Eating New Orleans*; Kolb, "Shopping at Solari's"; Lipsitz, "Learning from New Orleans"; Mullener, "Charmed Historian"; Mullener, "The Palace Guard"; Norman, *Norman's New Orleans and Environs*; T. Price, "Backstage at Emeril's"; Salaam, "Banana Republic"; Starr, *Inventing New Orleans*; Starr, *New Orleans Unmasked*.

The history of various markets is found in Novak, "Public Economy and the Well-Ordered Market"; Reeves, "Making Groceries"; Sauder, "The Origin and Spread of the Public Market System in New Orleans"; and Seaburg and Paterson, *The Ice King*.

Restaurant histories are found in *African Americans in New Orleans*; Brennan, Brennan, and Brennan, *Breakfast at Brennan's and Dinner Too*; Brennan, "Ralph's on the Park, History of the Building at 900 City Park Avenue"; Brennan's Restaurant Web site, "Owen Edward Brennan, Founder"; Guste, *Antoine's Restaurant since 1840 Cookbook*; Guste, *The Restaurants of New Orleans*; and Tujague's Restaurant, "History."

3	"ingredients, techniques, and flavorings": Farb and Armelagos, 190.
4	"the Kolly concession on the Chapitoulas coast New Orleans": G. M. Hall, 122–123.
4	"the great triumvirate of southern vegetables . . . turnips, cowpeas, and sweet potatoes": Taylor and Edge, 4.
6	"setting": Belasco, 15.
7	"new to the southern French and Spanish colonies" or "born here": Tregle, "Creoles and Americans," 137–139.
8	"lots of red beans and rice, . . . and crawfish bisque": Laudeman
9	"By the mid-1700s the riverfront . . . pushcart": Sauder, 282.
10	"refugees from West Indian uprisings": Cowan, 208.
10–11	"The difficulties one encountered . . . amusement below our galleries": Laussat, 48–49.
11	"disgusting," "perfectly," "greatly prized," and "the best fruit . . . the orange": Laussat, 49.
11	"enterprising spirit . . . itself in Louisiana": Laussat, 99.
11	"grand reservoir of the great West": Whipple, 118.
11	"It was with pardonable pride . . . at their doors" and "kegs of lard, . . . 'mountains of grain sacks'": Stephenson, 303, 302.
12	"roughly evenly divided . . . black," "revived," and "city's Francophone culture": Campanella, *Geographies*, 9.
13	"the greatest market day . . . delightful confusion": Norman, 135.
14	"everything coming from Louisiana . . . and so forth" and "the home-raised . . . or from Europe": Deiler, 113–114.
14	"Even New Orleans . . . and very nearly as good": Busstry, 326.
14	"free lunch . . . for a noontime potion": Cowan, 208.
17	"fancy and staple groceries": Solari and Solari.
17	"fine wines and liquors," "no reading . . . between 12 and 1," and "elephants, violins, or watches": Kolb, 124–125.
17	"decidedly unfussy space . . . main dining room": Johnson, 51.
18	"In New Orleans I walked . . . creative cooking?": Toklas, 131.
19	"Negro" and "old-time Mammy": PCCB, 1901, 6.
19	"Scarcely one person . . . American dictionary makers": PCCB, 1901, 97–98
19	"The Creoles will never eat a broiled pork chop": PCCB, 1901, 111.
19	"Drink while effervescing. . . . for generations": PCCB, 1901, 636.
20	"fine—yea, . . . gone all gone!": Galsworthy, 129.
20–21	"the restaurants and eating houses . . . even in far Paris": Hammond, 122.
21	"small ma-and-pa family restaurants . . . for a dollar or so," and "not rationed . . . or expensive": Widmer, 186–187.
22	"Nowhere else in the world . . . by legend": Paddleford, 1948, 2.
22	"boosterism": Lewis, 3–4.
23	"alive and vigorous . . . traditional dishes": Collin, *Revised New Orleans Underground Gourmet*, 125–126.
23	"Nouvelle Creole": T. Price.

24   "a traditional flocked-velvet dining room": Lovegren, 355.

24   "actually cook": Walker, "Reporting on New Orleans Food."

25   "food arrived ... atop shaved ice": Reeves, "History of Markets."

25   "beers when they walked into Schwegmann's": Mullener, "Charmed Historian."

25   "increasing standardization and devitalization" and "the American people ... at least ate decent
        food": Mencken, 172.

26   "Living poor and Black ... laughter make it seem": Salaam, 45.

26   "a population that eats ... very large community": Mintz, *Tasting Food*, 96.

SAZERAC

General information on absinthe is found in Wittels and Hermesch, *Absinthe, Sip of Seduction*. Late-nineteenth- and early-twentieth-century sources on the Sazerac are Hearn, *La Cuisine Creole*; Arthur, *Famous New Orleans Drinks and How to Mix 'Em* and *Old New Orleans*; and Kinney, *The Bachelor in New Orleans*. Cookbooks consulted include Bremer, *New Orleans Recipes*; Deutsch, *Brennan's New Orleans Cookbook*; Guste, *Antoine's Restaurant since 1840 Cookbook*; and Land, *Louisiana Cookery*. Oral history interviews and lectures of help were Evans, "Bartenders of New Orleans"; Wondrich, "You Call That a Sazerac?"

Recent interest in cocktails in general has meant more attention to the Sazerac. See Greene, "Antoine Amedee Peychaud"; Grimes, *Straight Up or On the Rocks*; McCaffety, *Obituary Cocktail*; Miester, "Good to the Last Drip"; and Wittels and Hermesch, *Absinthe, Sip of Seduction*. The absinthe regulations in the United States are changing by the day. See this link: http://newage.suite101.com/blog.cfm/absinthe_is_legal_in_the_us.

28–29   "an admixture of fact ... George Washington": Greene, 121.

29   "joiner" and "cronies": Greene, 124; Arthur, *Old New Orleans*, 47.

30   "New Orleans Style" and "Two dashes of Boker's ... into a cocktail glass": Hearn, *La Cuisine
        Creole*, 248.

30   "It's the usual story of commerce coming into it": Wondrich, telephone interview, November
        2007.

31   "Because in New Orleans they ... stuck to it" and "The problem is ... so entrenched":
        Wondrich interview.

31   "the popularity of the drink ... New Orleans" and "New Orleans and absinthe ... abhorred by
        others": Wittels and Hermesch, 5.

33   "Early observers seem to agree ...'line of demarcation'": Durrell, quoted in Grimes, 40.

34   "cordial introduced into general use": Greene, 132–133.

34   "As time passed brandy ... infiltrated the Creole city": Land, *Louisiana Cookery*, 307.

34–35   "In my opinion, ... Not pale": Sawyer, quoted in Evans.

35   "before commercial ice harvesting ... maintained icehouses" and "Production soared ... preparation of mixed drinks": Grimes, 46.

35   "At 300 Carondelet Street ... on Mardi Gras Day": Kinney, 20.

36   "Original Sazerac Cocktail," "a lump of sugar ... to moisten it,' and "crush the saturated lump ...
        put it in the drink": http://www.sazerac.com/bitters.html.

36   "The Sazerac" [recipe]: Land, *Louisiana Cookery*, 78.

37   "Sazerac" [recipe]: Culinary History Group's modification of various recipes.

FRENCH BREAD

One excellent source for the early history of bread in the city is an unpublished history written for the guild of master bakers in 1953, Baudier, "Boss Bakers' Protective Association: New Orleans Master Bakers Protective Association Together with a General Review of Origin and Development of the Baking Industry in Old New Orleans, 1722–1892," found in Special Collections, Tulane University Library, and the Newcomb Archives, NCCRW. Other sources for information on early bakeries are found in various newspapers of the city. Sources used for this essay include the *Louisiana Gazette* from 1810 to 1815, the *Daily Southern Star* from the 1860s, the *Daily Picayune* from the 1860s, the *Deutsche Zeitung* from 1850 to 1880, *Tagliche* from 1850 to 1880, the *New Orleans Tribune* from 1865 and 1866, and the *Daily Item* from 1892. See also Vandal, "Black Utopia in Early Reconstruction New Orleans."

Scholarly works that touch upon bread history are Woodward, *Tribute to Don Bernardo de Gálvez*; Ingersoll, *Mammon and Manon in Early New Orleans*; and Vandal, "Black Utopia in Early Reconstruction New Orleans." An early legal case is noted in *D'Aquin et al. v. Barbour*, 1849. Legal sources governing baking and bread are found in Baudier, in "Bakeries, Alphabetical and Chronological Digest of the Acts and Deliberations of the Cabildo, 1769–1803, A Record of the Spanish Government in New Orleans," found in the City Archives, NOPL; and in *Succession of Race*, No. 22965, Supreme Court of Louisiana, 144 La. 157: 80 o. 234; 1918 La. Lexis 1716.

NOPL, Louisiana Division, also maintains a vertical file on "Bakeries" in its business files; see at NOPL, "Compilation of Health Ordinances and Resolutions Regulating the Operation of Dairies, Butchers, Bakeries, Ice Cream Manufacturers, Restaurants, Laundries, City Board of Health."

For information on the numbers of bakers and the locations of bakeries see various editions of the city directories and the "Bread notebook" at Newcomb Archives, NCCRW. More recent history found in newspaper articles include Amoss, "Gendusa's Bakery"; Litwin, "Secrets of a Master Baker"; Walker, "New Orleans' French bread is tough to make at home."

General accounts of bread, French Bread, and sandwiches are found in Brown, Brown, and Brown, *10,000 Snacks*; Davidson, *The Oxford Companion to Food*; Harlow, *The Art of the Sandwich*; Kaplan, *The Bakers of Paris and the Bread Question, 1700–1755*; Mariani, *Encyclopedia of American Food and Drink*; Montagné, *Larousse Gastronomique*; PCCB; Randolph, *The Virginia House-Wife*; Smith, "Bread"; Ward, *The Grocer's Encyclopedia*; and Wason, *Cooks, Gluttons, and Gourmets*.

Information on the Gendusa Bakery was obtained by Michael Mizell-Nelson via a personal interview with John Gendusa in 1995. See also Amoss, "Gendusa's Bakery"; and "Poor Boy Gets Rich." Contemporary bread in the city was explored through interviews by Mizell-Nelson with Sandy Whann. The life of Margaret Haughery is explored in Gehman, *Women and New Orleans*; McGrath, "Margaret Haughery and the Establishing of St. Vincent's Orphan Asylum in New Orleans, 1858."

The history of the poor boy sandwich is a rich one. Probably the most reliable and earliest research is found in the work of linguist Cohen, "The History of Poor Boy, the New Orleans Bargain Sandwich"; Cohen interviewed Bennie Martin. The HNOC features a large variety of restaurant menus, including sandwich shops. Help in dating the oyster poor boy is a 1933 display ad for an African American restaurant, which states: "Specializing in Sandwiches and Oyster Loaves for twenty (20) years." See Souvenir Program, National Medical Association, August 11–17, 1935, Subseries XVI.2: Programs, Marcus Christian Collection, Special Collections, University of New Orleans, Earl K. Long Library.

One journalist's account of the poor boy origins is especially worth consulting. Bunny Matthews's "The Making of a Po-Boy" (*Times-Picayune*, Dixie Magazine, November 29, 1981) remains the most detailed article regarding the sandwich origins as well as the rapid demise of the sandwich shops and corner groceries that once provided New Orleanians with the majority of their food eaten away from home. Writing in 1970 for the *Clarion Herald*, Mel Leavitt interviewed the surviving Martin brother, Bennie. See vertical files, "Po-Boy Sandwiches," Louisiana Collection, NOPL.

For more of poor boy sandwich history, see Collin, *The Revised New Orleans Underground Gourmet*; Eames and Robboy, "The Submarine Sandwich: Lexical Variations in a Cultural Context"; and various dictionaries under the terms *pistolete*, *pourboire*, and *poor boy*. For comparisons of other sandwiches and poor boys, see Wason, *Cooks, Gluttons, and Gourmets*; Eames and Robboy, "The Submarine Sandwich." Harlow argues in favor of the pourboire account in *The Art of the Sandwich*.

The story of the Martins, their bakery, and the streetcar strike are explored in Matthews, "Making of a Po-Boy"; Amoss, "Gendusa's Bakery"; Hearty, "Po 'Boy No Mo'"; Mizell-Nelson, "Challenging and Reinforcing White Control of Public Space"; Mizell-Nelson, *Streetcar Stories*; Street Railway Union Collection, Special Collections, Tulane University. The interviews with William McCrossen, Sandy Whann, and John Gendusa were obtained by Mizell-Nelson, and more information about them is available in Mizell-Nelson, "Challenging and Reinforcing White Control of Public Space."

38	"running short-weight loaves": Baudier, 2–6.
39	"stick" and "cap": Baudier, 2–6.
40	"bitt": *Louisiana Gazette*, June 4, 1810, October 17, 1815; Baudier, 14–15.
40	"The round shape . . . little crust as possible" and "dough required . . . thus became elongated": Kaplan, 70–73.
41	"stick loaf" and "the very thin long baguette": Kaplan, 70–73.
41	"peerless baked goods": Montagné, 146.
41	"working Viennese-style bakery": Smith, "Bread," 116.
41	"made of the same dough . . . the *pain riche*": Ward, 79.
41	"shortening or sugar . . . in New Orleans" and "Some of the New Orleans . . . it does taste different": Poupart, quoted in Litwin.
41	"use a special hard wheat flour": Rima Collin, quoted in Litwin.
42	"chewy, slightly sour . . . room temperature": Amoss.
43	"loads": "Pistolet."
43	"Gizmo": "Pistolet."
43	"body humors from a sick worker": Baudier, 21.
44	"Breadwoman of New Orleans," "sea biscuits," and "mechanically equipped . . . by a steam engine": Gehman, 42.
45	"a sharp die . . . as we see in biscuits": *Daily Southern Star*, February 8 and 21, 1866.
45	"eight certain negroes, and certain other property": *D'Aquin et al. v. Barbour*.
45	"Commercial Association of the Laborers of Louisiana" and "People's Bakery": "People's Bakery," *New Orleans Tribune*, December 24 and 28, 1865.
46	"an amelioration of their hard conditions," "Boss Bakers Union," "give and take half an hour" and "his journeymen to board . . . employer's premises": *Daily Item*, August 19 and 25, 1892.
48	"welfare capitalism," "company unions," and "Progressive Benevolent Association": Mizell-Nelson, "Challenging and Reinforcing White Control."
48	"strike breakers": Mizell-Nelson, *Streetcar Stories*.
48	"Our meal is free . . . Division 194" and "We are with you . . . keep you warm": Martin and Martin.
49	"We fed . . . 'Here comes another poor boy'": B. Martin, quoted in Hearty.

49   "Between 900 and 1,100 loaves . . . 24 hours a day" and "On a Carnival Day . . . loaves of bread
      were used": Martin, quoted in Hearty.

50   "ten-cent fried-potato sandwich . . . lunch hour," "lettuce and tomatoes sandwiches," and
      "sloppy": Martin, quoted in "Poor Boy Gets Rich."

50   "borrowed" and "Improved Poor Boy Sandwich": Burke, Compilation, advertisements 22 and 25.

51   "Red": Eames and Robboy, 282.

51   "The story goes that Martin . . . 'sandwich fo' a po' boy'" and "in retelling . . . pronouncing 'po'
      boy'": Brown and Brown, 187–188.

51   "po-boy" and "to mock black dialect": "New Orleans Bread."

51   "The instruction . . . free for poor boys": Succession of Race.

53   "Another story says the term . . . goes back to 1875": Mariani, 246.

SHRIMP REMOULADE

For information on remoulade sauce in general, see Montagné, Larousse Gastronomique; and Escoffier,
Ma Cuisine. For information on mustard, see Davidson, The Oxford Companion to Food. New Orleans
cookbooks consulted for this chapter include, especially, Bégué, Mme. Bégué's Recipes of Old New Or-
leans; Bremer, New Orleans Recipes; Burton and Lombard, Creole Feast; CWE, The Creole Cookery Book;
DeMers, Arnaud's Creole Cookbook; Guste, Antoine's Restaurant since 1840 Cookbook; Hearn, Creole
Cook Book; Jones and Scott, The Gourmet's Guide to New Orleans; Junior League of New Orleans, The
Plantation Cookbook; A. Leslie, Chez Helene House of Good Food Cookbook; Mitcham, Creole Gumbo and
All That Jazz; PCCB; Rodrigue, Galatoire's Cookbook; Stanforth, The New Orleans Restaurant Cookbook.
      The place of shrimp in New Orleans history and diet is explored in Campanella, "Chinatown
New Orleans"; Harris, The Welcome Table; Landry, "Louisiana's Living Traditions"; and Prudhomme,
Chef Paul Prudhomme's Louisiana Kitchen.

55   "milder in character . . . preferred by many connoisseurs": Mitcham, 72.

56   "a good sauce for fish": Hearn, Creole Cook Book, 41.

56   "always served with cold meats" and "fish, or salads": PCCB, 168.

56   "fine mayonnaise sauce": PCCB, 67.

56   "it is all a matter of taste and imagination": Escoffier, 41.

57   "New Orleans is famous . . . used for cooking purposes": PCCB, 66.

57   "Shrimp's tendency to spoil . . . styles of New Orleans, and deep-fried": Harris, The Welcome
      Table, 255.

57   "My family had this . . . and we loved it": Prudhomme, Chef Paul Prudhomme's Louisiana
      Kitchen, 199.

57   "Crews of eight to twenty men . . . as great as 1,800 feet": Landry, 2.

57–58 "While a crew sailed the lugger . . . dampened palmetto leaves": Landry, 2.

58   "Shrimping as a way of life . . . stories of the fishermen": Landry, 4.

58   "who was said . . . French and Spanish food": Stanforth, The New Orleans Restaurant Cookbook,
      21.

58   "For the record . . . took off from them both" and "His recipe . . . remains a secret": DeMers,
      Arnaud's Creole Cookbook, 71.

58   "Enthrone on crisp, chopped lettuce": Bremer, 22.

59　"shrimp remoulade" and "favorite way . . . shrimp in New Orleans": Bégué, *Mme. Bégué's Recipes of Old New Orleans*, 22.

59　"Use a mayonnaise jar . . . and you are a chef": Burton and Lombard, 31.

59　"It is distinguished . . . of prepared horseradish": Rodrigue, 81.

60　"Shrimp Remoulade" [recipe]: New Orleans Junior League, 109.

61　"White Remoulade in the Style of Chez Helene" [recipe]: adapted by the Culinary History Group from Leslie, *Chez Helene House of Good Food Cookbook*.

OYSTERS ROCKEFELLER

Eighteenth- and nineteenth-century visitors to New Orleans left candid views on life in the city, including eating habits. Their writings are found in Whittington, "Dr. John Sibley of Natchitoches"; French, *Historical Collections of Louisiana and Florida* (found at the Louisiana State University Special Collections), Grimshaw; *Journal of Jonathan Grimshaw, 1818-1889*; A. O. Hall, *The Manhattaner in New Orleans*; and Laussat, *Memoirs of My Life*. An amusing glimpse of oyster vendors comes from an anonymous local resident who wrote a letter to the editor of the *Louisiana Gazette* in January 1805. Cookbooks documenting early oyster recipes include Hearn, *La Cuisine Creole*; Mayo, *Mme. Bégué and Her Recipes*; *PCCB*; and Richard, *Lena Richard's Cookbook*. Later cookbooks that offer currently popular recipes are Guste, *Antoine's Restaurant since 1840 Cookbook*; and Fitzmorris, *New Orleans Food*.

　　For a transcript of the oyster industry's assessment of devastation caused by Hurricanes Katrina and Rita, see Voisin, "Testimony before the Subcommittee on Water Resources and Environment." General information on the Louisiana oyster industry and oyster consumption is found in Feibleman, *American Cooking: Creole and Acadian*; Root, *Food*; Stall, *Buddy Stall's French Quarter Montage* and "Oysters no longer prohibited in months without an 'R'"; and Basso, *The World from Jackson Square*. Bellande's "The Seafood Industry at Ocean Springs" gives an excellent synopsis of the development of the seafood-processing industry on the Mississippi Gulf Coast. The Croatians are often overlooked in Louisiana history, and the story of their immigration and their contribution to the state's oyster industry is chronicled in Vujnovich, *Yugoslavs in Louisiana*. Information for this chapter was also obtained in an interview with Mike Sansovich, July 13, 2006.

62　"open[ing] the eyes . . . form of cooking": *PCCB*, 58.

62　"How ya like dem erstas, Mr. President?": Maestri, quoted in Marcus.

64　"palm and pleasure of the table": Pliny, quoted in Root, *Food*, 310.

64　"found a great quantity of oysters, which are not of so good a quality as those of Europe": French, 54.

64　"very well tasted": Feibleman, 188.

65　"New Orleans I am informed . . . half a dollar": Sibley, quoted in Whittington, 480.

65　"An Amateur," "noise and bawling," "konk shell," and "morning to night": *Louisiana Gazette*, January 18, 1805, letter to the editor, 3.

65　"tako," "so-so," and "how are you?": Vujnovich, 99–101.

66　"luggermen" and "smack": Vujnovich, 114–122.

66　"called at an oyster saloon and got some oyster soup and wine": Grimshaw.

66　"Manhattaner" and "garnished with oyster saloons": A. O. Hall, 2.

66–67　"Maunsell White" and "hard-tack": *PCCB*, 58.

69 "Oyster Pickle. Very Easy and Nice" [recipe]: Hearn, *La Cuisine Creole*, 30.

69 "Madame Bégué's Oyster Soup" [recipe]: Bégué, *Old Creole Cookery*, 64.

70 "In winter ... exceptionally palatable oysters ... style known to epicures and caterers": PCCB, 47.

70 "Oyster Loaf/*La Médiatrice*" [recipe]: PCCB, 66.

71 "Stewed Eggs and Oysters" [recipe]: Richard, *Lena Richard's Cook Book*, 36.

DAUBE GLACÉE

The history of the butchers is found through the study of city directories and other guides to the city, notably Braun, *Business Guide of New Orleans and Vicinity*, and Federal Writers' Project of the Works Progress Administration, *New Orleans City Guide*. Other sources include Block, "The Evolution of the Cuisine in New Orleans" (including a listing of many travel accounts); Bruce, transcribed interview, Newcomb Archives, NCCRW; Leathem, *Three Women and Their Restaurants*; and research materials gathered for the exhibit *Three Women and Their Restaurants*, Newcomb Archives, NCCRW.

Travel accounts and guides were also consulted. See especially, Horner, *Not at Home*; Collin, *The Revised New Orleans Underground Gourmet*; Kolb, *The Dolphin Guide to New Orleans*. Historical and autobiographical accounts consulted include Tinker, *Creole City*, and Hellman and Feibleman, *Eating Together*. General histories of food that are helpful in the study of meat and its preparation are David, *French Provincial Cooking*; Lee, *Taste of the States*; Montagné, *Larousse Gastronomique*; and Root and de Rochemont, *Eating in America*. Theories on food consulted include Appadurai, "How to Make a National Cuisine"; and Beoku-Betts, "We Got Our Way of Cooking Things." Food writers consulted were Anderson, "The Classic Hamburger Is Hard to Beat"; Bourg, "New Orleans Food"; Feibleman, *American Cooking: Creole and Acadian*, as well as notes from lectures and talks by Marcelle Bienvenu, Gene Bourg, and Nora Ephron, in the Culinary History Study Notebooks, Newcomb Archives, NCCRW.

Many cookbooks were consulted as noted within the essay. For an overall history of cookbooks, see Brown and Brown, *Culinary Americana*. For a history on New Orleans cookbooks since the 1960s, see Kaltwasser, "The Cookbook as an Indicator of Social History." Most helpful for further study of nineteenth- and early-twentieth-century food are Friedel, *La Petite Cuisinière Habile*; CWE, *The Creole Cookery Book*; Hearn, *La Cuisine Creole*; and Land, *New Orleans Cuisine*. Other cookbooks consulted are listed in the text and in the bibliography. James Beard's praise for Land's *Louisiana Cookery* is found in publicity for the book and in comments solicited by Louisiana State University Press (Mary Land Collection, scrapbook 1, Newcomb Archives, NCCRW).

Information on Corinne Dunbar's was obtained in interviews with her family. A collection of memorabilia on Corinne Dunbar can also be found within the Corinne Loeber Dunbar Collection, Newcomb Archives, NCCRW. Interviews conducted in 1999 with several people are mentioned in the text.

73 "Daube Froide à la Créole ... to be repeated": PCCB, 83.

73 "chopped sliced meats ... individual molds the day before": Feibleman, 8.

73 "some excellent steak and beef restaurants": Collin, *The Revised New Orleans Underground Gourmet*, 172.

73 "fairly rich hamburger history": Anderson, "The Classic Hamburger."

74 "By and by I worked ... his own particular meats": Horner, 46f.

76   "When bouilli is cooked . . . and other seasonings": Maylie, 7.

76   "This famous Creole dish is . . . fondly remembered": DeMers, *Food of New Orleans*, 112.

76–77   "Cold Jelly Daube" [recipe]: CWE, 52.

77   "Daube Glacée of Beef, for Cold Suppers" [recipe]: Hearn, *La Cuisine Creole*, 60–61.

77   "This is one . . . luncheons in winter": PCCB, 82.

78   "beautiful limpid appearance" and "polished": David, 401–402.

78   "The basis of a cold buffet . . . perfectly transparent": Carême, quoted/translated in Montagné, 288.

79   "practically anything": Women's Republican Club, 41.

80   "gift of champion daube glacé . . . ardent culinary enthusiasm" and "Ef yo' gonna stint . . . time en' trouble": Scott, *200 Years*, 99.

80   "an aging coquette, with a spicy past": Kolb, *The Dolphin Guide*, ix.

80   "in ancient cookery . . . to be eaten cold": Montagné, 1961 edition, 341.

80   "It is customary to serve . . . with its jelly": Friedel, 43; copy available at NCCRW.

81   "the cooking of the daubes" and "grandmother spoke no English at all": Feibleman, 80.

81   "daube wasn't something you ever ate in restaurants": Bourg, "New Orleans Food."

81   "Part of the pride . . . keep a few for the future": Feibleman, 80.

82–83   "Even though food preparation . . . group survival": Beoku-Betts, 536.

85   "poor man's elegant dish": Blake, 20.

85–86   "Daube Glacé" [recipe]: Junior League of New Orleans, 177–178.

TURTLE SOUP

Turtle meat in general and its history in Europe and the United States is discussed in Davidson, *Oxford Companion to Food*; Escoffier, *Ma Cuisine*; E. Leslie, *Directions for Cookery, In Its Various Branches*; Montagné, *Larousse Gastronomique*; Parsons, "Sea Turtles and Their Eggs"; Root and de Rochemont, *Eating in America*; Simmons, *American Cookery*. Turtle soup on early New Orleans tables is documented in Laussat, *Memoirs of My Life*; CWE, *The Creole Cookery Book*; Eustis, *Cooking in Old Créole Days*; Hearn, *La Cuisine Creole*, and the 1902 edition of the *PCCB*. Later accounts are found in Collin, *The Revised New Orleans Underground Gourmet*; Galatoire, *Galatoire's Cookbook*; and other cookbooks mentioned in the chapter and listed in the bibliography.

For information on African American cooks, see Andrews, "Soul Food, Baby"; and Burton and Lombard, *Creole Feast*. The 1899 suggestion for turtle soup is documented in the February 16, 1890, edition of the *Daily Picayune*, and in Laudeman, "A Preliminary Report," 11. Information on turtle soup today was obtained in interviews with Harlon Pearce and Paul Prudhomme.

87   "rooted in the creolized . . . tradition of New Orleans": Harris, *The Welcome Table*, 52.

87   "many of the restaurant's patrons . . . a soup course": Rodrigue, 99.

88   "was so important . . . 'buffalo of the Caribbean'": Root and de Rochemont, 21.

88   "To Dress a Turtle" and "To Dress a Calve's Head. Turtle fashion": Simmons, 22.

90   "I knew black people . . . Broussard's and Galatoire's" and "I couldn't name names . . . who they were": Andrews.

90   "French, Spanish, Cajun, Italian . . . restaurants in the city" and "The single, lasting . . . the Black element": Burton and Lombard, xv.

91   "The Mississippi furnished . . . prepare these animals perfectly": Laussat, *Memoirs of My Life*, 49.

137   "The secret is known to you . . . than like a vegetable": Feibleman, 43.

137   "will produce a creamy smoothness": Soniat, 200.

138   "Pickled pork is hard to get . . . a special taste": A. Leslie, quoted in Burton and Lombard, 32.

138   "I don't think anybody is really . . . and some bay leaf ": Chase, quoted in Burton and Lombard, 15–16.

139   "way red beans and rice were cooked . . . rich, natural gravy": Collin, *The New Orleans Cookbook*, 33.

139   "Red Beans and Rice for Eight Persons" [recipe]: Collin's recipe combined with changes by the Culinary History Group.

MIRLITON AND SHRIMP

Information on the mirliton is available in sources published by explorers and naturalists and, later, agricultural agents. For the former, see Browne, *The Civil and Natural History of Jamaica in Three Parts*; and Jacquin, *Selectarum Stirpium Americanarum Historia*. For the latter, see Cook, "The Chayote"; and Hoover, *The Chayote*. Both of these include various ways of serving as well as a discussion of names. Later descriptions of the mirliton and other vegetables are found in various cookbooks, some of which are quoted in this essay.

For information on colonial Louisiana, farming, and hunger, see Conrad, "Reluctant Imperialists: France in North America"; G. M. Hall, *Africans in Colonial Louisiana*; and Merrill, *Germans of Louisiana*. For information on artichokes see Ann Bruce Papers, Newcomb Archives, NCCRW; and Johnson, *Eating New Orleans*. Sources on vegetables and fruits and connections to Europe, South America, and the Caribbean are Montagné, *Larousse Gastronomique*; Seelig, *Fruit & Vegetable Facts & Pointers*; and Ward, *The Grocer's Encyclopedia*.

140   "Stuffed Mirliton" [recipe]: Leslie and Posey, *Austin Leslie's Creole-Soul*, 133.

141   "Here's what happens when Caribbean squash meets with pure Creole-Soul!": Leslie and Posey, *Austin Leslie's Creole-Soul*, 133.

142   "this class of peasants . . . the Rhine and Bavaria": Laussat, quoted in Merrill, 46.

142   "fastidious": N. V. Scott, *Mirations and Miracles*, 40.

143   "Artichokes prepared in this manner . . . or luncheon dainty": Watts and Watts, 116.

145   "It is claimed" and "the famous analytical chemist Chevreul": Montagné, 769.

145   "Creole method of making poor potatoes palatable": Washington, 204.

147   "commonly grown around Creole homes": PCCB, 247.

147   "having been grown for many years": Cook, 15

148   "for more than a generation": Hoover, 27-28.

148   "for creeping . . . The fruit is eaten cooked" and "even the bean . . . sweet potatoes or chestnuts": Hernandez, quoted in Cook, 14–15.

149–50   "the maverick vegetable of South Louisiana" and "the illegitimate offspring . . . somewhere in its ancestry": Feibleman, 99.

150   "a vegetable somewhat like . . . pepper and squash": Collin, *Revised New Orleans Underground Gourmet*, 18.

150   "price which certainly would not be paid . . . vegetable marrow": Fairchild, quoted in Cook, 21.

151   "The mirliton doesn't look . . . a hint of sweetness": Rombauer, Becker, and Becker, 269.

151 "a delicate flavor . . . full of life": Welty, quoted in Cheney, 100.

152 "the cook has shown it what it should have tasted like in the first place": Feibleman, 99.

152 "cover fences, sheds, or anything else which it is desired to conceal": Hoover, 5.

CREOLE TOMATO SALAD

One of the most helpful sources on Creole tomatoes is a pamphlet distributed by the Saint Bernard Office of the Louisiana Cooperative Extension Service, "Creole Tomatoes." For other general information on tomatoes across the world, see Davidson, "Tomato"; Hall, *Travels in North America in the Years 1827 and 1828*; Janick, "The Tomato: Vegetable or Fruit?"; Lelièvre, *New Louisiana Gardener*; Long, "Tomatoes"; Santich, "*A la recherche de la tomate perdue:* The First French Tomato Recipe?"; Smith, "Tomatoes"; and Wright, *A Mediterranean Feast*.

Articles by food writers provide some of the most complete local information. See Anderson, "Back in Business"; Bienvenu, "Creole Lullaby"; Bourg, "King Creole"; Dees, "I Say Tomato"; DeMers, "Creole Tomatoes"; Kemp, "There's Nothing Quite like a Creole Tomato"; Langenhennig, "Creole Tomatoes Are Welcome Storm Survivors"; Mahne, "Ripe for Fun"; Perrow, "You Say Tomato"; and Severson, "Slices of a Southern Summer." Cookbooks consulted on tomatoes include Bailey, *Lee Bailey's New Orleans*; Bremer, *New Orleans Recipes*; CWE, *The Creole Cookery Book*; Galatoire, *Galatoire's Cookbook*; Harris, *Beyond Gumbo*; Hearn, *Creole Cook Book* (1990); Junior League of New Orleans, *The Plantation Cookbook*; Kaufman and Cooper, *The Art of Creole Cookery*; PCCB (1901); and Rodrigue, *Galatoire's Cookbook*.

Sources on Italians, Italian and French foods and products, and other farmers in southern Louisiana are Boneno, "From Migrant to Millionaire"; Cram, *Old Seaport Towns of the South*; Dennett, "The Italian on the Land"; Harrison and Kollmorden, "The Place of French-Speaking Farmers of Southern Louisiana in Future Land Development and Reclamation Projects"; Solari and Solari, "Fancy and Staple Groceries"; Thackeray, *Roundabout Papers*; and Twain, *Life on the Mississippi*. The factory owned by the Bologna family is featured in a 1928 illustration by J. Woodley Gosling showing street lighting for the French Quarter. See Anthony J. Stanonis, "Saving the Vieux Carré," *Louisiana Cultural Vistas* 18, 2 (Summer 2007): 20. Information on the Italians was also obtained from Sal Serio at the Italian American Museum in New Orleans.

153 "I was born in Louisiana . . . best in the world": Bailey, 166.

153 "We have the absolute joy . . . the Creole tomato": Galatoire, 75.

153–54 "not *pretty* . . . with reds, yellows and greens": Bourg, "King Creole," 11.

154 "imperfectly shaped": Bienvenu.

154 "the juiciest, most luscious tomatoes I can remember eating": Bourg, "King Creole," 11.

154 "the alluvial soil and the climate" and "Everything grown in this soil . . . Irish potato": Becnel, quoted in Bourg, "King Creole," 11.

155 "plump fruit": Long, 351.

156 "all of which are used in cooking and equally good": Lelièvre, 104.

157 "We went over to the French Market . . . unintelligible Calabrese": Cram, 311.

158 "economy" and "Nowhere is the Italian's economy . . . stimulated to the utmost": U.S. Department of Labor, 487, 490.

158 "Let the people of Louisiana appreciate . . . immigrate to her waste places": Dennett, 37.

159   "drummers," "energetic of movement . . . dollar their god," and "We turn out the whole thing . . .
        dirt-cheap there": Twain, 347–348.

159   "the South of Europe": Solari and Solari.

160   "king of Creole tomatoes": Kemp.

160   "long ago": Bourg, "King Creole," 13.

160   "determinant, hybrid tomato variety": Saint Bernard Office.

161   "At Ben and Ben Becnel's . . . sold by the box": Anderson, "Back in Business."

161   "sun-drenched, river-washed flavor": Kemp.

161   "the flavor and the acidity . . . not so sweet and not so mealy": Pfeifer, quoted in Perrow.

161   "lower acid content than ordinary tomatoes . . . much more flavor": Prudhomme, *Chef Paul
        Prudhomme's Louisiana Kitchen*, 19.

162   "stuffed tomatoes . . . a slice of fat bacon": Hearn, *Creole Cook Book*, 86.

162   "raw tomato aficionados recommended . . . mustard, or milk" and "most common way to eat . . .
        salt, and pepper.": Smith, "Tomatoes," 77, 83.

163   "great family salad among the Creoles" and "the Creoles follow . . . salad disagreeable and
        coarse": *PCCB*, 164–165.

163   "Combining them demands a simplicity . . . speak for themselves": Harris, *Beyond Gumbo*, 12.

163   "nothing more to enhance them than a little salt and a grind of pepper": Bailey, 166.

163   "When Louisiana Creoles are in season . . . surpass that": Mahne.

163   "Serve nicely with a plain French Dressing or any . . . dressings": *PCCB*, 164.

CREOLE CREAM CHEESE

Interviews with cooks, chefs, and dairy owners offered a wealth of information. Recipes and/or
discussions on Creole cream cheese can be found in Carey, *Creole Nouvelle*; Bienvenu, Brasseaux, and
Brasseaux, *Stir the Pot*; Collin and Collin, *The New Orleans Cookbook*; Feibleman, *American Cooking:
Creole and Acadian*; Folse, *The Encyclopedia of Cajun and Creole Cuisine*; and Kaufman and Cooper, *The
Art of Creole Cookery*. Historical cookbooks give insight into the early popularity of dairy recipes. See
PCCB; Hearn, *La Cuisine Creole*; and, on the Internet, see the Library of Congress "Exhibit" for Mar-
tha Jefferson's handwritten cookbook (http://www.loc.gov/exhibits/treasures/trio33.html). Although
fiction, Chopin's *The Awakening* gives an accurate depiction of nineteenth-century Louisiana life,
including dining habits. Memoirs that mention dining on Creole cream cheese are Ripley, *Social Life in
Old New Orleans: Being Recollections of My Girlhood*; and Gore, *Memories from the Old Plantation Home*.
        Several newspaper, magazine, and Internet articles attest to the nostalgic popularity of Creole
cream cheese, including Curry, "Cream at the Top"; Elie, "Louisiana Delicacy Endangered"; Gaudin,
"Whey Down Yonder"; Griener, "Creole Cream Cheese"; Laborde, "The Cream Team"; and Schneider,
"Holy calas! No Creole cream cheese?" The *Daily Picayune's* article "Street Hawkers" gives insight
into the numerous nineteenth-century street vendors that roamed the streets of New Orleans. For an
understanding of foods that were part of the tables of Louisiana's free people of color, see Kein, *Creole*.
The Kraft Foods Web site has a good history of their products. Merrill's *Germans of Louisiana* documents the importance of the German immigrants to the Louisiana dairy industry.

164   "make a wonderful, wakening taste . . . did for your head": Feibleman, 118.

166   "Philadelphia quality": Kraft Foods Web site.

167   "The 'Green Sass' men. . . . 'cheeses! Ear! Ear!'": *Daily Picayune,* July 24, 1846.

167–68 "in the early morning, when one . . . pall on one's appetite": Ripley, 26.

169   "the actual active enzyme is . . . (true) stomach of calves": Carey, 179.

170   "Take the stomach from the calf . . . injure the rennet" and "Arcadian dishes; very delicious, cheap, and easily prepared": Randolph, 150.

170   "Biscuit Cream in Moulds" [recipe]: Hearn, *La Cuisine Creole,* 179.

171–72 "Cream Cheese/*Fromage à la Crème*" and "Cream cheese is always made from clabbered milk . . . corresponds to the German 'Schmier Kase.'": PCCB, 199–200.

173   "sprinkle cinnamon" and "add blueberries:" Laborde, 136.

177–78 "Creole Cream Cheese" [recipe]: Folse, 678.

BREAD PUDDING

For information on the international use of bread pudding and other desserts, see Acton, *Modern Cookery for Private Families;* Audot, *La Cuisinière de la Campagne et de la Ville;* Davidson, *The Oxford Companion to Food;* Montagné, *Larousse Gastronomique;* DePratz, *French Home Cooking;* and Escoffier, *The Escoffier Cook Book.* For information on bread pudding and other desserts in North America, see Clark, *French-American Cooking from New Orleans to Quebec;* Egerton, *Southern Food;* Farmer, *The Boston Cooking-School Cook Book;* Hamilton, *Two Hundred Years of Charleston Cooking;* Jenkins, *Bananas;* Moritz, *The Twentieth Century Cookbook and Practical Housekeeping;* Parloa, *Miss Parloa's Kitchen Companion;* Rombauer, Becker, and Becker, *Joy of Cooking* (1997 and 2006); and Ronald, *Mary Ronald's Century Cook Book.*

New Orleans cookbooks amply document various desserts. See especially various editions of the PCCB; CWE, *The Creole Cookery Book;* Eustis, *Cooking in Old Créole Days;* Barnes and Landry, *New Orleans Jazz and Heritage Festival Cookbook;* Barnes, *Creole New Orleans;* Bremer, *New Orleans Recipes;* Feibleman, *American Cooking: Creole and Acadian;* Guste, *Antoine's Restaurant since 1840 Cookbook;* Hearn, *La Cuisine Creole;* Lagasse, *From Emeril's Kitchens: Favorite Recipes from Emeril's Restaurant;* Land, *Louisiana Cookery* and *New Orleans Cuisine;* N. V. Scott, *200 Years of New Orleans Cooking;* Scott and Jones, *The Gourmet's Guide to New Orleans;* Soniat, *La Bouche Creole;* Dillard Women's Club, *The Dillard Women's Club Cookbook;* Stanforth and Deutsch, *Brennan's New Orleans Cookbook;* and Usher and Gray, *Food for Gourmets.*

An informative source on bread is the unpublished account in the Newcomb Archives of Baudier, giving the history of the baking trade in the city from the 1700s to the 1950s, *Boss Bakers' Protective Association.* Guides to the city also offer a wealth of information. For these, see Collin, *The Revised New Orleans Underground Gourmet;* and Kolb, *The Dolphin Guide to New Orleans.* Information on sugar is available in Conrad and Lucas, *White Gold: A Brief History of the Louisiana Sugar Industry;* Futsch, "Louisiana Sugar Industry," Newcomb Archives; and U.S. Department of Agriculture, *Sugar and Sweeteners Yearbook Tables.*

Theories on food are explored in Bourdieu, *Distinction;* and Mintz, *Tasting Food, Tasting Freedom.* Two newspaper articles to discuss bananas are Stouse, "Making the Belt or a Splash in the Lake"; and Waud, "Sunday in New Orleans—The French Market." The Barnes papers are part of the Newcomb Archives, NCCRW, Tulane University. The reference to the Ephron comment comes from notes taken by the author.

179–80 "Bread Pudding with Amaretto Sauce" [recipe]: Lee Barnes Papers, Newcomb Archives, NCCRW, Tulane University.

181   "Butter some slices of bread . . . with currants and citrus between" and "with 4 well-beaten eggs . . . taste and bake": Hearn, *La Cuisine Creole*, 204.

183   "a transition from a common version . . . simplicity of the dish": Acton, 359.

183–84 "The Creole housewife often makes . . . by the extravagant servant": Hearn, *La Cuisine Creole*, n.p.

185   "the colored *marchandes* . . . sugar no one sees now": Ripley, 24–25.

185   "raisins, which had been plumped . . . confection from the blaze": Land, *New Orleans Cuisine*, 221–238.

187   "Joy is one of the duties of life": Scott and Jones, v.

187   "The characteristic nature of the city . . . is a feeling of enchantment": Land, *New Orleans Cuisine*, 7.

187–88 "taking advantage of the smoothness . . . not too sweet taste": Feibleman, 123.

188   "inferior": Waud, 256.

189   "a magic potion" and "cure almost anything": Collin, *Revised New Orleans Underground Gourmet*, 150.

191   "archetype of all taste": Bourdieu, 466.

CAFÉ BRÛLOT

The history of coffee in general can be found in many cookbooks. See especially Hearn, *La Cuisine Creole*. For general information on coffee, see Davidson, *The Oxford Companion to Food*; Flandrin and Montarri, "The Rise of the Restaurant"; Montagné, *Larousse Gastronomique*; and Saint-Arroman, *Coffee, Tea, and Chocolate*. The latter two especially deal with French interpretations of coffee and its influence on health. For the history of New Orleans coffee, see Brannon, "Maritime Bean Counters"; Duke, "Coffee and the Coffee Trade"; M. B. Reed, "Louisiana Cookery, Its History and Development"; Robin, *Voyage to Louisiana*; Starr, *Inventing New Orleans*; Steckler, "Beverages"; and Saxon, *Fabulous New Orleans*. For more recent history and recipes see any edition of *PCCB*; Collin, *The New Orleans Underground Gourmet*; Egerton, *Southern Food*; "Duncan Hines Repents Calling New Orleans Coffee 'Syrupy Mud'"; and MacCash, "The Night They Raided the Quorum."

For information on chicory, see Dumas, *Dumas on Food*; Huber, *Creole Collage*; Montagné, *Larousse Gastronomique*; Saint-Arroman, *Coffee, Tea, and Chocolate*; Stilgenbauer, "Chicory: Michigan's Infant Monopoly Crop"; and Thorne, *Serious Pig*. For the controversy over coffee labeling, see *New Orleans Coffee Co. Ltd. v. American Coffee Co. of New Orleans*. For coffee labels themselves, HNOC offers examples. See especially Feahney, "Roasted Coffee and Chicory." For market history and coffee, see Reeves, "Making Groceries," in *Cultural Vistas*; and "French Market Coffee Stands." For Hearn's view of the markets, see Starr, *Inventing New Orleans*. For the history of the port and the coffee trade, see Louisiana State Museum, "From the Louisiana State Museum"; *Gardner's New Orleans Directory*; and Brannon, "Maritime Bean Counters." For directions and recipes, see Feibleman, *American Cooking: Creole and Acadian*; Jacobs, "Ceremony of Café Brulot Was Awesome Spectacle"; and M. B. Reed, "Louisiana Cookery, Its History and Development." For information on the sale of coffee in exchanges and other public places, see Bradley, *Interim Appointment*; and Holmes, "O'Reillly's Regulations on Booze, Boarding Houses and Billiards."

192   "Café Brûlot Diabolique" [recipe]: from the Culinary History Group.

192   "A good cup of Creole Coffee! . . . compared with it?": *PCCB*, 9–11.

192   "powerful aid" and "the sense of oppression": *PCCB*, 11.

193   "Café au lait . . . apotheosis of coffee" and "The visitor to the city . . . experiences New Orleans has to offer": Collin, *The New Orleans Underground Gourmet*, 176.

193   "Southern Louisiana prefers pure coffee as does northern Louisiana": Land, *Louisiana Cookery*, 277.

193   "Few persons can distinguish one from the other": An 1805 edition of the *Louisiana Gazette*, published in New Orleans, n.d., NOPL.

193   "prevents caffeine poisoning . . . and they are justified": Montagné, 270.

194   "succory . . . agrees with the bilious . . . causing any excitement" and "bad nourishment": Saint-Arroman, 70, 66.

194   "The addition of chicory was . . . and neither do I" and "Some Creoles looked upon it . . . invention of *les Américains*": Gandolfo, quoted in Huber, 41.

194   "Beet sugar was substituted . . . tasted better and was healthier": Dumas, 106.

194   "The most important aspect . . . impression of a conscious choice," "It is the preferred choice . . . cut off regular coffee shipments," and "Even so if one can trust . . . affection for it": Thorne, 262–263.

194   "Java blend," "a cheap grade of Rio coffee mixed with chicory," and "Strange to say . . . deceive the public": *New Orleans Coffee Co. Ltd. vs. American Coffee Co.*

195   "mellows, enriches and helps make coffee go twice as far": Coffee Partner Natural Ground Chicory, Reily Foods Co., New Orleans.

195   "The Louisianian drinks coffee all day," "It is claimed . . . fifteen cups a day," and "a thick liquid strong enough to stain a china cup": M. B. Reed, 35–38.

195   "These are called 'small blacks.' . . . a Café Brulot": Steckler, 17.

195–96 "Taken in large quantities . . . early in the morning, in New Orleans": Drake, quoted in Egerton, 205.

196   "Since the procedure may . . . filled with boiling water" and "Never set the drip pot . . . heat the coffee": Feibleman, 149.

196   "a respectable retreat for idle . . . mollahs their sermons" and "seminaries of sedition": Saint-Arroman, 23, 25–27.

197   "master lemonadier [*sic*]" and "lemonade, liquors . . . good quality & well-made": Holmes, 300.

197   "sugar, coffee, tafia . . . principal victuallers of the city" and "The Louisianians, whose palates . . . or stimulating nature": Robin, *Voyage to Louisiana*, 118, 44.

197   "New Orleans is destined, unquestionably . . . the United States" and "Twelve years ago . . . must very soon be ours": Duke, *DeBow's Commercial Review*, November 1846.

198   "The keepers of these stands . . . the coffee-vendor is all politeness": Hearn, quoted in Starr, 29.

198   "marbled-topped tables suspended . . . columns of the hall" and "replete with chairs and tables . . . all around Europe": Reeves, "Making Groceries," 34.

199   "All night long Decatur . . . with automobiles" and "From 11 to 3 is the most popular . . . on their way to work": "French Market Coffee Stands."

199   "syrupy mud," "New Orleans–type coffee," and "good old American coffee": "Duncan Hines Repents Calling New Orleans Coffee 'Syrupy Mud.'"

200   "Visitors never fail to comment . . . American cities, I believe": Saxon, 261–262.

200   "for offenses apparently no greater . . . people of other races": MacCash.

Bradshaw, Jim. "Cajuns Didn't Always Cook with Hot Sauce." *Lafayette (LA) Daily Advertiser*, April 27, 1999.

Brannon, Keith. "Maritime Bean Counters." *BizNewOrleans.com*, July 1, 2004. http://www.wavcis.csi .lsu.edu/news/Biz.html.

Braun, John F. *Business Guide of New Orleans and Vicinity*. Baltimore, MD: Flamm, n.d. [1881?].

Bremer, Mary Moore. *New Orleans Recipes*. New Orleans: General Printing, 1932; 10th ed., New Orleans: Dorothea Forshee [Thompson], 1944; 1932 reprint, *New Orleans Creole Recipes*, Dorothea Thompson, Waveland, MS, 1969.

Brennan, Ralph. "Ralph's on the Park, History of the Building at 900 City Park Avenue." http://www.ralphsonthepark.com/news_detail.php?id=4.

Brennan, Pip, Jimmy Brennan, and Ted Brennan. *Breakfast at Brennan's and Dinner Too*. New Orleans: Brennan's, 1994.

Brennan's Restaurant. "Owen Edward Brennan, Founder." http://www.brennansneworleans.com/ history.html.

Brillat-Savarin, Jean Antheleme. *The Physiology of Taste: Meditations on Transcendental Gastronomy*. Trans. Charles Monselet. New York: Liveright Publishing Company, 1948.

Brown, Cora, Rose Brown, and Bob Brown. *10,000 Snacks: A Cookbook of Delicious Canapes, Relishes, Hors D'Oeuvres, Sandwiches, and Appetizers for All Occasions*. Garden City, NY: Halcyon House, 1937.

Brown, Eleanor, and Bob Brown. *Culinary Americana: Cookbooks Published in the Cities and Towns of the United States of America during the Years from 1860 through 1960*. New York: Roving Eye Press, 1961.

Browne, Patrick. *The Civil and Natural History of Jamaica in Three Parts*. London: B. White and Son, 1789.

Bruce, Ann Maylie. Papers. Old Salem Talk file. Newcomb Archives, Newcomb College Center for Research on Women, Tulane University.

———. Transcribed interview, February 1, 2000. Three Women Exhibit Files, Newcomb Archives, Newcomb Center for Research on Women, Tulane University.

Bryan, Mrs. Lettice. *The Kentucky Housewife*. Cincinnati: Shepard & Stearns, 1839.

Burke, Ulic J., comp. *Compilation of Health Ordinances and Resolutions Regulating the Operation of Dairies, Butchers, Bakeries, Ice Cream Manufacturers, Restaurants, Laundries*. City Board of Health, ca 1932. Copy available in New Orleans Public Library, Louisiana Collection.

Burton, Nathaniel, and Rudy Lombard. *Creole Feast: 15 Master Chefs of New Orleans Reveal Their Secrets*. New York: Random House, 1978.

Busstry, Catherine. *Men and Manners in America*. Philadelphia: Carey, Lea & Blancard, 1833.

Cabildo. *Records and Deliberations of the Cabildo*. Vol. 4, no. 1, April 24, 1795–July 7, 1797. Translated by Joaquin Barcenas and Charles M. Ormond, 1936. Microfilm.

Cable, Mary. *Lost New Orleans*. New York: American Legacy Press, 1980.

Camellia Brand Foods. "The Story of Camellia." http://www.camelliabeans.com/story.html.

Campanella, Richard. "Chinatown New Orleans." *Louisiana Cultural Vistas* 18, no. 3 (fall 2007): 50–59.

———. *Geographies of New Orleans: Urban Fabrics before the Storm*. Lafayette: Center for Louisiana Studies, 2006.

Carey, Joseph. *Creole Nouvelle*. Lanham, MD: Taylor Trade Publishing, 2004.

Carney, Judith A. *Black Rice: The African Origins of Rice Cultivation in the Americas*. Cambridge, MA: Harvard University Press, 2001.

Carter, Susannah. *The Frugal Housewife*. 1792. A facsimile edition edited by Jean McKibben. Garden City, NY: Dolphin Books, 1976.

Chase, Leah. *The Dooky Chase Cookbook*. Gretna, LA: Pelican Publishing, 1990.

Chehardy, Melanie. *My Prize Winning Recipes*. New Orleans: A. F. Laborde and Sons, 1941.

Cheney, Winfred Green. *The Southern Hospitality Cookbook*. Birmingham, AL: Oxmoor House, 1976.

Chopin, Kate. "At the Cadian Ball." In *The Awakening and Selected Stories*, ed. Sandra M. Gilbert, 179–188. New York: Penguin, 1984.

———. *The Awakening*. New York: Avon, 1982.

Christian Woman's Exchange of New Orleans. *The Creole Cookery Book*. New Orleans: T. H. Thomason, 1885. Reprint, facsimile of original publication, Gretna, LA: Pelican Publishing, 2005.

Clark, John G. "New Orleans as an Entrepot." In *The Louisiana Purchase and Its Aftermath, 1800–1830*, ed. Dolores Egger Labbé, 387–409. Vol. 3. Louisiana Purchase Bicentennial Series in Louisiana History. Lafayette: Center for Louisiana Studies, University of Southwestern Louisiana, 1998.

Clark, Morton Gill. *French-American Cooking from New Orleans to Quebec*. New York: Funk and Wagnalls, 1967.

Cohen, Hennig. "The History of Poor Boy, the New Orleans Bargain Sandwich." *American Speech* 25, no. 1 (February 1950): 67–69.

———. "'Poor Boy' as an Old Field Term." *American Speech* 25, no. 3 (October 1950): 233–234.

Collin, Richard H. *The New Orleans Underground Gourmet*. New York: Simon and Schuster, 1970.

———. *The Revised New Orleans Underground Gourmet*. New York: Simon and Schuster, 1973.

Collin, Rima, and Richard Collin. *The New Orleans Cookbook*. New York: Alfred A. Knopf, 1975.

Conrad, Glenn R. "Reluctant Imperialists: France in North America." In *La Salle and His Legacy*, ed. Patricia K. Galloway, 93–105. Jackson, MS: University Press of Mississippi, 1982.

Conrad, Glenn R., and Ray F. Lucas. *White Gold: A Brief History of the Louisiana Sugar Industry, 1795–1995*. Lafayette: Center for Louisiana Studies, University of Southwestern Louisiana, 1995.

Cook, O. F. "The Chayote: A Tropical Vegetable." *Botanical Bulletin*. Washington, DC: U.S. Dept. of Agriculture, 1901.

Cooper, Anderson. Transcript, *Anderson Cooper 360 Degrees*. http://www.transcripts.cnn.com/TRANSCRIPTS/0509/16/acd.01.html.

Cowan, Walter G., et al. *New Orleans: Yesterday and Today*. 3rd ed. Baton Rouge: Louisiana State University Press, 2001.

Cram, Mildred. *Old Seaport Towns of the South*. New York: Dodd, Mead, 1917.

Crété, Lilian. *Daily Life in Louisiana, 1815-1830*. Trans. Patrick Gregory. Baton Rouge: Louisiana State University Press, 1981.

Cruickshank, Ruth. "Accounting for Taste: The Triumph of French Cuisine." *French Studies* 60, no. 1 (January 2006): 166–167.

Curry, Dale. "Cream at the Top." *New Orleans Times-Picayune*, April 3, 2003.

Curtin, Philip D. *Economic Change in Precolonial Africa*. Madison: University of Wisconsin Press, 1988.

D'Aquin et al. v. Barbour [no number in original]. Supreme Court of Louisiana, 4 La. Ann. 441; 1849 La. Lexis 263.

David, Elizabeth. *French Provincial Cooking*. Harmondsworth, England: Penguin Books, 1970.

Davidson, Alan, ed. *The Oxford Companion to Food*. New York: Oxford University Press, 2006.

Dees, Diane E. "I Say Tomato." *Somerset Review*, 2002. http://www.summersetreview.org/02fall/tomato.html.

Deiler, J. Hanno. *The Settlement of the German Coast of Louisiana and the Creoles of German Descent*. Baltimore: Genealogical Publishing, 1975.

DeLatte, Carolyn E., ed. *The Louisiana Purchase Bicentennial Series in Louisiana History.* Vol. 4, *Antebellum Louisiana, 1830-1860; Part A: Life and Labor.* Lafayette: Center for Louisiana Studies, 2004.

DeMers, John. *Arnaud's Creole Cookbook.* New York: Simon and Schuster, 1988.

———. "Creole Tomatoes." *Emeril's Notes from the Kitchen,* June 28, 2000. http://www.emerils .com/cooking/archives/000204.html.

———. *The Food of New Orleans.* Boston: Periplus Editions, 1998.

DeMers, John, and Rhonda Findley. *The Top 100 New Orleans Recipes of All Time.* Lafayette, LA: Acadian House Publishing, 2003.

Dennett, David. "The Italian on the Land." *U.S. Department of Labor Bulletin 70.* Washington, DC: GPO, 1907.

Dennis, Jana. *Palmyra Street.* Brooklyn: Soft Skull Press, 2005.

Denuzière, Jacqueline, and Charles Henri Brandt. *Cuisine de Louisiane: Histoire et Recettes.* Paris: Editions Denoël, 1989.

DePratz, Claire. *French Home Cooking.* New York: E. P. Dutton, 1956.

Dethloff, Henry C. *A History of the American Rice Industry, 1685–1985.* College Station: Texas A&M University Press, 1988.

Deutsch, Hermann B. *Brennan's New Orleans Cookbook . . . And the Story of the Fabulous New Orleans Restaurant.* New Orleans: Robert L. Crager, 1964.

Dillard University Women's Club. *The Dillard Women's Club Cookbook: A Collection of Fine Recipes Including Louisiana Cuisine, Foreign Dishes, and Favorite Family Recipes.* Kansas City, MO: Circulation Service, 1958.

Dimitry, John. *Lessons in the History of Louisiana.* New York: A. S. Barnes, 1877.

Din, Gilbert C., and John E. Harkins. *The New Orleans Cabildo: Colonial Louisiana's First City Government, 1769–1803.* Baton Rouge: Louisiana State University Press, 1996.

Dominguez, Virginia R. "Social Classification in Creole Louisiana." *American Ethnologist* 4, no. 4 (November 1977): 589–602.

Duke, J. S. "Coffee and the Coffee Trade." *DeBow's Review, Agricultural, Commercial, Industrial Progress and Resources* 2, no. 5 (November 1846): 303–322.

Dumas, Alexandre. *Dumas on Food: Selections from Le Grand Dictionnaire de Cuisine by Alexandre Dumas.* Originally published in 1873. Trans. Alan and Jane Davidson. London: Folio Society, 1978.

"Duncan Hines Repents Calling New Orleans Coffee 'Syrupy Mud.'" *New Orleans Times–Picayune,* August 17, 1954.

Eames, Edwin, and Howard Robboy. "The Submarine Sandwich: Lexical Variations in a Cultural Context." *American Speech* 42, no. 4 (December 1967): 282.

Egerton, John. *Southern Food: At Home, on the Road, in History.* New York: Alfred A. Knopf, 1993.

Elie, Lolis Eric. "Creole Cuisine's Roots." *New York Times,* April 10, 2005, letter to the editor.

———. "Louisiana Delicacy Endangered," *New Orleans Times-Picayune,* June 25, 1997.

Ellis, Kate, and Stephen Smith. "Routes to Recovery." Transcript, *American RadioWorks.* Part 1. Aired August 2007. http://www.americanradioworks.publicradio.org/features/nola/ transcript.html.

Escoffier, Auguste. *The Escoffier Cook Book: A Guide to the Fine Art of Cookery.* New York: Crown Publishers, 1941.

———. *Ma Cuisine.* Trans. Vyvyan Holland and ed. Marion Howells. London: Hamlyn, 1965.

Eustis, Célestine. *Cooking in Old Créole Days/La Cuisine Créole à l'Usage des Petits Ménages.* New York: R. H. Russell, 1904.

Evans, Amy. "Bartenders of New Orleans." Oral history interview with Martin Sawyer, for the South-

ern Foodways Alliance, March 2005. http://www.southernfoodways.com/oral_history/
    bartenders/martin_sawyer.shtml.

Farb, Peter, and George Armelagos. *Consuming Passions: The Anthropology of Eating*. Boston: Houghton
    Mifflin, 1980.

Farmer, Fannie Merritt. *The Boston Cooking-School Cook Book*. 1896; facsimile edition, New York, Hugh
    Lauter and Crown Publisher, 1973.

Feahney, Charles. "Roasted Coffee and Chicory." Coffee Label Collection. Accession no. 1979. 369.18.
    Historic New Orleans Collection, New Orleans.

Federal Writers' Project of the Works Progress Administration. *New Orleans City Guide*. Boston:
    Houghton Mifflin, 1938.

Feibleman, Peter S. *American Cooking: Creole and Acadian*. Foods of the World Series. New York:
    Time-Life Books, 1971.

Fertel, Randy. "Katrina Five Ways." *Kenyon Review* 28, no. 3 (summer 2006): 71–84.

Fisher, Abby. *What Mrs. Fisher Knows about Old Southern Cooking: Soups, Pickles, Preserves, Etc.* Fac-
    simile edition with historical notes by Karen Hess. Bedford, MA: Applewood Press, 1995.

Fitzmorris, Tom. *Eclectic Gourmet Guide to New Orleans*. Birmingham, AL: Monasha Ridge Press, 2001.

———. "New Orleans Could Have the Most Distinctive Soups in the Nation." *New Orleans City Busi-
    ness*, November 20, 2006.

———. *The New Orleans Eat Book*. New Orleans: New Orleans, Big Bend & Pacific Company, 1991.

———. *New Orleans Food*. New York: Stewart, Tabori & Chang, 2006.

Flandrin, Jean-Louis, and Massimo Montarri. "The Rise of the Restaurant." In *Food: A Culinary
    History from Antiquity to the Present*, ed. Montarri Flandrin and Albert Sonnenfeld and trans.
    Albert Sonnenfeld, 471–480. New York: Columbia University Press, 1999.

Folse, John D. *The Encyclopedia of Cajun and Creole Cuisine*. Gonzales, LA: Chef John Folse and
    Co. Publishing, 2004.

French, B. F. *Historical Collections of Louisiana and Florida, including translations of original manuscripts
    relating to their discovery and settlement, with numerous historical and biographical notes*. New York:
    A. Mason, 1875.

"French Market Coffee Stands." *New Orleans Morning Tribune*, June 10, 1928, Metro sect.

Friedel, Louise. *La Petite Cuisinière Habile*. Toulouse, France, 1840.

Futsch, Catherine. "Louisiana Sugar Industry." Unpublished paper. Newcomb Archives, Newcomb
    Center for Research on Women, Tulane University.

Galatoire, Leon. *Galatoire's Cookbook*. Gretna, LA: Pelican Publishing, 1994.

Galsworthy, John. *The Inn of Tranquility: Studies and Essays*. New York: Charles Scribner's Sons, 1913.

Gamefish Profiles. http://www.thejump.net/fishlist/fishlist.htm.

Gardner's New Orleans Directory. New Orleans: C. Gardner, 1858–1869.

Gaudin, Lorin. "Whey Down Yonder." *Emerils.com*, August 28, 2000. http://www.emerils.com/
    cooking/archives/00231.html.

Gehman, Mary. *Women and New Orleans: A History*. New Orleans: Margaret Media, 1988.

Genovese, Eugene. *Roll Jordan, Roll: The World the Slaves Made*. New York: Pantheon Books, 1974.

Giraud, Marcel. *A History of French Louisiana*. Vol. 2: *Years of Transition, 1715–1717*. Trans. Brian
    Pearce. Baton Rouge: Louisiana State University Press, 1993.

Gore, Laura Locoul. *Memories from the Old Plantation Home*. Vacherie, LA: Zoe Company, 2000.

Gothard, Jackie Pressner. Interview with Mildred Covert, March 14, 2001. Transcript. Newcomb
    Archives, Newcomb Center for Research on Women, Tulane University.

Green, Aliza. *Beans: More than Two Hundred Delicious, Wholesome Recipes from around the World.* Philadelphia: Running Press, 2004.

Greene, Phil. "Antoine Amedee Peychaud, Pharmacist and New Orleans Cocktail Legend." *Mixologist: The Journal of the American Cocktail* (2005): 113–146.

Griener, Maria. "Creole Cream Cheese: A New Orleans Tradition That Refuses to Die." *Louisiana Cookin'* 4, no. 6 (August 2001): 13.

Grimes, William. *Straight Up or On the Rocks: The Story of the American Cocktail.* New York: North Point Press, 2001.

Grimshaw, Jonathan. *Journal of Jonathan Grimshaw, 1818–1889.* [Original manuscript in the possession of Carroll Binder, Minneapolis, Minnesota.] http://www.grimshaworiginorg/WebPages/JonaEliza.html.

Guste, Roy F., Jr. *Antoine's Restaurant since 1840 Cookbook.* New Orleans: Carbery-Guste, 1979; New York: W. W. Norton, 1980.

———. *The 100 Greatest Dishes of Louisiana Cookery.* New York: W. W. Norton, 1988.

———. *The 100 Greatest New Orleans Creole Recipes.* Gretna, LA: Pelican Publishing, 1994.

———. *The Restaurants of New Orleans.* New York: W. W. Norton & Sons, 1992

Gutierrez, C. Paige. *Cajun Foodways.* Jackson: University Press of Mississippi, 1991.

Haas, Edward F. "New Orleans on the Half-Shell: The Maestri Era, 1936–1946." *Louisiana History* 13 (1972): 289–297.

Hall, A. Oakey. *The Manhattaner in New Orleans; or, Phases of "Crescent City" Life.* Clinton Hall, NY: J. S. Redfield, 1851.

Hall, Basil. *Travels in North America in the Years 1827 and 1828.* Vol. 3. 3rd ed. Edinburgh: Robert Cadell, 1830.

Hall, Gwendolyn Midlo. *Africans in Colonial Louisiana: The Development of Afro-Creole Culture in the Eighteenth Century.* Baton Rouge: Louisiana State University Press, 1992.

Hamilton, Elizabeth. Introduction to *Two Hundred Years of Charleston Cooking*, by Blanche Rhett. Columbia: University of South Carolina Press, 1976.

Hammond, John Martin. *Winter Journeys in the South.* Philadelphia: J. B. Lippincott, 1916.

Hanger, Kimberly S. *Bounded Lives, Bounded Places: Free Black Society in Colonial New Orleans.* Durham, NC, and London: Duke University Press, 1997.

"Haricot Bean." In *The Oxford Companion to Food*, ed. Alan Davidson, 370–371. Oxford: Oxford University Press, 1999.

Harland, Marion. *Common Sense in the Household: A Manual of Practical Housewifery.* Rev. ed. New York: C. Scribner's Sons, 1889.

Harlow, Jay. *The Art of the Sandwich.* San Francisco, CA: Chronicle Books, 1990.

Harris, Jessica B. *Beyond Gumbo: Creole Fusion Food from the Atlantic Rim.* New York: Simon & Schuster, 2003.

———. *The Welcome Table: African-American Heritage Cooking.* New York: Fireside, 1995.

Harrison, Robert W., and Walter M. Kollmorden. "The Place of French-Speaking Farmers of Southern Louisiana in Future Land Development and Reclamation Projects." *Journal of Land & Public Utility Economics* 22 (August 1946): 223–231.

Hearn, Lafcadio. *Creole Cook Book, with the addition of a collection of drawings and writings by Lafcadio Hearn during his sojourn in New Orleans from 1877 to 1887: a literary and culinary adventure.* Gretna, LA: Pelican Publishing, 1990.

———. *Gombo Zherbes.* New York: Will H. Coleman, 1885.

————. *La Cuisine Creole: A collection of culinary recipes from leading chefs and noted Creole housewives who have made New Orleans famous for its cuisine.* New York: Will H. Coleman, 1885. 2nd ed. New Orleans: F. F. Hansel & Bro., Ltd., 1885.

Hearty, James. "Po' Boy No Mo'; He's Celebrating," *New Orleans States-Item,* May 3, 1969.

Hellman, Lillian, and Peter S. Feibleman. *Eating Together: Recollections and Recipes.* Boston: Little, Brown, 1984.

Hess, John, and Karen Hess. *The Taste of America.* Champaign, IL: University of Illinois Press, 2000.

Hess, Karen. *The Carolina Rice Kitchen: The African Connection.* Columbia: University of South Carolina Press, 1992.

Holmes, Jack D. L., ed. "O'Reilly's Regulations on Booze, Boarding Houses and Billiards." *Louisiana History* 6, no. 3 (summer 1965): 293–300.

Hoover, L. G. 1923. *The Chayote: Its Culture and Uses.* USDA Dept. Circ. 286:1–11.

Horner, Hattie. *Not at Home.* New York: John B. Alden, 1889.

Huber, Leonard V. *Creole Collage: Reflections on the Colorful Customs of Latter-Day New Orleans Creoles.* Lafayette: Center for Louisiana Studies, University of Southwestern Louisiana, 1989.

Ingersoll, Thomas. *Mammon and Manon in Early New Orleans: The First Slave Society in the Deep South, 1718–1819.* Knoxville: University of Tennessee, 1999.

Jackson, Waukesha. *What Would the World be Without Women: Stories from the 9th Ward.* Brooklyn: Soft Skull Press, 2005.

Jacobs, Howard. "Ceremony of Café Brulot Was Awesome Spectacle." *New Orleans Times-Picayune,* November 11, 1958.

Jacquin, Nikolaus von. *Selectarum Stirpium Americanarum Historia.* Vindobonae: Ex officina Krausiana, 1763.

Janick, Jules. "The Tomato: Vegetable or Fruit?" In *Encyclopedia of Food and Culture,* ed. Solomon H. Katz and William Woys Weaver, vol. 3: 404. New York: Scribner, 2003.

Jefferson, Martha. Holograph Manuscript Notebook, 1772–1782. Manuscript Division, Library of Congress.

Jenkins, Virginia Scott. *Bananas: An American History.* Washington, DC: Smithsonian Press, 2000.

Jim Lehrer News Hour, December 15, 2005. http://www.pbs.org/newshour/bb/weather/july-dec05/evacuees_12-15.html#.

Johnson, Pableaux. *Eating New Orleans: From French Quarter Creole Dining to the Perfect Poboy.* Woodstock, VT: Countryman Press, 2005.

Jones, Caroline Merrick, and Natalie Vivian Scott. *The Gourmet's Guide to New Orleans.* 19th ed. New Orleans: self-published, 1967.

Junior League of Baton Rouge. *River Road Recipes.* 72nd printing. Baton Rouge, LA: Junior League of Baton Rouge, 2000.

Junior League of Denver. *Colorado Cache Cookbook.* Denver: Junior League of Denver, 1978.

Junior League of Lafayette. *Talk About Good.* Lafayette, LA: Junior League of Lafayette, 1967.

Junior League of New Orleans. *The Plantation Cookbook.* Garden City, NY: Doubleday, 1972.

Kaltwasser, Jennifer. "The Cookbook as an Indicator of Social History: New Orleans, Louisiana, c. 1960–1970." Honors thesis, Newcomb College, Tulane University, 1998.

Kaplan, Steven. *The Bakers of Paris and the Bread Question, 1700–1755.* Durham, NC: Duke University Press, 1996.

Kaufman, William I., and Sister Mary Ursula Cooper. *The Art of Creole Cookery.* Garden City, NY: Doubleday, 1962.

Kein, Sybil. *Creole: The History and Legacy of Louisiana's Free People of Color*. Baton Rouge: Louisiana State University Press, 2000.

Kemp, Jon, "There's Nothing Quite Like a Creole Tomato." *New Orleans Times-Picayune*, June 7, 2007, Vieux Point.

Kinney, Robert. *The Bachelor in New Orleans*. New Orleans: Bob Riley Studios, 1942.

Kolb, Carolyn G. *The Dolphin Guide to New Orleans*. Garden City, NY: Dolphin Books, 1984.

———. "Shopping at Solari's: A Grocery like None Other." *New Orleans Magazine* 38, no. 10 (July 2004): 124–125.

Kraft Foods. http://www.kraft.com/archives/brands/brands_cream.html.

Laborde, Errol. "The Cream Team." *New Orleans Magazine*, May 1998.

Lagasse, Emeril. *Every Day's a Party: Louisiana Recipes for Celebrating with Family and Friends*. New York: William Morrow, 1999.

———. *From Emeril's Kitchens: Favorite Recipes from Emeril's Restaurants*. New York: HarperCollins, 2003.

Land, Mary. *Louisiana Cookery*. Baton Rouge: Louisiana State University Press, 1954.

———. *New Orleans Cuisine*. New York: A. S. Barnes, 1969.

Landry, Laura. "Louisiana's Living Traditions." In *Louisiana Folklife Festival Booklet 1990*. http://www.louisianafolklife.org/LT/Articles_Essays/creole_art_shrimping_overv.html.

Langenhennig, Susan. "Creole Tomatoes Are Welcome Storm Survivors." *New Orleans Times-Picayune*, May 21, 2006, Algiers-Picayune.

Latrobe, Benjamin Henry. *The Journal of Latrobe: Being the Notes and Sketches of an Architect, Naturalist and Traveler in the United States from 1796 to 1820*. New York: D. Appleton, 1905.

Laudeman, Sue. *Elegant Entertaining along St. Charles Avenue: Authentic Menus and 1890's Recipes from the Garden District of New Orleans*. New Orleans: Historic New Orleans Collection, 1994.

———. "A Preliminary Report on the Historic New Orleans Collection (HNOC) project, *A Dollop of History in Every Bite, 2005-2007*." New Orleans: HNOC, 2007.

Laussat, Pierre-Clément de. Archives Nationales, Ministère des Colonies, Messidor (June 19-July 18, 1803) 11, Col., C 13 A, vol. 52, fol. 199.

———. *Memoirs of My Life*. Trans. Agnes-Josephine Pastwa and ed. Robert Bush. Baton Rouge: Louisiana State University Press, 1978.

Lawrence, John H., Pamela D. Arcenaux, Susan R. Laudeman, John Magill, and Gerald Patout. *What's Cooking in New Orleans? Culinary Traditions of the Crescent City*. Exhibition catalog. New Orleans: Historic New Orleans Collection, 2007.

Le Page du Pratz, Antoine Simon. *History of Louisiana*. 1774. Reprint, trans. and ed. Joseph C. Tregle. Baton Rouge: Louisiana State University Press, 1975.

Leathem, Karen Trahan. *Three Women and Their Restaurants: Elizabeth Bégué, Marie Esparbé, and Corinne Dunbar: An Exhibition Guide*. New Orleans: Newcomb Center for Research on Women, 2000.

———. *Two Women and Their Cookbooks: Lena Richard and Mary Land: An Exhibition Guide*. New Orleans: Newcomb Center for Research on Women, 2001.

Lee, Hilde Gabriel. *Taste of the States: A Food History of America*. Charlottesville, VA: Howell Press, 1992.

Lelièvre, Jacques-Felix. *New Louisiana Gardener*. Trans. and introduction by Sally Kittredge Reeves. Baton Rouge: Louisiana State University Press, 2001.

Les Vingts Quatre Club. *First—You Make a Roux*. Lafayette, LA: Les Vingts Quatre Club, 1954.

Leslie, Austin. *Chez Helene House of Good Food Cookbook*. New Orleans: De Simonin Publications, 1984.

Leslie, Austin A., and Marie Rudd Posey. *Austin Leslie's Creole-Soul: New Orleans' Cooking with a Soulful Twist*. New Orleans: De Simonin Publications, 2000.

Leslie, Eliza. *Directions for Cookery, In Its Various Branches*. Philadelphia: E. L. Carey & Hart, 1840.

Lewis, Peirce F. *New Orleans: The Making of an Urban Landscape*. 2nd ed. Santa Fe, NM: Center for American Places, 2003.

Lipsitz, George. "Learning from New Orleans: The Social Warrant of Hostile Privatism and Competitive Consumer Citizenship." *Cultural Anthropology* 21, no. 3 (August 2006): 451–468.

Litwin, Sharon. "Secrets of a Master Baker." *New Orleans States-Item*, March 29, 1979.

Logsdon, Joseph. *Ice and Refrigeration in New Orleans*. Panel Discussion, August 20, 1998. Newcomb Center for Research on Women, Tulane University.

Long, Janet. "Tomatoes." In *The Cambridge World History of Food*, ed. Kenneth F. Kiple and Kriemhild Coneè Ornelas, vol. 1. Cambridge: Cambridge University Press, 2000.

Louisiana State Museum. "From the Louisiana State Museum: Richly Brewed New Orleans Coffee Legacy." *Cultural Vistas* 8, no. 1 (spring 1997): 4–7.

Louisiana State University Agricultural Center. http://lsuagcenter.com.

Louisiana State University Department of Animal Sciences. http://lsuagcenter.com/en/our_offices/departments/Animal_Science/.

Lovegren, Sylvia. *Fashionable Food: Seven Decades of Food Fads*. New York: Macmillan, 1995.

MacCash, Doug. "The Night They Raided the Quorum." *New Orleans Times-Picayune*, June 27, 2004.

Mahne, Theodore P. "Ripe for Fun: The Creole Tomato Festival Expands to Two Days." *New Orleans Times-Picayune*, June 8, 2007, Lagniappe.

Marcus, Frances Frank. "Antoine's Celebrates 150 Years of Cuisine." *New York Times*, May 23, 1990.

Mariani, John. *Encyclopedia of American Food and Drink*. New York: Lebhar-Friedman, 1999.

Martin, Bennie, and Clovis Martin. Letter to Division 194, Box 6, Street Railway Union Collection, Special Collections, Tulane University.

Matthews, Bunny. "The Making of a Po-Boy." *New Orleans Times-Picayune*, November 29, 1981, Dixie Magazine.

Maylié, Eugénie Lavedan. *Maylie's Table d'Hote Recipes: The History and Some Facts Concerning La Maison Maylie et Esparbe*. 5th ed. New Orleans: Anna May Maylie, 1986.

Mayo, H. M. *Mme Begué and Her Recipes*. San Francisco, CA: Southern Pacific Co., Sunset Route, 1900.

McCaffety, Kerri. *Obituary Cocktail: The Great Saloons of New Orleans*. New Orleans: Vissi d'Arte Books, 2001.

McCrossen, William. Retired New Orleans Fire Superintendent. Interview, May 1995.

McGrath, Marci. "Margaret Haughery and the Establishing of St. Vincent's Orphan Asylum in New Orleans, 1858." Thesis, University of New Orleans, 1993. Special Collections, Earl K. Long Library, University of New Orleans.

McWilliams, Richebourg G. *Iberville's Gulf Journal*. Tuscaloosa: University of Alabama Press, 1981.

Mencken, H. L. "The Home of the Crab." In *American Food Writing: An Anthology with Classic Recipes*, ed. Molly O'Neill, 171–172. New York: Penguin Putnam, 2007.

Merrill, Ellen C. *Germans of Louisiana*. Gretna, LA: Pelican Publishing, 2005.

Metairie Garden Club. *Favorite Recipes from Old Metairie*. Waverly, IA: G & R Publishing, 1938.

Miester, Mark. "Good to the Last Drip." *Gambit Weekly*, December 17, 2002.

Mintz, Sidney W. "Cuisine and Haute Cuisine: How Are They Linked?" *Food and Foodways* 3 (1989): 185–190.

———. *Tasting Food, Tasting Freedom: Excursions into Eating, Culture, and the Past.* Boston: Beacon, 1996.

Mitcham, Howard. *Creole Gumbo and All That Jazz.* Reading, MA: Addison-Wesley, 1978.

Mizell-Nelson, Michael. "Challenging and Reinforcing White Control of Public Space: Race Relations on New Orleans Streetcars, 1861–1965." PhD diss., Tulane University, 2001.

———. *Streetcar Stories.* Video Documentary. Matthew Martinez, Director. WYES, New Orleans Public Broadcasting System affiliate, 1995.

Mme. Begue and Her Recipes/The Picayune's Creole Cook Book. Facsimile of 2nd ed., 1901. Birmingham, AL: Oxmoor House, 1984.

Montagné, Prosper. *Larousse Gastronomique: The Encyclopedia of Food, Wine, and Cookery.* Trans. Nina Froud and others. New York: Crown Publishers, 1961, 1977.

Moritz, Mrs. C. F. *The Twentieth Century Cookbook and Practical Housekeeping.* New York: G. W. Dillingham/Alhambra, 1898.

Mullener, Elizabeth. "Charmed Historian." *New Orleans Times-Picayune,* September 21, 1994.

———. "The Palace Guard." *New Orleans Times-Picayune,* June 6, 1998.

National Research Council (U.S.). *Lost Crops of Africa: Vegetables.* Washington, DC: National Academy Press, 2006.

Nelson, Mary Hutson. Papers. Newcomb Archives, Newcomb Center for Research on Women, Tulane University.

"New Orleans Bread." Research Binder. Culinary Research Group. Newcomb Archives, Newcomb Center for Research on Women, Tulane University.

New Orleans Coffee Co. Ltd. v. American Coffee Co. of New Orleans. Ltd. Supreme Court of Louisiana. 124 La. 19; 49 So. 730; 1909 La. LEXIS 418.

Norman, Benjamin. *Norman's New Orleans and Environs.* New Orleans: B. M. Norman, 1845.

Northup, Solomon. *Twelve Years a Slave.* Ed. Sue Eakin and Joseph Logsdon. The Library of Southern Civilization. Baton Rouge: Louisiana State University Press, 1968.

Nossiter, Sharon Stallworth. "Food Supply and Markets in Colonial New Orleans." Unpublished paper. Culinary History Files: New Orleans Notebook. Newcomb Archives, Newcomb Center for Research on Women, Tulane University.

Novak, William J. "Public Economy and the Well-Ordered Market: Law and Economic Regulation in 19th-century America." *Law & Social Inquiry* 18, no. 1 (winter 1993): 1–33.

O'Neill, Molly. *American Food Writing: An Anthology with Classic Recipes.* New York: Penguin Putnam, 2007.

Ormond, Suzanne, Mary E. Irvine, and Denyse Cantin. *Favorite New Orleans Recipes.* Gretna, LA: Pelican Publishing Company, 1979.

Paddleford, Clementine. *How America Eats.* New York: Scribner, 1960.

———. "New Orleans Is Keeping the Croxignolle Secret." *New York Herald Tribune,* March 10, 1954.

———. *Recipes from Antoine's Kitchen: The Secret Riches of the Famous Century-Old Restaurant in the French Quarter of New Orleans.* New Orleans: This Week Magazine, 1948.

Parks, William. *The Williamsburg Art of Cookery; or Accomplish'd gentlewoman's companion . . .* Ed. Helen Claire Duprey Bullock. Williamsburg, VA: Colonial Williamsburg, 1938.

Parloa, Maria. *Miss Parloa's Kitchen Companion: A Guide for All Who Would Be Good Housekeepers.* Boston: Estes and Lauriat, 1887.

Parsons, James J. "Sea Turtles and Their Eggs." In *Cambridge World History of Food*. Vol. 1: 567–573. Cambridge: Cambridge University Press, 2000.

Patout, Alex. *Patout's Cajun Home Cooking*. New York: Random House, 1986.

"Peoples Bakery." Incorporation. *New Orleans Tribune*, February 23, 1866.

Perrow, Jonathan. "You Say Tomato; However You Say It, the French Market Sings Praises of the Creole Tomato." *New Orleans Times-Picayune*, June 10, 2005, Lagniappe.

The Picayune's Creole Cookbook. 2nd ed. New Orleans: Picayune, 1901.

Pintard, John. "New Orleans, 1801: An Account by John Pintard." Ed. David Lee Sterling. *Louisiana Historical Quarterly* 34, no. 3 (July 1951): 217–233.

"Pistolet." *Oxford English Dictionary*. 2nd ed. http://www.oed.com.

"Po-Boy Sandwiches." Louisiana Collection, New Orleans Public Library.

"Poor Boy." In *Dictionary of American Regional English*. Cambridge, MA: Belknap Press, 1995.

———. In *Oxford English Dictionary*. 2nd ed. http://www.oed.com.

———. In *Random House Unabridged Dictionary*, 2nd ed. Online.

"Poor Boy Gets Rich." *New Orleans Item?* 1949 news clipping, Michael Mizell-Nelson personal collection, gift from Gendusa family memorabilia.

"Pourboire." In *The Oxford Dictionary of Foreign Words and Phrases*, ed. Jennifer Speake. New York: Oxford University Press, 1997.

Price, Jacob. "Economic Function and the Growth of American Port Towns in the Eighteenth Century." *Perspectives in American History* 8 (1974): 123–186.

Price, Todd A. "Backstage at Emeril's." *Offbeat, Louisiana Music & Culture Magazine* 20, no. 9 (September 2007). http://www.offbeat.com/artman/publish/article_2470.shtml.

Prudhomme, Paul. *Chef Paul Prudhomme's Louisiana Kitchen*. New York: William Morrow, 1984.

———. *Prudhomme Family Cookbook: Old-Time Louisiana Recipes*. New York: William Morrow, 1987.

Randelman, Mary Urrutia, and Joan Schwartz. *Memories of a Cuban Kitchen*. New York: Macmillan, 1992.

Randolph, Mary. *The Virginia House-Wife*. 1860. Reprint, ed. Karen Hess. Columbia: University of South Carolina Press, 1985.

Reed, Julia. "In Creole Kitchens." *New York Times*, February 20, 2005.

Reed, Mary Barton. "Louisiana Cookery: Its History and Development." M.A. thesis, Louisiana State University, 1931.

Reeves, Sally K. "The History of Markets." Lecture, April 15, 2000. Oral History Collection, Newcomb Center for Research on Women, Tulane University.

———. "Making Groceries." *Cultural Vistas* 18, no. 3 (fall 2007): 25–35.

———. "Making Groceries: Markets and Market Folk in 19th-Century New Orleans." Lecture, January 19, 2007. Food for Thought: Culinary Traditions of New Orleans. Historic New Orleans Collection, New Orleans.

Richard, Lena. *Lena Richard's Cookbook*. New Orleans: Rogers Printing, 1939.

———. *New Orleans Cook Book*. Boston: Houghton Mifflin, 1940.

Richman, Alan. "Yes, We're Open." *GQ* 76, no. 11 (November 2006): 294–299, 337–338.

Ripley, Eliza. *Social Life in Old New Orleans: Being Recollections of My Girlhood*. New York: D. Appleton, 1912.

Roberts, Florence. *Dixie Meals*. Nashville, TN: Parthenon Press, 1934.

Robin. C. C. *Voyage to Louisiana, 1803–1805*. Trans. and ed. Stuart O. Landry Jr. New Orleans: Pelican Publishing, 1966.

———. *Voyages Dans l'Interieure de la Louisiane*. Trans. Irene Blanche Pujol. M.A. thesis translation, Louisiana State University, 1939.

Rodrigue, Melvin, with Jyl Benson. *Galatoire's Cookbook: Recipes and Family History from the Time-Honored New Orleans Restaurant*. New York: Clarkson Potter/Publishers, 2005.

Rombauer, Irma S., Marion Rombauer Becker, and Ethan Becker. *Joy of Cooking*. New York: Scribner, 1997. 75th anniversary ed., New York: Simon and Schuster, 2006.

Ronald, Mary. *Mary Ronald's Century Cook Book*. New York: Century Company, 1895.

Root, Waverley. *Food*. New York: Simon and Schuster, 1980.

———. *The Food of France*. 1958. Reprint, New York: Vintage Books, 1992.

Root, Waverly, and Richard de Rochemont. *Eating in America: A History*. New York: William Morrow, 1976. Reprint, Hopewell, NJ: Ecco Press, 1981.

Rose, Judy. "Real New Orleans Cooking is a stunning blend of ingredients and ethnic traditions." *Detroit Free Press*, February 25, 1998.

Rozin, Elisabeth. "The Structure of Cuisine." In *The Psychobiology of Human Food Selection*, ed. Lewis M. Barket, 189–203. Westport, CT: AVI, 1982.

Saint-Ange, Evelyn. *La Bonne Cuisine de Madame E. Saint-Ange: The Original Companion for French Home Cooking*. Trans. Paul Aratow. Berkeley, CA: Ten Speed Press, 2005.

Saint-Arroman, Auguste. *Coffee, Tea, and Chocolate: Their Influence Upon the Health, the Intellect, and the Moral Nature of Man*. Philadelphia: Townsend Ward, 1846.

Saint Bernard Office of the Louisiana Cooperative Extension Service. "Creole Tomatoes." *Louisiana State University Extension Service Special Information Sheets*. Baton Rouge, 1999. Copy available at Newcomb Center for Research on Women, Tulane University.

Saint Matthew's Guild. *De Bonnes Choses à Manger (Good Things to Eat)*. Houma, LA: The Guild, 1939.

Salaam, Kalamu ya. "Banana Republic." *Cultural Vistas* 4, no. 3 (fall 1993): 40–49.

Salt Institute. http://www.saltinstitute.org.

Santich, Barbara. "*A la recherche de la tomate perdue*: The First French Tomato Recipe?" *Gastronomica* 2 (spring 2002): 68–71.

Sauder, Robert A. "The Origin and Spread of the Public Market System in New Orleans." *Louisiana History* 22 (1981): 281–297.

Saxon, Lyle. *Fabulous New Orleans*. New York: The Century, 1928. Reprint, New York: D. Appleton/Century, 1938.

Schneider, Frank. "Holy Calas! No Creole Cream Cheese?" *New Orleans Times-Picayune*, April 30, 1986: Second Cup sect.

Scott, Liz. "Tempest in a Bean Pot." *New Orleans Magazine* (July 1987): 62–64.

Scott, Natalie Vivian. *Mirations & Miracles of Mandy*. New Orleans: R. H. True, 1929.

———. *200 Years of New Orleans Cooking*. New York: Jonathan Cape & Harrison Smith, 1931.

Scott, Natalie Vivian, and Caroline Merrick Jones. *The Gourmet's Guide to New Orleans*. New Orleans: Scott & Jones, 1933. Reprint, New Orleans: by the authors, 1951.

Seaburg, Carl, and Stanley Paterson. *The Ice King: Frederic Tudor and His Circle*. Boston and Mystic, CT: Massachusetts Historical Society and Mystic Seaport Museum, 2003.

Seelig, Raymond A. *Fruit & Vegetable Facts & Pointers: Bananas*. Washington, DC: United Fresh Fruit & Vegetable Association, 1969.

Severson, Kim. "'Faerie Folk' Strike Back with Fritters." *New York Times*, December 6, 2006.

———. "Slices of a Southern Summer." *New York Times*, March 15, 2006.

Simmons, Amelia. *American Cookery*. Hartford: Printed by Hudson and Goodwin for the author, 1796.

Sins, Amy Cyrex. *The Ruby Slippers Cookbook: Life, Culture, Family and Food after Katrina.* New Orleans: by the author, 2006.

Smith, Andrew F., ed. "Bread." *The Oxford Encyclopedia of Food and Drink in America*, ed. Andrew Smith, vol. 1, 116–124 New York: Oxford University Press, 2004.

———. "Sandwiches." *The Oxford Encyclopedia of Food and Drink in America*, ed. Andrew Smith, vol. 2, 397–400. New York: Oxford University Press, 2004.

———. "Tomatoes." In *The Oxford Encyclopedia of Food and Drink in America*, ed. Andrew Smith, vol. 2, 603–645. New York: Oxford University, 2004.

Snellings, Marie Louise. *Cook with Marie Louise.* Monroe, LA: Tom Gates, 1966.

Soard's New Orleans City Directory, 1928–1939. New Orleans: Soard's Directory Company, 1874–1935.

Solari, A. M., and J. Solari. *Fancy and Staple Groceries.* Brochure. Historic New Orleans Collection, New Orleans.

Soniat, Leon E., Jr. *La Bouche Creole.* Gretna, LA: Pelican Publishing, 1981.

Spera, Keith. "On the Bandstand or on the Air, Bob French Pulls No Punches." *New Orleans Times-Picayune*, May 6, 2007.

Stall, Buddy. *Buddy Stall's French Quarter Montage.* Detroit: Harlo Printing, 1992.

———. "Oysters no longer prohibited in months without an 'R.'" *New Orleans Clarion Herald*, April 20, 2005.

Stanforth, Deirdre. *Creole! The Legendary Cuisine of New Orleans.* New York: Simon and Schuster, 1969.

———. *The New Orleans Restaurant Cookbook.* Rev. ed. Garden City, NY: Doubleday, 1976.

Stanforth, Deirdre, and Hermann Deutsch. *Brennan's New Orleans Cookbook.* New Orleans: Robert L. Crager, 1961.

Starr, S. Frederick. *New Orleans Unmasked: Being a Wagwit's Sketches of a Singular American City.* New Orleans: Dedeaux, 1985.

———. ed. *Inventing New Orleans: Writings of Lafcadio Hearn.* Jackson: University Press of Mississippi, 2001.

Steckler, Mrs. Henry A. "Beverages." In *Sauce for the Goose: A New Orleans Cook Book.* Louisiana Pond Auxiliary of Blue Goose International. Self-published, 1948.

Stephenson, Wendell H. "Antebellum New Orleans as an Agricultural Focus." In *The Louisiana Purchase Bicentennial Series in Louisiana History.* Vol. 4, *Antebellum Louisiana, 1830–1860; Part A: Life and Labor*, ed. Carolyn E. DeLatte, 301–314. Lafayette: Center for Louisiana Studies, 2004.

Stilgenbauer, Floyd A. "Chicory: Michigan's Infant Monopoly Crop." *Economic Geography* 7, no. 1 (January 1931): 84–100.

Stoney, Louisa C. *Carolina Rice Cook Book.* Charleston, SC: Carolina Rice Kitchen Association, 1901.

Stouse, Suzanne. "Making the Belt or a Splash in the Lake." *New Orleans Times-Picayune*, July 10, 1983.

"Street Hawkers." *New Orleans Daily Picayune*, July 24, 1846.

"Stuffed Roll aka pistolet." http://www.LouisianaCajun.com.

Succession of Race. No. 22965, Supreme Court of Louisiana, 144 La. 157: 80 0. 234; 1918 La. Lexis 1716.

Tarr, Yvonne Young. *The Tomato Book.* New York: Vintage Books, 1977.

Taylor, Joe Gray, and John T. Edge. "Southern Foodways." In *Foodways*, ed. John T. Edge, vol. 7: 1–14. *The New Encyclopedia of Southern Culture.* Chapel Hill: University of North Carolina Press, 2007.

Thackeray, William Makepeace. *Roundabout Papers.* New York: Harper & Brothers, 1863.

Thorne, John, with Matt Lewis Thorne. *Serious Pig: An American Cook in Search of His Roots.* New York: Farrar, Strauss and Giroux, 1996.

Tinker, Edward Larocque. *Creole City: Its Past and Its People.* New York: Longmans, Green, 1953.

Tobias, Ruth. "Beans." In *The Oxford Encyclopedia of Food and Drink in America*, ed. Andrew F. Smith, 70–72. New York: Oxford University Press, 2004.

Toklas, Alice. "Food in the United States in 1934 and 1935." In *The Alice B. Toklas Cookbook*, 123–135. New York: Harper, 1954.

Tregle, Joseph G., Jr. "Creoles and Americans." In *Creole New Orleans: Race and Americanization*, ed. Arnold R. Hirsch and Joseph Logsdon, 131–185. Baton Rouge: Louisiana State University Press, 1992.

———. "Early New Orleans Society: A Reappraisal." *Journal of Southern History* 18, no. 1 (February 1952): 20–36.

Trubek, Amy. *Haute Cuisine: How the French Invented the Culinary Profession*. Philadelphia: University of Pennsylvania Press, 2000.

Tujague's Restaurant. "History." http://www.tujaguesrestaurant.com/history.html.

Turley, Alan C. "The Ecological and Social Determinants of the Production of Dixieland Jazz in New Orleans." *International Review of the Aesthetics and Sociology of Music* 26, no. 1. (June 1995): 107–121.

Twain, Mark. *Life on the Mississippi*. Montreal: Dawson Brothers, 1883.

Tyree, Marion Cabell. *Housekeeping in Old Virginia*. Louisville, KY: John P. Morton and Co., 1879.

United States Department of Agriculture. *Sugar and Sweeteners Yearbook Tables*. Economic Research Service, 2005. http://www.ers.usda.gov/Briefing/Sugar/Data.html.

———. Economic Research Service. http://www.ers.usda.gov/Briefing/Rice/questionsAndAnswers.html.

United States Department of Labor. "The Italian on the Land." *Bulletin 70*. Washington, DC, Government Printing Office, 1907.

Ursuline Convent Cookbook. New Orleans: Franklin Printing, 1981.

Usher, Ethel Mae Wight, and Matilda Geddings Gray. *Food for Gourmets*. New Orleans: by the authors, 1940.

Usner, Daniel H. *American Indians in the Lower Mississippi Valley*. Lincoln and London: University of Nebraska Press, 1998.

Vandal, Gilles. "Black Utopia in Early Reconstruction New Orleans: The People's Bakery, a Case-Study," *Louisiana History* 38, no. 4 (fall 1997): 437–470.

Vaucresson, Vance. Interviewed by Amy Evans, August 9, 2006. Transcript. http://www.southerngumbotrail.com/vaucresson.shtml.

Voisin, Michael. "Testimony before the Subcommittee on Water Resources and Environment." U.S. House of Representatives, October 18, 2005.

Vujnovich, Milos M. *Yugoslavs in Louisiana*. Gretna, LA: Pelican Publishing, 1973.

Walker, Judy. "New Orleans' French bread is tough to make at home," *New Orleans Times-Picayune*, March 16, 2006.

———. "Reporting on New Orleans Food." Lecture, October 8, 2007. Historic New Orleans Collection, New Orleans.

Ward, Artemas. *The Grocer's Encyclopedia*. New York: American Grocer, 1911.

Washington, Mrs. *The Unrivalled Cook-book and Housekeeper's Guide*. New York: Harper and Brothers, 1885.

Wason, Elizabeth. *Cooks, Gluttons, and Gourmets: A History of Cookery*. Garden City, NY, 1962.

Watts, Edith, and John Watts. *Jesse's Book of Creole and Deep South Recipes*. New York: Weathervane Books, 1954.

Waud, A. "Sunday in New Orleans—The French Market." *Harper's Weekly*, August 18, 1866: 256.

Whipple, Henry Benjamin. *Bishop Whipple's Southern Diary, 1843–1844*. Ed. and with introduction by Lester B. Shippee. Minneapolis: University of Minnesota Press, 1937.

Whittington, G. P. "Dr. John Sibley of Natchitoches, 1757–1837." *Louisiana Historical Quarterly* 10, no. 4 (October 1927): 467–512.

Widmer, Mary Lou. *New Orleans in the Forties*. 3rd ed. Gretna, LA: Pelican Publishing, 1990.

Wilson, James Grant. *Thackeray in the United States, 1852–3, 1855–6*. New York: Dodd, Mead, n.d.

Wittels, Betina J., and Robert Hermesch. *Absinthe, Sip of Seduction: A Contemporary Guide*. Denver, CO: Corvus Publishing, 2003.

Wolfert, Paula. *The Cooking of South-West France*. New York: Harper & Row, 1983.

Women's Republican Club of Louisiana. *New Orleans Carnival Cookbook*. New Orleans: Women's Republican Publications, 1951.

Wondrich, David. "You Call That a Sazerac? The Curious and the Contradictory History of New Orleans' Signature Cocktail." Lecture, Southern Foodways Alliance symposium. Oxford, MS, October 26–28, 2007.

Woodward, Ralph Lee, Jr., *Tribute to Don Bernardo de Gálvez: Royal Patents and an Epic Ballad Honoring the Spanish Governor of Louisiana*. Baton Rouge: Historic New Orleans Collection, 1979.

Wright, Clifford A. *A Mediterranean Feast: The Story of the Birth of the Celebrated Cuisines of the Mediterranean, from the Merchants of Venice to the Barbary Corsairs, with More Than 500 Recipes*. New York: William Morrow, 1999.

Young Men's Gymnastic Club. *Menu for Twenty-Fifth Anniversary, September 2, 1897*. New Orleans: Walle and Company, 1897.

CONTRIBUTORS

Karen Trahan Leathem is Museum Historian at the Louisiana State Museum and has curated, written, edited, and assisted with many exhibits and publications about food. She is co-editor of *The American South in the Twentieth Century* (University of Georgia Press, 2005).

Patricia Kennedy Livingston is a writer who edited and tested recipes for five cookbooks for Chef Paul Prudhomme. Since 1987, she has written a weekly column and occasional articles for the *New Orleans Times-Picayune*.

Michael Mizell-Nelson is Assistant Professor in the Department of History at the University of New Orleans. His research interests focus upon the social and cultural history of New Orleans, and he is completing a study of race relations within the New Orleans public transit system.

Cynthia LeJeune Nobles is a recent graduate from the University of New Orleans. She holds a certification in *boulangerie* from Le Cordon Bleu, Paris, and she is the author of *Dining on the Delta Queen: A Culinary History 1926–2008* (American Foodways Press, forthcoming).

Sharon Stallworth Nossiter is a former newspaper reporter and has attended culinary classes at home and abroad. She is co-author of "Food," one of six major sections in *American Regional Cultures: The South* (Greenwood Press, 2004).

Sara Roahen is a freelance writer and oral historian. She is author of the book *Gumbo Tales: Finding My Place at the New Orleans Table* (Norton, 2008). She also served as food critic for the *New Orleans Gambit Weekly* from 2001 until 2004.

Susan Tucker is the author of *Telling Memories among Southern Women* (Lousiana State University, 1989) and co-editor of *The Scrapbook in American Life* (Temple, 2006). She is an archivist and librarian at the Newcomb Center for Research on Women.

INDEX

Entries in **boldface** refer to recipes.